The Press and Race: Mississippi Journalists Confront the Movement

The Press and Race
Mississippi Journalists
Confront the Movement

Edited by David R. Davies

University Press of Mississippi *Jackson*

www.upress.state.ms.us

Copyright © 2001 by University Press of Mississippi
All rights reserved
Manufactured in the United States of America

Print-On-Demand Edition
∞

Photo credits: Percy Greene, courtesy of the Beadle Collection, Mississippi Department of Archives and History; Jimmy Ward, courtesy of *The Clarion-Ledger*; J. Oliver Emmerich, courtesy of J. O. Emmerich Papers, Special Collections, Mississippi State University Library; George A. McLean, *Northeast Mississippi Daily Journal*; Ira B. Harkey, Jr., courtesy of Ira B. Harkey, Jr.; Wilson F. Minor, courtesy of Wilson F. "Bill" Minor Papers, Special Collections, Mississippi State University Library; Hazel Brannon Smith, courtesy of Wilson F. "Bill" Minor Papers, Special Collections, Mississippi State University Library; and Hodding Carter, Jr., courtesy of Hodding and Betty Werlein Carter Papers, Special Collections, Mississippi State University Library.

Library of Congress Cataloging-in-Publication Data

The press and race : Mississippi journalists confront the movement / edited by David R. Davies.
    p. cm.
Includes bibliographical references and index.

    1. Afro-Americans—Civil rights—Mississippi—History—20th century. 2. Press and politics—Mississippi—History—20th century. 3. Journalists—Mississippi—History—20th century. 4. American newspapers—Mississippi—History—20th century. 5. Mississippi—Race relations. 6. Civil rights movements—Mississippi—History—20th century. I. Davies, David R. (David Randall), 1957–

F350.N4 M57 2001
323.1′1960730762—dc21   00047730

British Library Cataloging-in-Publication Data available

ISBN 1-934110-52-3

Contents

Acknowledgments vii

Introduction 3
David R. Davies

Mississippi's Daily Press in Three Crises 17
Susan M. Weill

Percy Greene and the *Jackson Advocate* 55
Caryl A. Cooper

Jimmy Ward and the Jackson *Daily News* 85
David R. Davies & Judy Smith

J. Oliver Emmerich and the McComb *Enterprise-Journal* 111
David R. Davies

George A. McLean and the *Tupelo Journal* 137
Laura Nan Fairley

Ira B. Harkey, Jr., and the *Pascagoula Chronicle* 173
David L. Bennett

Wilson F. (Bill) Minor and the New Orleans *Times-Picayune* 209
Lawrence N. Strout

Hazel Brannon Smith and the *Lexington Advertiser* 233
Arthur J. Kaul

Hodding Carter, Jr., and the *Delta Democrat-Times* 265
Ginger Rudeseal Carter

About the Contributors 295

Index 297

Acknowledgments

This book is the cumulative effort of nine people—eight co-authors and myself—as well as the numerous people who contributed to the gathering of the information in the five-year maturation of the project. I make a modest effort here to offer thanks.

Of course, the book would not have been possible without the generous contributions of the many archivists and librarians who helped us navigate the primary source material that is the basis for the volume. In particular, Mattie Sink, Manuscripts Librarian at Mitchell Memorial Library, Mississippi State University, offered consistent help (from 1994 onward), as did the librarians at the State Historical Society of Wisconsin in Madison.

Others read versions of the manuscripts and offered valuable suggestions, including Hodding Carter III, Neil R. McMillen, Charles Dunagin, and Dub Shoemaker. I am deeply grateful to David Bennett, who not only contributed a chapter to this volume but who read all other chapters and offered detailed suggestions. This book is his project as much as mine.

The University of Southern Mississippi offered generous financial assistance to make the research for the book possible. In particular, the Aubrey Keith Lucas and Ella Ginn Lucas Endowment for Faculty Excellence provided valuable research funds.

Encouragement came from all corners: from Wm. David Sloan at the

Acknowledgments

University of Alabama; Seetha Srinivasan and Anne Stascavage at University Press of Mississippi; Arthur J. Kaul of the USM Journalism Department; and my colleagues and friends associated with the American Journalism Historians Association.

An editorial note: My colleagues and I chose to use the designation [*sic*] sparingly—only to denote a spelling error in original text. While a few extended quotations include stylistic errors, they were reproduced as originally written for accuracy's sake.

The book is dedicated to my wife, Ellen, and our son Graham. As always, to them I owe the greatest thanks.

Introduction

David R. Davies

For Southern newspapers as for American Southerners, the social upheaval in the years following *Brown v. Board of Education* were, as *Time* magazine put it on 20 February 1956, the "region's biggest running story since the end of slavery." The Southern press struggled with the region's difficult accommodation with the school desegregation ruling and with black Americans' demand for civil rights before and after. Desegregation would indeed prove a difficult story to tell.

In Mississippi newspapers did no better. This volume illuminates the broad array of print journalists' response to the Second Reconstruction in Mississippi, a state that was one of the nation's major civil rights battlegrounds. The volume covers the press from 1954, when the Supreme Court struck down school segregation as unconstitutional, to 1965, the year Congress approved the Voting Rights Act. The period encompasses some of the most important media events of the civil rights movement—the South's resistance to school desegregation through the 1950s and 1960s; the Freedom Rides to desegregate bus transportation in 1961; James Meredith's admission into the University of Mississippi in 1962; the assassination of Medgar Evers in 1963; and the events of Freedom Summer in 1964.

Press response was far from monolithic. A handful of Mississippi editors and newspapers defended blacks and challenged the racial mores of

Introduction

Mississippi society in the 1950s and early 1960s, a time when extreme racism dominated the state. Others responded to the Second Reconstruction by redoubling their support of Mississippi's segregated society. Still others responded with a defense of black Americans' legal rights tempered with a defense of segregation. The shades of editorial opinion were multifaceted, illustrating a broader range of journalistic response than usually described by Northern reporters who reported the South at the time or by historians. Both groups have tended to divide journalists into two camps—the segregationists and the integrationists, the villains and the heroes. In fact, only a handful of journalists in the South, and only Pascagoula's Ira B. Harkey, Jr., in Mississippi, publicly proclaimed themselves as integrationists. And segregationist sentiment varied widely even among so-called "moderate" editors such as Hazel Brannon Smith of Lexington and Hodding Carter, Jr., of Greenville. In sum, both the villains of the segregationist press and the heroes of moderation were complex. This volume attempts to explain why.

Susan M. Weill begins the volume with an overview of daily press response to three important challenges to the racial status quo in Mississippi—the *Brown* decision, Meredith's desegregation of all-white Ole Miss, and Freedom Summer. Defense of Mississippi's closed society was firm but nonetheless varied, she writes, through the three crises. Caryl A. Cooper examines the segregationist Percy Greene of the *Jackson Advocate*, Mississippi's dominant black newspaper through these years. David R. Davies and Judy Smith explore the staunchly segregationist Jackson *Daily News* and its outspoken editor, Jimmy Ward. Davies profiles J. Oliver Emmerich of McComb, the patriarch of the Mississippi press whose *Enterprise-Journal* ultimately helped end the bombings in south Mississippi in 1964. Laura Nan Fairley offers a thorough account of George McLean, Tupelo's renowned civic booster whose *Tupelo Journal* steered the region away from racial turmoil toward civic improvement. David L. Bennett explores the complicated integrationist and Pulitzer Prize-winning Harkey and his *Pascagoula Chronicle*, particularly his spirited and lonely defense of Meredith. Lawrence N. Strout chronicles the career of Wilson F. (Bill) Minor, still the dean of Mississippi's capital correspondents, who observed the breadth of the civil rights movement as the New Orleans *Times-Pica-*

Introduction

yune's Jackson correspondent. Arthur J. Kaul explicates the Progressive mind of Hazel Brannon Smith of Lexington, also a Pulitzer Prize winner, a crusader against the elite power structure in Holmes County until she lost her newspaper in the 1980s. And Ginger Rudeseal Carter explores the career of Mississippi's best-known journalist, Carter, and his Greenville *Delta Democrat-Times.*

Mississippi's journalistic response to the civil rights movement can only be understood in the context of the national press' treatment of black Americans in this period. Before the Supreme Court transformed desegregation into a national imperative, black Americans had long been virtually invisible in the pages of the nation's daily press. By and large, blacks did not merit a mention in most white-owned newspapers unless they committed a crime or died a violent death. On the rare occasions when blacks did merit a mention in the newspaper, they were further identified by race, and in many journals "black news" was segregated from "white news." In the late 1940s and early 1950s, however, journalists' treatment of blacks began to improve, if only by degrees.

In the early postwar years, some newspapers had retreated from their policy of identifying blacks by race in news articles, and a few had even begun to use courtesy titles. This development was in response to the pleas of black leaders, who believed that racial identification of blacks in crime stories had hurt the public image of the entire black race. The *New York Times* had announced a new policy of omitting racial designations in an editorial 11 August 1946. "This may seem like a small thing," the *Times'* editorialist wrote. "The Negroes don't think so." The *Times*, echoing the complaints of black leaders, said that racial designations, particularly in crime articles, increased ill will toward blacks. "The press, we believe, has a special and heavy responsibility, not merely editorially . . . but in its treatment of news." The *Times'* policy was not to refer to race unless doing so would serve a legitimate purpose, as in articles about a race riot or the search for a suspect in a crime. The new policy was enough of a departure from standard newspaper procedure to attract coverage by *Time* magazine.

A 1952 survey of thirty-four Deep South dailies by the *Columbus* (Ga.)

Introduction

Ledger found that only half were using courtesy titles for blacks or running regular columns or pages of black news. Still, that represented progress. *Editor & Publisher* magazine reported 13 December 1952 that the figures reflected "a significant change in [the] attitude of the press toward the Negro in the last decade." But a report on Southern newspapers' coverage of racial news released in 1949 by the Southern Regional Council (SRC), a biracial group of educators based in Atlanta, gave Southern newspapers mixed reviews. "The past ten years have seen a marked improvement in the coverage of racial news by Southern newspapers," the report said. Still, while the vast majority of Southern newspapers eschewed the explicit racism evident in news and comment in previous decades, the Council reported in *Race in the News*, blacks continued to be ignored in most newspapers unless they committed a crime against a white. And many newspapers persisted in inequitable treatment of news of the two races.

"North and South, most newspapers are consistently cruel to the colored man," observed the 1946–47 class of Harvard University's Nieman fellows—nine veteran reporters from around the country—in a 1947 book, *Your Newspaper*. "As pictured in many newspapers, the Negro is either an entertaining fool, a dangerous animal, or (on the comparatively rare occasions when a Negro's achievements are applauded) a prodigy of astonishing attainments, considering his race" (pp. 23–24). More often, blacks were simply ignored. Simeon Booker of *Jet*—a black-oriented magazine—in 1955 examined the numerous daily newspapers *Jet* received and found that most in both North and South included no obituaries or local social, civic, church, or business news about blacks. "It is shocking to appraise the sum total of so-called Negro news," Booker concluded in the January 1955 *Nieman Reports* (pp. 12–13).

"[T]he only time a black man ever got in the paper was if he were in trouble," recalled Harkey, editor and publisher of the *Pascagoula* (Miss.) *Chronicle* from 1948 to 1963. "He'd been arrested for something, he'd been accused of something, he'd been executed, he was being searched for as a fugitive. Particularly in the smaller newspapers, there was never a positive story about a black—blacks winning honors, graduating from school, getting scholarships and so on, nothing of that sort appeared in the newspapers." Such policies applied at most daily newspapers in cities both large and small, North and South. At the New Orleans *Times-Picayune*, where Harkey worked before and after World War II, photographers had standing instructions not to publish pictures of minorities. "If there was a crowd shot, and black faces were here or there," Harkey recalled in a 28 October 1992 speech at the University of Southern Mississippi, "they would be cut out or they would be airbrushed out or airbrushed white."

The few Southern newspapers that did print black news often segregated it on special pages, as the *Pascagoula Chronicle* had done before Harkey bought it, or relegated it to "colored editions" delivered only to black neighborhoods. The *St. Petersburg Times*, for example, started its "Negro makeover" page in 1939, remaking one newspaper page a week of black news in editions distributed only in black neighborhoods. The special page, printed daily beginning in 1948, was defended on the ground that it gave blacks a dignity not afforded them elsewhere. Such "Negro editions" were not uncommon. The *Montgomery Advertiser* and the *Alabama Journal* each published separate editions for blacks for more than thirty years, finally discontinuing them in the 1960s because they were too costly to produce. Southern newspapers' lack of interest in blacks was reflected in the racial makeup of daily newspapers: Most journals had virtually all-white staffs. Blacks were rare in both newsrooms and in journalism organizations, though black reporters made a few important inroads into print journalism in the early postwar years.

The United States Supreme Court's desegregation decision in 1954 pushed newspapers into writing more about blacks and about desegregation. The *Brown* case, a consolidation of school desegregation lawsuits in Kansas, South Carolina, Virginia, and Delaware, struck down segregation in public schools as unconstitutional. Segregation, the court found, violated the equal protection clause of the Fourteenth Amendment. The 1954 Supreme Court decision, coupled with the court's 1955 decision ordering desegregation to proceed "with all deliberate speed," transformed race relations and school desegregation into one of the most important running news stories of the postwar years. The thorny story of long-term societal change would eventually strain relations between Northern and

Introduction

Southern editors, exacerbate journalists' questions about objectivity, and sharpen newspapers' competition with television news.

A few of the nation's leading newspapers responded admirably to the challenge of covering desegregation, devoting considerable attention and resources to this complex and continuing story. In breadth and depth of coverage of civil rights, the *New York Times* was the undisputed leader among newspapers. The *Times* covered the *Brown* decision in detail from the beginning. The *Times* had first assigned a correspondent to cover the South in 1947, when *Times* editor Turner Catledge, a Mississippi native, had tapped Virginia-born John N. Popham to report on the tremendous social change brewing in the region. Popham quickly established himself as the premier journalistic authority on the South. "There was hardly a cow patch or a shade-tree mechanic below the Mason-Dixon line he did not know or a mayor or sheriff who did not know him, his Jim Dandy hat, and his extraordinary Tidewater Virginia accent," recalled Popham's colleague at the *Times*, Harrison E. Salisbury, in his autobiography, *A Time of Change* (1988) (p. 44).

But while the *New York Times* led the way in desegregation coverage, the vast majority of other daily newspapers followed far behind. In both the quality of their news coverage and the vitality of their editorial leadership, many daily newspapers were lacking. Newspaper editors in both South and North reflected the biases of white society and of their readership in racial matters. James McBride Dabbs, longtime director of the Southern Regional Council, said Southern newspapers' bias was to be expected. "Local newspapers, with exceptions so small as to be negligible, are owned, published and edited by Southern whites," Dabbs once wrote, as quoted in Harry Ashmore's *Civil Rights and Wrongs*. "Their subscribers are white; their advertisers are white. Is it not going a little far to expect complete objectivity and candor of a white Southern editor in discussing the duties of his subscribers and advertisers to members of a race that brings him no bread and butter?" (p. 63).

But beyond an opposition to violence, most of the nation's daily newspapers had been slow to exercise editorial leadership on the race issue. *Time* magazine's media correspondent concluded 20 February 1956 that, with a few exceptions, Southern newspapers in particular were doing "a patchy, pussyfooting job" of covering civil rights-related issues. Jere Moore, editor of the weekly *Union Register* in Milledgeville, Georgia, said newspapers had failed to exercise much leadership. "They have been weak-kneed when they should have been strong," Moore said (p. 76).

Southern newspapers were indeed offering little support for the law of the land, in sharp contrast to the enthusiastic support offered by Northern dailies, the black weeklies, and the nation's one black daily, the *Atlanta World*. Of the thirty largest dailies in the South and border states, the SERS concluded in *With All Deliberate Speed* (1957), all were hostile to *Brown* except for a dozen in the border states of Arkansas, Georgia, North Carolina, and Tennessee. "Once away from the border states," the Southern Education Reporting Service found, "no single large newspaper has emerged as enthusiastically integrationist." However, a few large and influential newspapers, such as the *St. Louis Post-Dispatch* and the *Louisville Courier-Journal*, had urged compliance with *Brown*. Others, such as the *Nashville Tennessean* and Carter's *Delta Democrat-Times*, had favored gradual integration (pp. 31–34).

Fewer than a dozen Southern newspapers were openly integrationist in these years, recalled Ashmore, editor of the *Charlotte* (N.C.) *News* in the late 1940s and the *Arkansas Gazette* in the 1950s, in *Civil Rights and Wrongs* (p. 63). Carter of Greenville said Southern newspapers reflected the conformist attitudes of the towns and small cities of the South, a factor that diminished the number of Southerners willing to challenge the racial status quo. Those who did were not necessarily in favor of integration; they were simply more likely to support obeying the law of the land in the Supreme Court's decision, or to favor to some degree the equal treatment of black citizens. The South, as Carter wrote in the *Delta Democrat-Times* of 7 November 1948, was the "only place in the western world where a man could become a liberal simply by urging obedience to the law."

As for newspapers' reporting of the civil rights movement, journalists in the 1950s agreed that the desegregation story after *Brown* was difficult and that the press had a spotty record of covering it. Press coverage generally concentrated on crises of desegregation as opposed to explanations of social change, a long-term process hard to chronicle for event-oriented daily newspapers. As desegregation efforts increased in the late 1950s, Northern newspapers turned greater attention to the South, prompting an influx of reporters from Northern news organizations into the region. "There are as many Yankee reporters dropping off planes and trains as there were carpetbaggers in the 1860s," complained the segregationist Thomas R. Waring, editor of the *Charleston* (S.C.) *News and Courier*, in the *Newsweek* of 2 April 1956. Sixty reporters were on hand at the University of Alabama riots in 1956. Seventy-five had flocked in 1955 to the Sumner, Mississippi, trial of the men accused of killing fourteen-year-old Emmett Till.

The Till trial had been a turning point in increasing coverage of racial friction in the South. The murder, as journalist David Halberstam has observed in *The Fifties* (1993), was "the first great media event of the civil rights movement" (p. 437). The brutality of the crime "electrified the large black communities in the nation's Northern industrial cities," Halberstam writes (p. 436), and Northern journalists sensitized to Southern racial issues by the *Brown* decision jumped on the story. Reporters, photographers, television cameramen, radio announcers, and newspaper columnists from across the country crowded into tiny Sumner for the trial of Roy Bryant and J.W. Milam, half-brothers accused of killing young Till. The Chicago youth had been visiting relatives in Money, Mississippi, when he had either whistled at or spoken suggestively to a white woman in a grocery. For violating the rules of white supremacy, he was kidnapped from his uncle's home, his body tied to a cotton-gin fan and thrown into the Tallahatchie River.

Southern resentment against Northern journalists who came South to report racial unrest was widespread. Southern editors, particularly those conservative on racial matters, deeply resented the influx of Northern reporters covering Southern racial news after *Brown*. A schism developed among some editors, who divided according to North vs. South and moderate vs. conservative. Southern editors, particularly those who defended Southern racial practices, considered Northern newspapers as overplaying Southern racial strife while ignoring Northern racial problems. Southerners also resented many Northern editors' agreement with the Supreme

Introduction

Court's decision that segregation was inherently unequal and unjust. This North vs. South dispute was evident in public feuds between editors and in spirited, sometimes heated debates at editors' meetings.

The segregation story proved especially vexing for the wire services, which served both Northern and Southern newspapers, whose editors were always scanning the wires for evidence of bias. So many Southern editors complained that the wire services were overplaying Southern racial problems that both the United Press and Associated Press assigned reporters on several occasions to cover race problems outside of the South. Editors in both North and South wanted the wire services to cover racial problems outside their region, on the assumption that racial problems far from home were being downplayed.

Editor & Publisher magazine, the newspaper trade journal, noted with dismay the emotional dispute over desegregation coverage. "[W]e have rarely seen the heat that is now being generated between editors of two sections of the country over the desegregation issue," editor Robert U. Brown observed in 12 November 1955, after the trial in the Till case. Northern and Southern differences, a 1957 editorial said, were compounded by the rise of interpretive reporting and by the intense emotionalism evident on both sides. The editorial added that the two camps should recognize differences in their points of view and desist from name-calling. "We do not condone this situation," *Editor & Publisher*'s editorialist wrote. "Neither side helps its own case by charging the other with errors."

Mississippi journalists not only reflected the journalism profession of which they were a part but also the state and communities they served. The Magnolia State's journalistic response to the civil rights movement must also be understood, then, in the context of Mississippi's treatment of black Americans in this period. Well into the second half of the twentieth century, Mississippi had a deplorable record of mistreating black Americans.

Mississippi in the postwar years was "the closed society," as historian James Silver put it in his 1964 book of the same name. Segregation was entrenched, and blacks were relegated to second-class citizenship. As Weill explains in the first essay in this book, Mississippi's blacks—most of them impoverished—attended poorly funded, inferior schools. Blacks and whites had little contact with one another, separated by Jim Crow laws which kept lunch counters, buses, restaurants, hotels, beaches—virtually all public areas—strictly segregated. A complex web of Mississippi laws required tests of would-be voters, but whites always seemed to pass the tests, and blacks always seemed to fail them. With no political power, blacks had little avenue but their own activism to fight the society that oppressed them.

It's not surprising that most Mississippi newspapers reflected the orthodoxy of the closed society to one degree or another. Each of the editors profiled in this volume was Southern by birth; most were born in Mississippi or the Deep South. All came of age before mid-century and before serious challenges to the hegemony of the closed society had ever been mounted. Moreover, the editors were not only journalists but businessmen and women deeply dependent upon the advertisers and readers of their respective communities. "For the most part, they were fully as honest, hard-working, upstanding, and God-fearing as their harshest critics," historian Neil R. McMillen wrote of the segregationists he profiled in *The Citizens' Council* (1971), an observation that could equally be applied to Mississippi journalists. "That they often exhibited the ignoblest prejudices even as they professed the loftiest ideals should surprise only beginning students of human behavior" (p. ix). For these journalists, to question the basic tenets of the closed society was to fall out of step with the guiding principles of their Southern upbringing and the mores of their communities.

But some editors did. Why? A few common threads run through the background of editors who challenged some elements of the closed society. Some, like Carter and McLean, had attended college outside of Mississippi and came to question the "Southern way of life." Others, such as Smith and Emmerich, saw the negative impact upon their communities by civil-rights related violence against blacks and were prompted to speak out. Many of the editors deplored the tactics of the worst elements of the segregationists, particularly the economic reprisals favored by the Citizens' Councils, an anti-integration group formed just after *Brown*.

Several of the editors' shared viewpoints were rooted in the fact that

Introduction

all were Southerners commenting upon a Southern news story. For each of these editors, civil rights activism and white resistance to it were vital issues of the day that dominated politics and daily life in Mississippi and the South. To comment and report on any aspect of such a volatile topic was far riskier than editorializing, say, on the latest crisis in Afghanistan. ("Afghanistanism," a term coined by editor Jenkin Lloyd Jones of the *Tulsa World* in 1948, describes the editorialist's propensity to philosophize in print about insignificant, faraway issues rather than explosive local ones.) It was in recognition of this fact that virtually all of the editors profiled in this volume deeply resented what they saw as the hypocrisy of Northern reporters coming from racially troubled Northern cities to cover Southern racial problems. The fact that the Northern racial story differed substantially from the Southern—the former's segregation was de facto and the latter's was de jure—was not lost on these editors, but they resented it all the same.

The editors shared another view. No matter the extent to which they challenged segregation, they tended to reflect white viewpoints of the civil rights struggle rather than the black. An obvious point, it had far-reaching effects journalistically. After all, if even Northern editors were painfully slow to recognize and print black perspectives, it should come as no surprise that Southern editors were just as sluggish to do so. Southerners by birth and members of their community's elite, even the most outspoken of the journalistic critics of the closed society relied almost exclusively upon white officialdom for their news sources. Reporters and editors, as any beginning reporting textbook will explain, are far too prone to overrely upon officialdom in any case, but for Mississippi journalists this constituted a fatal journalistic lapse. By and large Mississippi journalists failed to recognize and to print the black perspective on the civil rights story; their news stories and editorial views about the movement usually reflected the dominant white viewpoint. Northern reporters, critical of Mississippi racial orthodoxy and covering a region that, to them, was as foreign as Afghanistan, saw the civil rights activists as central components of the Southern story. As a result, Northern journalism tended to be more balanced, as did wire service accounts, which were written for both Northern and Southern media outlets.

Introduction

One last, important commonality was the courage each exhibited to differ with the closed society. Though some of these editors were derided by civil rights activists for not going far enough to support black rights, it took genuine courage to speak against the closed society; the commonplace violence of Mississippi in these years was a constant reminder of the risks of speaking out.

In Mississippi as in the nation, the newspaper editors who challenged racial orthodoxy were awarded the journalism profession's most prestigious prizes, a recognition by their peers of the courage implicit in challenging racial norms. Three editors profiled in this volume were awarded the Pulitzer Prize, journalism's most prestigious honor. Carter of the Greenville *Delta Democrat-Times* won the Pulitzer for his editorials in 1946. Harkey of the *Pascagoula Chronicle* won the same award in 1963, and the following year so did Hazel Brannon Smith of the *Lexington Advertiser*, the first woman to win the editorial writing award. Other Southern editors who won the Pulitzer for their civil rights stands were Buford Boone of the *Tuscaloosa* (Ala.) *News*, who won in 1957; Ashmore of the *Arkansas Gazette*, 1958; Ralph McGill of the *Atlanta Constitution*, 1959; and Lenoir Chambers of the *Norfolk Virginian-Pilot*, 1960.

These editors, and all others in the South in these years, faced daily decisions on covering and commenting on the most important running news story since slavery. In Mississippi some parted with their neighbors, advertisers, and readers to defend some element of black rights. Others mirrored their white readership with even greater resolve. All of the editors responded to the civil rights movement according to the particular circumstances of their communities and the contours of their own individual personalities. Most importantly, in community after community, all reflected Mississippi's painfully slow accommodation with the Second Reconstruction.

References

Ashmore, Harry. *Civil Rights & Wrongs*. (New York: Pantheon Books, 1994).

Davies, David R. An Industry in Transition. Ph.D. diss., University of Alabama, 1997. A portion of this introduction is derived from sections of chapter 6.

Introduction

Halberstam, David. *The Fifties.* (New York: Villard Books, 1993).

McMillen, Neil R. *The Citizens' Council.* (Urbana, Il.: University of Illinois Press, 1971).

Salisbury, Harrison. *A Time of Change.* (New York: Harper & Row, 1988).

Shoemaker, Don. *With All Deliberate Speed.* (New York: Harper, 1957).

Southern Regional Council. *Race in the News.* (Atlanta: Southern Regional Council, 1954).

Svirsky, Leon, ed. *Your Newspaper.* (New York: Macmillan, 1947).

The Press and Race: Mississippi Journalists Confront the Movement

Mississippi's Daily Press in Three Crises

Susan M. Weill

"The majority of Southern editors and publishers have been cynically defending a myth they know to be untrue," media analyst Ted Poston wrote in 1967, "—white superiority, Negro indolence, and a baseless contention that the region's magnolia-scented values would triumph over the moral and legal might of the federal government" (*Race and the News Media*, p. 63).

Hodding Carter III, a reporter and editor at the Greenville (Mississippi) *Delta Democrat-Times* during several decades of the civil rights movement, had a different interpretation. He defended his fellow editors in 1968 as people who were products of their time. "My point is that this was not a case of an evil conspiracy of bad men," Carter wrote, "but of men totally reflecting the community in which they moved in the same way that most other newspaper publishers do" ("Comment on Coverage in the Domestic Press," *The Black American and the Press*, Jack Lyle, editor, p.39).

The manner in which the Southern press has dealt with the issue of civil rights and the black struggle for equality has been a subject of much debate. Critics have condemned Southern newspapers for their erratic reporting and inflammatory interpretation. But other observers maintain that while most Southern newspapers were averse to racial integration, as espoused in their editorials, and while they failed to offer much interpretation of the issues, they generally did report the facts. Media researcher Sharon Bramlett concluded in "Southern vs. Northern Newspaper Coverage of a Race Crisis—The Lunch Counter Sit-In Movement, 1960–1964: An Assessment of Social Responsibility" (1987) that civil rights coverage did not differ substantially between newspapers of the two diverse regions.

Although the Southern press in general has often found itself the target of scorn, the Mississippi daily press is often viewed with particular disdain. Most of the state's press, according to James Silver in *Mississippi: The Closed Society* (1964), stood "vigilant guard over the racial, economic, political, and religious orthodoxy of the state" (p. 30). Hodding Carter III agreed with this analysis, conceding to Robert Hooker in "Race and the News Media in Mississippi, 1962–1964" (1971), "None of us began to meet our responsibilities in the media and most of us still don't" (p. 241).

Ensconced as they were within the "closed society," one of rigid and entrenched norms based on white supremacy and black oppression, the editors of the Mississippi daily press faced three major social crises in one turbulent decade: the 1954 *Brown v. Board of Education* Supreme Court decision; the 1962 federally mandated desegregation of the University of Mississippi; and the 1964 civil rights activism of Freedom Summer. Each was a crisis because it threatened Mississippi's entrenched racial segregation as well as the power structure that enforced it. *Brown v. Board of Education* ruled segregated public schools unconstitutional; James Meredith became the first black person of record to attend Ole Miss; and Freedom Summer signaled a changing national climate that would ultimately bring civil rights to all people regardless of race.

Most editors of the Mississippi daily press perceived these three events as major disruptions of Southern tradition, as evidenced by their editorials. But, as this chapter will demonstrate, that notion ranged in fervor. Many of the editors expressed outrage, and many encouraged outright nonviolent defiance, to any suggestion of racial desegregation. Several editors urged cautious acceptance of gradual desegregation, only to quickly reverse their position. Editorial response to all three crises was far from monolithic.

The state's daily press was nearly unanimous, however, in the view that no Mississippian, black or white, was ready for the reality of a racially integrated society. Many of the editors argued that federal civil rights laws unconstitutionally revoked the individual rights of the states. And according to the vast majority of the Mississippi daily press editorials written from 1954 through 1964, the notion that blacks and whites were equal as races of people remained unacceptable and inconceivable.

To evaluate the coverage given to these three events by the Mississippi daily press, a comprehensive analysis was conducted of every issue of the newspapers during the critical months of these crises: May 1954, the month of the *Brown* decision, and August 1954, the month before the state's public schools were to open that year; September 1962, when the first black of record enrolled at the University of Mississippi; and June through August 1964, Freedom Summer. In all, about four thousand issues of Mississippi daily newspapers were examined. From these newspapers, nearly a thousand editorials and six thousand news articles and headlines were evaluated. For purposes of this analysis, unsigned editorials published in a newspaper as that newspaper's opinion are credited to the editor of the newspaper in which it was published.

The daily newspapers included were the *Clarksdale Press Register*, Columbus *Commercial Dispatch*, Corinth *Daily Corinthian*, Greenville *Delta Democrat-Times*, *Greenwood Commonwealth*, Greenwood *Morning Star*, Grenada *Sentinel-Star*, *Gulfport Daily Herald*, *Hattiesburg American*, Jackson *Clarion-Ledger*, Jackson *Daily News*, *Laurel Leader-Call*, McComb *Enterprise-Journal*, *Meridian Star*, *Natchez Democrat*, Natchez *Times*, Pascagoula *Chronicle*, Pascagoula *Mississippi Press*, *Starkville Daily News*, Tupelo *Daily Journal*, *Vicksburg Herald*, *Vicksburg Evening Post* and the West Point *Times Leader*. The Jackson *State-Times*, a daily Mississippi newspaper that acquired a reputation for avoiding segregationist excesses during its brief existence, began publication in September 1954 and ceased publication in January 1961, thus being excluded from this analysis. Except for 1954, when there were twenty daily newspapers published in Mississippi, the other time periods totaled nineteen.

Most of the daily newspapers were published in Mississippi counties that had black and white populations of equal numbers. Washington County, where the Greenville *Delta-Democrat Times* is published, had the highest proportion of blacks at seventy percent; Alcorn County, where the *Daily Corinthian* is published, had the lowest proportion of blacks at fifteen percent. Hinds County, where the state capital is located and where the Jackson *Clarion-Ledger* and Jackson *Daily News* were published, had a population that was about forty percent black during the 1950s and 1960s.

To frame the findings of this study, the coverage of the three time periods by the Mississippi daily press was evaluated through the recommendations of social responsibility made by the Hutchins Commission to the media in 1947, just a few years before the *Brown* decision. Robert Hutchins, then chancellor at the University of Chicago, was contracted by Henry Luce of Time, Inc., to conduct an extensive study on the freedom and responsibility of the press. The ensuing Commission on Freedom of the Press, also known as the Hutchins Commission, was composed of notables Archibald MacLeish, a former Secretary of State, Arthur Schlesinger, a professor of history at Harvard, and Beardsley Ruml, chair of the Federal Reserve Bank of New York. After a five-year intensive study of American mass communication, they released *A Free and Responsible Press: A General Report on Mass Communication: Newspapers, Radio, Motion Pictures, Magazines and Books* (1947), a publication that recommended social responsibility to the news media in five ways: "providing a truthful, comprehensive, and intelligent account of the day's events in a context which gives them meaning; providing a forum for the exchange of comment and criticism; projecting a representative picture of the constituent groups in society; presenting and clarifying the goals and values of the society; and providing a full access to the day's intelligence" (p. ix).

Journalist Walter Lippmann, who was considered one of the most powerful opinion makers of his time, had expressed concern in his book, *Public Opinion* (1922), that editors often failed to be socially responsible, that is, they controlled public access to the news as it suited their purpose (p. 42). Social responsibility as an obligation of the press was also incorporated into the 1923 Canons of Journalism of the American Society of Newspaper Editors. A list of press requirements describing the specifics of social responsibility, however, was not drawn together and formally stated until 1947, by the Hutchins Commission. This chapter will explore whether the Mississippi daily press abided by these recommendations in their coverage of three major events that threatened the fabric of Southern society and the white power structure that controlled it.

Mississippi's History of Segregation and White Power

Press coverage of the civil rights era can only be understood in the context of the history of Mississippi's "closed society," a firmly established system of racial segregation and discrimination that developed during and after years of slavery. In 1860, just prior to the Civil War, Mississippi was inhabited by half a million blacks held in bondage who represented over fifty percent of the state's populace. In 1900, three decades after the Thirteenth Amendment to the United States Constitution terminated the South's "peculiar institution," free blacks, with few rights and privileges, constituted nearly sixty percent of Mississippi's people. After World War I, blacks began to migrate northward in hope of a better life, and by 1960, only forty percent of Mississippi's two million people were of African descent. Most of them faced a life of poverty, and the political process was closed to them.

The search for a better life included the pursuit of civil rights—access to legal, social and economic equality—and civil rights were slow in coming to people of color in the United States in general, and in the South in particular. Congress had granted black men suffrage with passage of the Reconstruction Acts in 1867, and that year more than sixty thousand emancipated slaves registered to vote in Mississippi. By 1954, however, because of intimidation, restrictive poll taxes, and violence by the Ku Klux Klan and other groups, the number of blacks registered to vote in Mississippi had dropped to twenty thousand. The "closed society" had no place for black voters, whose political power would certainly challenge established white control. "Most blacks were afraid to try to register, and to vote, and with reason," wrote John Dittmer in *Local People: The Struggle for Civil Rights in Mississippi* (1994). "Moreover, with all the state and local candidates for office pledged to maintain white supremacy, there was simply no one to vote for. No candidate dared to seek the black vote" (p. 28).

In the 1960s, a decade after *Brown* mandated the desegregation of the nation's public schools, Mississippi's white-controlled primary and secondary educational institutions remained segregated, as did most of the state's society. Movie theaters in Mississippi towns relegated blacks to a balcony known as the "colored section"; waiting rooms in Mississippi doctors' and dentists' offices were segregated. Blacks in Mississippi towns lived predominantly in poverty-stricken "quarters," and most rural Mississippi blacks lived in sharecropper hovels. White Mississippi's contact with black Mississippi was most often limited to relationships with black maids, black yardmen, black laborers or black field hands, and although usually cordial and polite on the surface, these relationships were almost always white controlled.

The economic repression and social discrimination faced by Mississippi blacks was not written into the state's laws; this was not necessary. As noted by historian Neil McMillen's *Dark Journey: Black Mississippians in the Age of Jim Crow* (1990), "Wherever the two races came together, the forces of social habit and white opinion were in themselves usually sufficient to ensure that the races knew their places and occupied them with neither statute nor a 'white' or a 'colored' sign to direct the way" (p. 10).

There was, of course, organized and "socially acceptable" protest to threats of racial integration. The Citizens' Council, founded in Mississippi in 1953 to maintain segregation in anticipation of *Brown v. Board of Education*, condemned the violence and terrorism of the Ku Klux Klan but shared its objective of preserving the traditional South. Established by Robert Patterson, the manager of a plantation in Leflore County, Mississippi, the Citizens' Council enjoyed a membership boom after the *Brown* decision. The Council, according to Neil McMillen in *The Citizens' Council: Organized Resistance to the Second Reconstruction, 1954–1964* (1971), "urged concerned and patriotic citizens to stand together forever firm against communism and mongrelization" (p. 17). The Council suggested, McMillen notes, that "the Negroes' ultimate motive for desegregating the schools was integration in the white bedroom" (p. 36). Consequently, the Citizens' Council advocated noncompliance to *Brown* and began to organize its own system of private schools around the state. An organization that greatly influenced Mississippi government well into the 1960s and claimed a membership of sixty thousand in more than two hundred groups around the state, the Citizens' Council was supported by most Mississippi legislators and by the Hederman family, who owned the Jackson *Clarion-Ledger* and the Jackson *Daily News* (McMillen, *Citizens'*

Council, p. 25). Extensive coverage of the Council and its activities by these major daily newspapers provided credibility as well as free advertising (Weill, p. 116).

When the *Brown v. Board of Education* decision was handed down in May 1954, Mississippi's white power elite, including the editors of the Mississippi daily press, was ready. *Brown* would stir the interest of the national media once again in the Magnolia State, and it would offer a ray of hope to Mississippi blacks seeking quality education for their children. But it would take more than a Supreme Court mandate to pry open the iron jaws of the "closed society."

Brown vs Board of Education and the Mississippi Daily Press

Mississippi's segregated school systems were funded inequitably for years. In the early 1900s, black children constituted more than fifty percent of Mississippi's public school students, but black schools received less than twenty percent of the state's public school allocation. That was not the only disparity. Many black schools in Mississippi were held in privately owned buildings such as churches and community centers and were thus not eligible for public funding for repairs or improvements. According to McMillen in *Dark Journey* (1990), one school official thought the majority of black school buildings during the early 1940s were "unfit even for cotton storage," and most had no water supply or outhouse (pp. 84–85).

School desegregation had been a longtime goal of the National Association for the Advancement of Colored People because black and white students in seventeen Southern states attended segregated schools that while separate were certainly not equal. By 1950, black students constituted nearly sixty percent of the public school students in Mississippi, but they received only thirty percent of public school funds. Annual salaries for black teachers were half of what white teachers earned.

There was a specific reason for this underfunding of black education in Mississippi. According to McMillen in *Dark Journey*, "Throughout the Jim Crow era, the single greatest impediment to better Afro-American schools was white fear of the revolutionary and economic implications of educating a subservient workforce" (p. 90).

The editors of Mississippi's daily press in 1954 knew the court's 1896

Plessy v. Ferguson "separate but equal" decree had been ignored in the state for more than half a century. Most of them probably thought, as did editor Fred Sullens of the Jackson *Daily News*, that *Brown* would not be enforced either. To these editors, *Brown* may have appeared as simply another token attempt at change by the federal government. As Sullens observed on 24 May 1954, "For the fifty-eight years the mandate of the Supreme Court was on the books declaring that separate facilities must be equal, this was never enforced. How much harder will it be if they try to enforce this most recent version?"

Reaction to *Brown* by the editors of the Mississippi daily press varied from outright defiance to cautious acceptance, the latter usually followed by a quick reversal. Most of the twenty Mississippi daily newspapers published only two or three editorials pertaining to *Brown*, though the issue was unquestionably a top news story on the front pages of the Mississippi daily press, usually through Associated Press (AP) and United Press International (UPI) reports. Following *Brown*, Mississippi editors were concerned that black and white children should not be schooled in the same facilities because this could lead to integrated socializing, which was unacceptable to most white, and some black, Mississippians at the time. The editors also warned that black and white children should not be schooled together because they believed black children would not be able to compete academically with white children. Many of the editors said that all Mississippi residents, both black and white, equally shared these concerns. Why the white editors believed they could speak for the black community, however, was never explained. No blacks were quoted, no black names mentioned as sources.

On 17 May 1954, Mississippi Governor Hugh White told the press he was "disappointed" and saddened by *Brown*. He also said, "We shall resist by every legal means at our command." The governor was quoted in the state's daily press saying that he doubted the schools in Mississippi would be affected by *Brown* for a half century, just as the state had not complied with *Plessy v. Ferguson* for fifty years. Other Mississippi elected officials were not so reserved. Senator James Eastland told readers of the state's daily newspapers on 18 May 1954, "The South will not abide by, nor obey, this legislative decision by a political court." Senator John Stennis agreed but offered a different criticism. He told readers, "The justices abandoned their role as judges of the law and organized themselves into a group of social engineers." Mississippi Lieutenant Governor Carroll Gartin resented federal interference in what he considered a local issue. "Segregation is our last, most important, states' right," he told the readership of the Jackson *Daily News* on 3 August 1954.

Editors of the state's daily newspapers gave the story front-page play, and several stepped outside their positions in the "closed society" to criticize state officials for their remarks. "Every responsible individual with whom we have talked about the matter is using his good sense and refuses to be stampeded into making damn fool remarks," Hodding Carter, Jr., of the Greenville *Delta Democrat-Times* wrote on 20 May 1954. "This isn't so of our politicians and state observers." George McLean at the Tupelo *Daily Journal*, though no supporter of school desegregation, disapproved of politicians using the issue for personal gain. On 20 May 1954, he wrote, "Southern politicians are occupied full time nowadays denouncing the Supreme Court. But when the novelty has worn off this sport, they will seek something more spectacular to keep their names before the public as guardians of Dixie education." Taking a different view was Harriet Gibbons of the *Laurel Leader-Call*, the only woman editor of a Mississippi daily in 1954. In her sole comment on the decision that summer, she encouraged Mississippi's public officials to stay calm. Gibbons did not openly support the desegregation of the state's public schools, but she also did not support violence or racially charged diatribes to maintain the traditions of the South. "Nothing is gained," she wrote on 18 May 1954, "by politicians taking this subject as an opportunity for inflaming passion and arousing prejudice."

Outright defiance of *Brown* was the approach taken in the state's capital, where the Jackson *Clarion-Ledger* was never hesitant to proclaim its convictions, particularly in support of the state's traditional conservatism. On 18 May 1954, an editorial in the *Clarion-Ledger* referred to *Brown* as "a black day of tragedy for the South, and for both races." Other than that one editorial, however, the only other staff-written comment in the *Clarion-Ledger* regarding *Brown* in May 1954 came in the form of a suggested alternative from Charles M. Hills in his "Affairs of State" column. "If integration becomes a painful fact one of these days and we of the white race just can't take it, why not look into television education?" He wrote on 25 May 1954. "Children could get their education right in their own homes, and certainly there is no law yet that could force us to invite negro children into our living rooms."

The Jackson *Daily News* made news itself in early August 1954 after being purchased by the rival Hedermans of the *Clarion-Ledger*. Fred Sullens, who continued as editor of the *Daily News* after the sale, voiced his interpretation of *Brown* as the final insult from a Supreme Court that was, he believed, determined to destroy the Southern way of life regardless of the confusion and carnage it caused. "The decision was the worst thing that has happened to the South since carpetbaggers and scalawags took charge," he wrote on 18 May 1954. "Mississippi will never consent to placing white and Negro children in the same public schools. White and Negro children in the same schools will lead to miscegenation. Miscegenation leads to mixed marriages and mixed marriages lead to mongrelization of the human race."

Sullens often elaborated on his traditional Southern belief that blacks were mentally inferior to whites as a means to bolster his continual criticism of the Supreme Court decision. He vowed on 23 May 1954 that *Brown* would be ignored in Mississippi. "There may be many doubts as to what other states intend to do," he wrote, "but the people of Mississippi have always had the intelligence and courage sufficient to manage their own destiny." Later in the summer, Sullens concluded that the high court's decision was illegal. "It is a flagrant defiance of an essential and firmly established social order," he declared on 8 August 1954. "No matter how the Supreme Court may phrase its final decree, that decree will not be obeyed by the people of Mississippi. Public sentiment is still the law and our minds are still governed by common sense." On 1 August 1954, Sullens praised "thinking" blacks who supported segregation and he claimed these "thinking" blacks were not concerned about equal rights. He did not, however, mention who these "thinking" blacks were by name. "The great masses of the Negroes in Mississippi are happy and contented in their schools, churches and social activities," he wrote. "Thoughtful, hardworking peace-loving Negroes prefer their own schools, churches and places of entertainment. They are not seeking social equality. Why not let them have what they want?"

In agreement with the Jackson daily newspapers was W. H. Harris, editor of the West Point *Times-Leader*. Harris believed school desegregation would not be enforced in Mississippi for many years. "None of us think for one minute that we are about to throw white schools open to Negro children now," he wrote on 18 May 1954. "Your writer firmly believes that he will some day see non-segregated schools in the South. But first, we must pass through a lengthy period of equalized school facilities which will lift the Negro onto a higher level—mentally, socially and morally." Harris, along with Sullens of the Jackson *Daily News*, was vehement in his denouncement of *Brown*.

Firm opposition came from several other newspaper editors. Andrews Harmon of the *Hattiesburg American* editorialized on 21 May 1954 that it was in the best interests of everyone, black and white, to keep the schools racially segregated. On 2 August 1954, just before the beginning of the 1954–55 school year, Harmon encouraged his readers to act on their beliefs. "If all the people of Mississippi want to retain racial segregation in the public schools they can do it simply by standing together," he wrote. "No power on earth can compel more than a million people to do something that is against the law of God and nature."

No one agreed more than James H. Skewes, editor of the *Meridian Star*. Two days after the *Brown* decision, on 19 May 1954, Skewes wrote, "We violently disagree with Supreme Court school segregation politics. Neither average Southern white, or Southern black, approves." The *Vicksburg Evening Post* supported segregation but urged calm. "Basically, we disagree with the decision," editor L. P. Cashman wrote on 21 May 1954. "We do not believe either colored or white Mississippians will ever be happy under a system of non-segregation. By their very natures, the races are apart."

Although not a proponent of *Brown* or desegregated schools, the Mississippi daily newspaper editor who devoted the most time and effort to offering his readers possible alternatives to the mandate was J. Oliver Emmerich, editor and publisher of the McComb *Enterprise-Journal*. An outspoken supporter of the traditional South, Emmerich called for his community to remain calm in the face of *Brown*, and on 17 May 1954 he voiced support for a measure under consideration by the Mississippi legislature that was aimed at providing more equitable funding to the state's black schools. The bill was a thwarted attempt to counteract *Brown*.

The next day, 18 May 1954, Emmerich announced in his front-page editorial column, "Neither race wants an integrated school system in Mississippi."

While seeking endorsement for his traditional Southern views, Emmerich sought blacks with segregationist views to substantiate his own. This was most likely an effort to validate his beliefs, and possibly a means, although probably ineffectual, to sway his black readers. Emmerich found such a person in Davis Lee, the black publisher of the *Newark* (New Jersey) *Telegraph*, whose editorial on *Brown* was reprinted on the front page of the McComb newspaper on 9 August 1954, and warned: "Southern Negroes may lose a lot more than they gain. Integration in the North and East is not a howling success. This movement to integrate the schools of the South is loaded with more racial dynamite than appears on the surface and the Negro will be the one who is blown away."

In the Mississippi Delta, editor Virgil Adams at the Greenwood *Morning Star* viewed *Brown* as inevitable and undesirable. He agreed that the consequences of the decision were detrimental to both blacks and whites. In an editorial published the day after the decision, 18 May 1954, Adams wrote: "This means that the South must adjust itself for the impact of the mixing of the races in at least part of the schools. We fully expect there will be a greater inter-marriage of the races and some other evil effects which are not good for either race."

The daily Mississippi newspapers in the Delta were not in editorial agreement, however. No editor of the Mississippi daily press rejected his state's outright defiance of *Brown* more than Hodding Carter, Jr., of the Greenville *Delta Democrat-Times*. On 18 May 1954, Carter displayed a global consciousness unusual for the times and urged his readers to consider the positive aspects of the mandate: "Whatever the South thinks of it, there is no doubt that [the decision] will raise America's prestige in the world, and especially in the world of brown and yellow and black people. And to us in the South, it gives a challenge to replace trickery and subterfuge in our educational structure with an honest realization that every American child has the right to an equal education."

Carter did not advocate school desegregation except at the college level. On 22 August 1954, as Greenville's public schools were enrolling students, the *Delta Democrat-Times* published a front-page editorial that clearly stated Carter's view of the situation. "A majority of Southerners," he wrote, "are not ready for the reality of integration."

Carter's son, Hodding Carter III, recalled in an interview that his father's published views about desegregation were often altered as a matter of survival. "He pushed the public as far as he thought possible, pushed it a little further, and then fell back for a while when the reaction blew hot." Carter III said his father believed desegregation would take at least a generation and was by necessity a gradual process. The elder Carter, according to his son, "thought that civic rights—voting, equal job opportunities—should be stressed ahead of those that involved a massive assault on the old social citadels, of which the public schools were a leading component in the rural South."

Carter briefly had an editorial ally on the banks of the Mississippi River in Adams County, where the *Natchez Democrat* published one of the few editorials supporting the Supreme Court's decision. An unnamed writer, perhaps editor Elliott Trimble, stepped beyond the traditional Southern views of the newspaper on 17 May 1954. "Certainly there can be pride that the Supreme Court has finally faced up to what has obviously been the law all the time," the editorial stated. "Administered with goodwill, it may prove an important step in clearing up the whole matter of segregation. Children growing up together can hardly maintain the deep suspicions which have so complicated this problem."

But two days later, on 19 May 1954, a different voice emerged. "It is our considered opinion that we shall live to regret this Supreme Court decision—not necessarily because formal segregation has been abolished, but because the court reasoned and acted capriciously without due regard to its position in the division of power among the three branches of government and because of the non-judicial considerations which guided it."

On 15 August 1954, just before the school year was to begin, the *Natchez Democrat* observed that blacks and whites agreed on segregation. "The only conflict is that which has been engendered by ratical [*sic*] minority elements seeking to impose their will upon the majority," The *Natchez Democrat* reported. Why the tone changed so drastically in the *Natchez Democrat* editorials may never be known. Hodding Carter III's recollection of his father's reaction to *Brown* may also have been true for Trimble. Perhaps advertisers pressured the newspaper, or threats of bodily harm were made, or community outrage was overwhelming. For whatever reason, the editorial pen at the *Natchez Democrat* that at first supported the concept of *Brown* was definitely refocused.

Another advocate of a calm approach to the inevitable changes in Southern society was George McLean, publisher of the Tupelo *Daily Journal*. McLean's immediate response to *Brown* was an editorial on 18 May 1954, in which he wrote, "The South will no doubt respond with a gradual reaction to the Supreme Court ruling rather than changing its school system overnight. This is not a time for high emotion or thoughtless action." McLean was the only editor of the Mississippi daily press in 1954 who discussed in print the economic implications of the Supreme Court decision. In an editorial on 18 August 1954, he suggested that federal funding for the state's schools might be threatened if *Brown* was ignored, and he would ultimately be proven correct.

As the Mississippi academic year began in late August 1954, none of the Mississippi public schools was racially desegregated. Nor was the Mississippi public school system abolished as threatened by the governor. In 1955, a Supreme Court directive known as *Brown II* ordered "prompt and reasonable," though not immediate, compliance to *Brown v. Board of Education*. It was not until a decade later, however, that a few schools in Mississippi began to comply, and then primarily because a federal court order threatened to revoke federal education funds from schools that refused.

Although the Mississippi daily press did not advocate violence to repudiate *Brown*, the newspapers did, as an aggregate, reject the *Brown* mandate. The usual rationalization by the editors was a desire to preserve the traditional Southern way of life, one they claimed was acceptable to all Mississippians, black and white. Less than a decade later, when the state was ordered by another federal decree in 1962 to desegregate its schools on the college level, similar arguments were set forth by the editors. The "closed society" was on the verge of being forced open.

The Desegregation of Ole Miss and the Mississippi Daily Press

Eight years after *Brown*, the Fifth Circuit Court of Appeals ordered the admission of a black applicant to the University of Mississippi. Governor Ross Barnett continued a long tradition of gubernatorial defiance toward desegregation when he exclaimed in response to the court order, "I'll go to jail before mixing schools!" That same day, 13 September 1962, the newspaper with the second largest circulation in the state, the Jackson *Daily News*, headlined a front-page editorial, "We Support Governor Barnett." On 30 September 1962, despite Barnett's initial stance, a bloody riot welcomed Air Force veteran James Meredith to campus as the first known black student.

In early September 1962, when the Fifth Circuit Court of Appeals ordered that James Meredith be admitted to Ole Miss, the decision was front-page news in every Mississippi daily newspaper. Unlike the *Brown* decision a few years earlier, the Ole Miss ruling threatened both immediate desegregation and a violent backlash. The editors were also dealing with a change in the racial climate, not only in Mississippi, but nationally, as civil rights issues were advancing to the forefront of political debate and activism. Unlike *Brown*, which took years to implement, the legal directive for Ole Miss to allow Meredith to enroll in September 1962 thrust Mississippi, and all its vestiges of Old South conservatism, into the spotlight of the national and international media.

The state's politicians led the defense of the "closed society." The day after the decision, Mississippi Governor Ross Barnett proclaimed that Meredith would never be admitted to Ole Miss and that the state would close the university system before it would allow racial integration of the campuses. Barnett addressed the Meredith decision on statewide television and radio the evening of 13 September 1962 and was praised by Jackson *Clarion-Ledger* staff writer Tom Ethridge the following day as "courageous." During his much-publicized speech, Barnett blamed professional agitators and an unfriendly liberal press for the state's problems, and with a staggering lack of foresight he pledged, "No schools in Mississippi will be integrated while I am your governor." Two chaotic weeks later, Meredith attended his first class at Ole Miss.

Barnett initially had the support of most editors of the Mississippi daily press. In the state's capital, front-page editorials at the Jackson *Clarion-Ledger* were common during the Ole Miss crisis. Editor T.M. Hederman, Jr., urged readers to back Barnett. State officials were directed to stand by the governor or resign. Schools are "state business," the paper exhorted on 14 September 1962. "By authority of the federal constitution this is true, regardless of misinterpretations of the constitution in recent years. As the governor said, it is apparent this state is the keystone in the battle for states' rights. We must neither falter nor fall in this supreme test." At the Jackson *Daily News*, editor James Ward had replaced Fred Sullens, who died in 1957. Ward maintained Sullens' propensity for segregationist Southern opinion but was not nearly so prolific. He praised the governor's defiant stand as "courageous" on 13 September 1962 and announced the newspaper's stance the next day, "We Support Governor Barnett." A week later, on 21 September 1962, Ward angrily suggested that the name "Ole Miss" be changed to "the United States Academy for Negroes."

J. Oliver Emmerich of the McComb *Enterprise-Journal* joined the majority of the Mississippi daily press editors in 1962 in voicing his support for Barnett. When the governor announced he would speak to the state on television to address the Ole Miss situation, Emmerich offered him front-page coverage in an editorial on 13 September 1962. "The people of Mississippi stand behind their officials in this crisis," he wrote. The next day, Emmerich praised Barnett's speech as "unflinchingly courageous" and expressed his veneration for the governor.

Many other editors of the Mississippi daily press offered their support to Barnett. Birney Imes, Sr., at the Columbus *Commercial Dispatch*, wrote on 14 September 1963: "Our freedom is in great danger. A federal government, growing ever more powerful, is slowly smothering the life from individual freedoms. The current move is an order to admit a negro to the University of Mississippi. Heretofore, the Southern cause has lacked unity and adequate leadership. Now it is provided by the stand of Governor Barnett."

James B. Skewes, who had replaced his father as editor and publisher of the *Meridian Star*, agreed. During the early 1960s, the younger Skewes was a member of the Citizens' Council, and he praised Barnett's stand on 8 September 1962: "We agree with the governor one hundred percent for racial integrity." In his final editorial column for the month, on 30 September 1962, Skewes voiced support for states' rights in matters of education and told his readers, "If the government uses force to bring about the integration of Mississippi, we will know that there is no longer a democratic government."

Thatcher Walt of the *Greenwood Commonwealth* joined in praising Barnett. Walt offered no editorial opinion regarding Meredith until the middle of the month, when his first comment was to praise Barnett, referring to him on 21 September 1962 as "a knight on a white charger." In his only front-page opinion on the Meredith decision in September, Walt placed a heavy burden on Barnett, albeit one the governor had been asking for, and called on Barnett to force the nation's hand. "The South needs a martyr of stature," Walt wrote on 25 September 1962. "You, Governor, are the South's last hope for one."

At the *Clarksdale Press Register*, editor Joseph Ellis, Jr., supported Barnett on states' rights but voiced some concerns. "As in a Greek tragedy, we know that a major disaster is impending," Ellis wrote on 26 September 1962, "and like the murmuring extras on the stage, are helpless to avert it. The doomed heroes in this case are several, the republican concept of a Federal government of limited powers, the rights of the people of several states to control and regulate, rightly or wrongly, wisely or unwisely, their own affairs, and most important, the status of a great university."

Barnett found one of his most outspoken supporters in one of the most traditional and angry Southerners among the editors of the Mississippi daily press in 1962. W. H. Harris, editor and publisher of the West Point *Times-Leader*, expressed his support of Barnett and was confident, on 11 September 1962, that if Meredith was admitted to Ole Miss he would prove unable to meet academic standards.

Another Barnett defender was Louis P. Cashman, Jr., of the *Vicksburg Evening Post*, who had replaced his father as editor. Cashman directed his angst toward the United States Supreme Court just as his father had directed his anger toward the court following *Brown* in 1954. Cashman praised Barnett's televised address, interpreting it as a call for states' rights, a political ideology the elder Cashman had often advanced. "This was no political tirade—no inflammatory appeal to passion," Cashman wrote on 14 September 1962. "The Meredith decision is a much deeper issue than integration. We must lead the fight."

The primary means by which Barnett proposed to defy the mandate to desegregate Ole Miss was "interposition," an antiquated legal argument in which a state places its sovereignty between a federal ruling and the state, thus forcing the disputed issue to be settled by Constitutional amendment. Southern states had argued unsuccessfully for interposition before the Civil War. Barnett's enthusiasm for the doctrine in 1962 was headline news in the Mississippi daily press, despite the fact that similar arguments had been rejected in Alabama following *Brown*. On 13 September 1962, when Barnett mentioned his determination to "interpose" himself between Meredith and Ole Miss, Alabama Governor James Folsom described the futility of the measure in the Clarksdale *Press Register*. "It's like a dog baying at the moon," Folsom quipped, "and claiming it's got it treed."

Only a few editors of the Mississippi daily press openly criticized Barnett's stand. Hodding Carter III had taken the helm as editor of the Greenville *Delta Democrat-Times* by 1962, and that year he was one of only two editors of the Mississippi daily press who endorsed allowing blacks to attend Mississippi's traditionally white institutions of higher learning. "There is no secret to what we believe is the proper course of action," he wrote on 12 September 1962. "When the Meredith case first came to the courts, this newspaper said the University of Mississippi should stay open no matter what occurred. And before the 1954 Supreme Court desegregation decree, we said that qualified Negro students should be admitted to our institutions of higher learning." Five days later, on 17 September 1962, Carter III said most white Mississippians supported Barnett, but few thought he could keep Meredith out of Ole Miss. Carter also raised the specter of sedition. "Few people really believe the federal government can be successfully defied," he wrote. "We even doubt that the Mississippi legislature, which yesterday voted with scarcely a dissenting voice to endorse Governor Barnett's position on interposition, is so blinded by political necessity as to be able to ignore the record which stands plainly in view. It will also take us to the edge of treason."

Carter III had a supporter on the Mississippi Gulf Coast, where Ira B. Harkey, Jr., had been at the editorial helm of the Pascagoula *Chronicle* since June 1949. Harkey was no traditional Southerner, and he, like the Hodding Carters, did not endorse the white supremacist view. In response to Barnett's televised speech regarding Meredith's admission to Ole Miss,

Harkey appealed to his readers' good sense. "Mississippians are mature enough to recognize the inevitable, to accept it and adapt to it with good enough grace," Harkey wrote on 14 September 1962. "The political faction that rules them, however, is not. We had always thought deep down inside when the moment arrived even Ross Barnett and his blazing advisers would make the best of it. Instead, the emotional nature of Barnett's address last night left little doubt that he intends to make the worst of it. He will drive Mississippi to chaos."

Some editors who supported Barnett initially were suspicious of his call for interposition. Emmerich in McComb, who had praised Barnett's stand against a federal decree to desegregate Ole Miss, began to doubt Barnett's ability to deal with the crisis, and he questioned the wisdom of Barnett's call for interposition. Despite his support for Barnett, Emmerich began to doubt whether the governor would be able to keep his promise of barring the doors of the state's universities to blacks, and on 28 September 1962, he wrote: "Will he be the first governor to brush aside a Supreme Court decision?"

Harry Rutherford, editor of the Tupelo *Daily Journal* now that George McLean had moved from that position to become the full-time publisher, advised against the use of interposition in one of his two editorials regarding the Meredith decision. "Governor Barnett is a good lawyer," Rutherford observed on 27 September 1962. "He knows that no person, agency or state has ever been able to defy the authority of the government of the United States." At the *Laurel Leader-Call*, Jay West had taken over as editor from Harriet Gibbons and shared her vague distrust of politicians. "Governor Barnett is trying his best to interpose himself between the announced law of the land and what some of our citizens think it should be," West wrote on 18 September 1962. "Barnett is a lawyer by profession. He knew, or should have known, that the theory of interposition has been rejected by the courts since 1792."

Several Mississippi editors were aghast at Barnett's threat to close Ole Miss, parting ways with the governor when his anti-desegregation positions began for the first time to hurt whites as well as blacks. Some editors even favored accepting desegregation if that's what it took to save the university, a view shared by many of the institution's students, faculty, and alumni. Rutherford at the Tupelo *Daily Journal* criticized the idea of closing the state's universities rather than desegregating them. In "No One has the Right to Destroy our Colleges," on 18 September 1962, Rutherford declared, "Surely, the Board of Trustees, regardless of pressure from the governor, will, at the last minute, stand up for the reasonable expectation of every young Mississippian to get an education." Carter III at the *Delta Democrat-Times* agreed with Rutherford and told his readers that he considered the suggestion by Barnett to close Ole Miss "a highflying burst of idiocy." He expressed his contempt for Barnett, "a governor who can tranquilly contemplate the destruction of a university for the sake of a philosophy which sees some men as inherently inferior to others." Emmerich in McComb said closing Ole Miss would be futile. "What good would it accomplish?" he asked 24 September 1962. "Would it keep Mississippi's schools all white, this year, and the next year and for the decade and the decades to come?"

In concurrence was Leonard Lowrey, who had replaced Andrews Harmon as editor at the *Hattiesburg American*. Despite his Southern conservatism, Lowrey thought the state's universities should remain open, no matter what. In a front-page editorial on 27 September 1962, Lowrey wrote: "We admire and applaud the tenacious effort of Governor Barnett to keep James Meredith from enrolling at Ole Miss. However, we feel there are considerations more important than barring one Negro from the university, and we hope the governor and those working with him will not lose sight of these things in their zeal for the battle at hand. No matter what else, Ole Miss, and all of our other state institutions of higher learning, should be kept open and in good standing." Another Southern traditionalist who argued in favor of keeping Ole Miss open was Bill Simpson, news director of the Corinth *Daily Corinthian*. Simpson agreed with Lowrey and the others, but for another reason. "Our students would be forced to seek their education in other states," Simpson reasoned in his "Talk of Town" editorial on 21 September 1962, "probably with negroes."

On 30 September 1962, Barnett backed down. Burdened by the threat of a ten thousand dollar-a-day fine, he finally agreed with federal authorities to have Meredith escorted onto campus that day. By early evening, a crowd began milling near the Lyceum Building, where several hundred United States marshals and several thousand federalized Mississippi National Guardsmen were positioned. As dusk settled over the campus, a riot broke out that lasted eight hours into the night. Most of the rioters were not students. Many had come from all over the country to heed the call of General Edwin A. Walker, a Texan and former major general in the United States Army who referred to the United States Supreme Court as "the anti-Christ," and was vehemently opposed to federal interference in what he considered states' rights. Walker had arrived in Mississippi in September, eager to do battle rather than allow the racial integration Ole Miss.

Many people were injured in the riot at Ole Miss that night, including a hundred and sixty marshals, and two people were killed—Roy Gunter, twenty-three, an Oxford resident, and Paul Guihard, a photographer for a French news agency. The following morning, the Ole Miss campus was littered with burned-out automobiles, tear gas canisters, and broken glass. Martial law had been declared, and seventy-five rioters were arrested, including several members of the American Nazi Party from Georgia.

On 1 October 1962, the day after the riot, Ellis at the Clarksdale *Press Register* had harsh words for Barnett and encouragement for the students at Ole Miss. "We must start looking for new leadership—on the national and state level," Ellis wrote. "Both have failed this nation and state to a miserable, shameful degree. A 'banzai' charge against an impregnable position is not an act of courage—it is an act of suicide and insanity. This is an appeal to reason. The students at the university must return to their classes and their books."

Despite the initial shock wave that roared through Mississippi in September 1962, Meredith remained at Ole Miss and attended classes. He graduated in August 1963.

In 1962, no other public schools in the state were desegregated in the wake of Ole Miss. There was no domino affect that rippled down into the state's secondary school system. It would take another federal court order to make that happen. But the "closed society" was never quite as impregnable again, and there were members who began to seriously question whether it should be, including a few editors of the Mississippi daily press.

When the *Brown v. Board of Education* decision was handed down, Mississippi's white majority, including the editors of the Mississippi daily press, had been prepared. They knew a Supreme Court decision could take years to implement. But when James Meredith's admission to Ole Miss was ordered by a federal court and backed by federal troops in 1962, there was no going back. The editors, and many other Mississippians, black and white, began to see that changes could be made, and would be made.

Freedom Summer 1964 and the Mississippi Daily Press

Only two years later, as the summer of 1964 began, the Mississippi daily press was issued another challenge—not only by the impending Freedom Summer project, but also by the passage of federal civil rights legislation. Signed into law in early July by President Lyndon Johnson, the Civil Rights Act of 1964 was intended to guarantee that blacks and other minorities had equal access to public facilities. The Act was approved by Congress in late June and sent to Johnson in the White House, where it was signed in a dramatic televised ceremony on 2 July 1964. Mississippi Governor Paul B. Johnson, Jr., who had assisted Ross Barnett in his attempt to bar Meredith from Ole Miss in 1962, labeled the Act unconstitutional and advocated noncompliance. His words were printed as headline news in the Mississippi press.

Editorial reaction among the Mississippi daily newspapers to the 1964 Civil Rights Act varied. Most expressed opposition. In the state's capital, the Jackson *Clarion-Ledger*, under the continued editorship of T. M. Hederman, Jr., reported disdain for and criticism of the measure. The mindset at the *Clarion-Ledger* on 16 June 1964 was that "the civil rights bill would take away far more rights than it would protect." In other words, it would threaten control by the state's white power structure. At the Jackson *Daily News*, editor James Ward warned his readers on 11 June 1964 that liberals would "rue the day" the bill became law. Ward also described "the evil consequences of the fiendishly-concocted civil rights legislation" on 25 June 1964, and detailed "the blackness of thorough and crushing domination."

In McComb, Emmerich at the *Enterprise-Journal* questioned the constitutionality of the Act. "Mississippi opposed the legislation," he wrote on 6 July 1964. "We still oppose the idea." Emmerich was an outspoken opponent of the 1964 Civil Rights Act and justified his stance by arguing that blacks and whites were inherently distinct and should not be forced to interact. In an editorial of 7 July 1964, he wrote, "Different races have different traits." Concurring with Emmerich was Birney Imes, Jr., at the Columbus *Commercial Dispatch*, who reprinted an editorial on 9 July 1964 from the *Dixie Lumberman*, which complained, "The Kennedy idea of civil rights is to take them from the majority and give them to the minority." Bill Simpson at the *Daily Corinthian* agreed and addressed the impending passage of the Civil Rights Act of 1964 on 1 July. "By tomorrow morning," he wrote, "Americans will have lost their right of jurisdiction over most private property with the exception of their homes—and possibly, that will be covered in a later bill." In Hattiesburg, Leonard Lowrey at the *Hattiesburg American* was also given to doomsaying. "We greatly fear that an era of federal control, strife and racial trouble such as this country has never seen before is ahead for the entire nation," he wrote on 11 June 1964. On the Gulf Coast, W. David Brown had taken the helm as editor of the Pascagoula *Chronicle*, and he was as staunchly segregationist on the race issue as former editor Ira Harkey, Jr., had been integrationist. Brown decreed on 24 June 1964 that to sign the Civil Rights Act near the Fourth of July was a "desecration" of that national holiday. He was, no doubt, speaking from the Southern conservative white tradition, not the black.

The only editorial support for the Civil Rights Act of 1964 came from Hodding Carter III at the Greenville *Delta Democrat-Times*, who was concerned about peaceful compliance with the legislation. Carter asked his readers to remain calm until the issue had been examined legally. "Let us today resolve that the testing ground for the law shall be in the courts and not in the streets," he implored on 4 July 1964. "Let us also resolve that as the law is applied, we demonstrate again that we are following the law, much as many may resent or dislike it." Carter III was also the only editor of the Mississippi daily press in 1964 to encourage his readers to give the Civil Rights Act the benefit of a doubt. On 19 July 1964, he wrote, "What civil rights groups and whites alike need to do now is to give the bill a chance to work before running pell mell into the streets with angry accusations, ultimatums and impassioned speeches."

Carter III found an element of support among several other Mississippi daily editors, who urged readers to obey the civil rights mandate whether they supported the concept or not. Lowrey of the *Hattiesburg American*, who opposed the legislation, asked his readers to be patient with local business people who complied with the Civil Rights Act. In an editorial on 6 July 1964, he wrote, "Above all else, fair-minded Mississippians should guard against unfair treatment and criticism of their long-time neighbors and proven good citizens who recognize that they have no choice, at this time under the law, but to comply." In agreement with Lowrey's approach was the *Vicksburg Evening Post*, where editor Louis P. Cashman, Jr., decried the "civil wrongs bill" but advised his readers on 12 July 1964 to comply with the law until it was tested in the courts, "although it seems unconstitutional."

Consequently, as the summer of 1964 began, white Mississippians were already skeptical and angry, and black Mississippians hopeful and apprehensive, when into this seething cauldron came the civil rights workers of Freedom Summer. Their efforts altered the fabric of Mississippi society—not so much in immediate civil rights gains for blacks, but by the national and world media attention Freedom Summer brought to the state. About six hundred volunteers, mostly white college students from Northern universities and colleges, arrived in June. The civil rights workers, as they were called, organized black voter registration and established "freedom schools." According to Charles Payne in *I've Got the Light of Freedom* (1995), the freedom schools offered instruction in traditional academic subjects, discussions on how to understand the white power structure and politics, and black cultural awareness programs (p. 301–306). John Dittmer noted in *Local People* (1994) that there were fifty freedom schools in Mississippi during Freedom Summer and more than two thousand black students attended, ranging in age from pre-school to the elderly (p. 259).

The civil rights workers who came to Mississippi as volunteers during Freedom Summer faced an uphill battle for acceptance among most black Mississippians, and hostility and opposition from most white Mississippians. They were considered outside agitators, part of an unwanted "invasion" on the state. Although calculations vary regarding the violence in Mississippi during the Freedom Summer campaign, there were at least three summer workers killed, eighty beaten, thirty homes and thirty churches in the black community burned or bombed, and more than a thousand arrested. Despite the fact that their home state was the center of national media attention, Mississippi daily newspapers often ignored local civil rights activities and usually did not send their staff reporters to cover them. Instead, they relied upon accounts from the wire services and national news organizations, which regularly documented civil rights-related beatings, bombings, arrests and church burnings. The state's pattern of race-related violence was finally being reported to a national and global audience. The summer's events put Mississippi's reporters and editors to the test and raised questions as to whether they acted responsibly in a time of crisis.

Mississippi newspaper editorials viewed the civil rights workers with skepticism and even loathing. They scorned the organizers of Freedom Summer, primarily the Congress of Racial Equality (CORE), the Southern Christian Leadership Conference (SCLC), the Student Nonviolent Coordinating Committee (SNCC), and the National Council of Churches (NCC), which was denounced by several Mississippi daily newspapers. The Pascagoula *Chronicle* criticized the NCC on 10 July 1964 for aiding "insurrectionists," and the *Hattiesburg American* opined on 25 July 1964, "We heatedly disagree that churches should be political." The SCLC was headed by Martin Luther King, Jr., and during Freedom Summer, King toured Mississippi briefly. The *Meridian Star* referred, on 12 June 1964, to "the miserable 'non-violent' street rabble led by the unspeakable Martin Luther King and his ilk." The Jackson *Daily News* dismissed King on 22 July 1964 as "the Reverend Dr. Extremist Agitator Martin Luther King junior." Rutherford at the Tupelo *Daily Journal* wrote that King was a "false leader" on 12 June 1964.

Although the civil rights workers were ridiculed and threatened by many Mississippians, few publicly celebrated the fate that befell Michael Schwerner of New York City, Andrew Goodman of Brooklyn, New York, and James Chaney of Meridian, Mississippi. The three vanished on 22 June 1964 after being jailed for investigating a church burning near Philadelphia, Mississippi. Widely covered in the state's daily press, editorial opinion regarding their disappearance varied. Carter in Greenville had no blame to lay, only fear for the future. "If our prayers are not answered, if murder has been committed," he wrote on 24 June 1964, "then the rest of this summer could well be pure hell." In Pascagoula, Brown showed no sympathy. "Nothing has been said about how much wiser the missing young men would have been had they stayed home and minded their own business," he wrote the same day.

The search for the missing trio lasted most of the summer and was widely covered in the Mississippi daily press, which criticized the federal government for becoming involved. President Lyndon Johnson ordered an extensive search by the Federal Bureau of Investigation, and FBI Director J. Edgar Hoover obliged by personally opening a Jackson office. The federal assistance was considered an "insult" by several of the Mississippi daily newspapers, including the Jackson *Clarion-Ledger* on 12 July 1964 and the Pascagoula *Chronicle* on 24 June 1964.

The civil rights workers in the state feared the three young men had been murdered, and within a few days of their disappearance, President Johnson sent United States Marines and sailors to comb the area. Mississippi Governor Johnson, as well as several editors of the state's daily press, were outraged that federal troops were sent to the state. "If they have met with foul play, it is certainly regrettable," Simpson in Corinth wrote on 24 June 1964. "But when talk of sending troops comes up there appears to be other parts of the country where they are needed more." Nash in Starkville concurred on 24 June 1964. "Why don't federal troops get sent to New York when someone there disappears?" Harris in West Point also protested on 25 June 1964: "There was more racial violence in New York City over the weekend than is experienced in Mississippi during an entire year. But no federal troops were sent to New York. Nor will there be."

After more than two months and three million dollars spent on the search, the decomposing bodies of Chaney, Schwerner, and Goodman were unearthed in the red clay of Neshoba County, just north of Meridian, the home of Chaney. James B. Skewes, editor of the *Meridian Star*, had been a harsh critic of Freedom Summer, referring to the civil rights movement on 4 July 1964 as "the so-called Negro revolution." He had ignored the disappearance of the three men in the editorial columns of the *Meridian Star* until their bodies were discovered in August. A staff-written report on 24 June 1964 had speculated that the disappearance was a publicity hoax. Readers were continuously led to believe the disappearance was a ruse. Three front-page stories addressed the finding of the bodies of Chaney, Schwerner, and Goodman in the *Meridian Star*. On 6 August 1964, Skewes placed the blame for the murders on the civil rights movement in general, and on the workers themselves. "The civil rights organizations share the blame for the murders," he wrote on 6 August 1964. "Because if the summer project had not been organized, the three young men would not have been murdered."

In the state capital, the Jackson *Daily News* was editorially silent regarding the deaths until late in the summer, when the national media's criticism of Mississippi apparently roused editor Ward's ire. "So far there is not a shred of evidence that a Mississippian laid a hand on either one of the three civil rights workers who went to Philadelphia to meddle in local affairs," Ward wrote on 30 August 1964. "But all over the nation, loud racial agitators, self-serving politicians, long-haired liberals, Communists, misguided preachers, the leftist news media and other assorted groups have joined in howls of ugly and unfounded criticism of our state and its people. It is as clear as the noonday sun that the integrationists, the vote hunting politicians, the Communists, and others are determined to punish Mississippi for its policies and way of life."

After the bodies were found, Governor Johnson told the press he "deplored" the killings but noted that Mississippi had a low crime rate, which he said proved that racial segregation resulted in peace. "Bunk," Carter III wrote on 14 August 1964. "If Johnson's remark was, in fact, accurate, the three civil rights workers' bodies would never have been found. In fact, the trio would never have come to Mississippi because there would have been no reason for a militant civil rights movement here."

Carter III in Greenville wanted the killers found. In "Justice Must Prevail," on 9 August 1964, he wrote, "Let's not let another murder go unpunished." Harris at the West Point *Times-Leader*, despite his usual harsh words for the civil rights movement, was in agreement. "Like millions of other Americans, we were hoping that the three civil rights workers missing for six weeks would turn up alive—and that the whole affair was a hoax," he wrote on 5 August 1964. "We must find who murdered them and bring them to justice." Several other Mississippi daily press editors spoke up publicly to condemn the murders. In Tupelo, Rutherford wrote on 7 August 1964, "The slaying is a crime, a tragedy, a blackeye for all Mississippi." Cashman in Vicksburg spoke out on 6 August 1964. "We must track down the murderers of these men and bring them to justice."

Although the disappearance and murders of Chaney, Schwerner, and

Goodman were daily front-page news in most Mississippi daily newspapers, other aspects of Freedom Summer were also newsworthy. Editorials addressing the civil rights workers during Freedom Summer primarily questioned the motives of the volunteers, criticized the organizations that supported them, requested patience from readers, and advocated nonviolence.

The lone exception to the negative approach was in Greenville, where the *Delta Democrat-Times* was never one to dodge an important social issue. Prior to the arrival of the civil rights workers, Carter III was determined to discourage violence. "The summer of 1964 should not go down in history as a synonym for violent discord in Mississippi," he wrote on 13 July 1964. "The time for militant opposition to the laws of the land are gone." In response to the burnings of several black churches in the Delta, Carter lambasted his white readers on 2 August 1964. "We white Mississippians talk righteously about the failure of citizens of the big cities of the East to offer aid as women are assaulted in the streets, or as men are mugged in broad daylight," he wrote. "But what of the one million whites of our own state who will do nothing as native-born thugs carry out a reign of terror against black fellow Mississippians, with the house of God as their favorite target?"

In the state's capital, the Jackson *Clarion-Ledger* referred to the civil rights project on 21 June 1964 as a "summer lark for youth." The *Clarion-Ledger* argued on 22 July 1964 that the North needed the summer volunteers to solve its own racial woes, not the South's. Few violent incidents against the summer volunteers in Jackson were reported in the *Clarion-Ledger*. In August, when blacks in Jackson reported Ku Klux Klan crosses burned at several locations, City Commissioner Tom Marshal was quoted on 12 August 1964 as saying the blacks themselves had probably burned the crosses to "agitate trouble." Unlike most other Mississippi daily newspapers, the *Clarion-Ledger* reported few civil rights activities from around the state, other than the disappearance and murder of Chaney, Schwerner, and Goodman. Other stories were usually buried, rarely front-page news unless included in the condensed "On the Racial Front" column. One of the few front-page articles concerning the summer project was written by staff reporter William Chaze, who visited the office of the civil rights workers in Hattiesburg. His article on 14 July 1964 was headlined, "Odor of

Sweat, Dirt, Fill Hattiesburg COFO Office." Chaze, who wrote several articles about Freedom Summer activities, reported on 23 August 1964 that in Marshall County, civil rights workers had threatened blacks to coerce them into registering to vote, telling them their "welfare checks would be cut if they didn't." No COFO response to the allegations was included in the article.

At the Jackson *Daily News*, the same negative attitude toward civil rights and the summer workers prevailed. The summer volunteers were described as "race mixing invaders" on 4 June 1964 and as "racial zealots" on 23 June 1964. Ward often denigrated the civil rights workers in his "Crossroads" column, as on 15 July 1964, when he dismissed them as "unkempt agitators." Ward often used "Crossroads" as a forum for poems and puns to ridicule the volunteers, and he was equally dismissive of the "liberal" media. On 10 July 1964, CBS was renamed the "Colored Broadcast System," ABC was the "African Broadcast Corporation," and NBC was the "Negro Broadcast Corporation."

In McComb, Emmerich's initial response to the summer project was to warn readers not to believe unsubstantiated rumors and to maintain calm. On 9 July 1964, Emmerich's front-page editorial column reported that civil rights workers were in the area only to help register voters, and he urged all residents to remain "peaceful." Emmerich never wrote derogatory statements about the civil rights workers during Freedom Summer. The antagonistic opinions of others were often quoted, however, such as a statement by former Mississippi Governor Ross Barnett headlined on 22 July 1964, "Ross Suggests Righters Bathe."

In the Mississippi Delta, readers of the *Clarksdale Press Register* were urged to "meet the summer project with dignity and patience" on 18 June 1964. Clarksdale was ready, Ellis wrote on 23 June 1964, for "the immature collegians and over-ripe missionaries," and he advised his readers to "leave the law to law enforcement officials." In Columbus, the *Commercial Dispatch* had only one published comment regarding the summer workers prior to August, when the bodies of Chaney, Schwerner, and Goodman were found. On 26 June 1964, Imes suggested that blacks unhappy with the Southern way of life should be given a free bus ticket so they could move to the North.

Freedom Summer was big news in Greenwood, a small Delta town that served as national headquarters for SNCC during the summer project. Editor Thatcher Walt of the *Greenwood Commonwealth* advised his readers on 22 June 1964 to keep calm. Like other Mississippi daily newspapers, the *Greenwood Commonwealth* reported wire service stories about other areas of the state more than it reported local activity. The newspaper's first mention of the local summer project was a headline story on 15 June 1964 from the wire services, "SNCC Says Headquarters Coming Here." No staff-written article ensued. The paper next commented on the project on 24 June 1964, after fourteen people were arrested for picketing a local store, and a week after that on 1 July 1964, when several summer workers were quoted as saying they were in town to help register voters and to open a freedom school, not to test the mandates of the Civil Rights Act. When Martin Luther King, Jr., came to Greenwood to encourage voter registration, his speech on 21 July 1964 was not reported in the *Greenwood Commonwealth*, although his arrival in Greenwood made front-page news in the form of an AP story. During King's speech to a thousand people, the Ku Klux Klan had an airplane fly over and drop threatening leaflets throughout the crowd and across town. But the *Greenwood Commonwealth* failed to cover the incident, which was reported in several other Mississippi daily newspapers.

In Hattiesburg, editor Lowrey of the *Hattiesburg American* expressed concern on 23 June 1964 about the "behavior" of the arriving summer volunteers: "We hope the NCC had someone on hand who advised the young people of morality for morality's sake, not for the sake of the project." The newspaper argued, on 12 August 1964, that the summer workers would have been much more useful working toward racial harmony in the North. As was the case with many other Mississippi daily newspapers, the *Hattiesburg American* regularly published wire service articles regarding civil rights activities in other parts of the state, but failed to report comprehensively about local events. Interestingly, the *Hattiesburg American* was one of the few Mississippi daily newspapers that offered the civil rights workers a chance to tell their side of Freedom Summer. On 7 July 1964, Terri Shaw, director of communications for COFO in Hattiesburg, reported in an article for the *Hattiesburg American* that the primary purpose of the summer project was to register voters. Shaw reported that fifty volunteers were in the Hattiesburg area and that nearly six hundred blacks, ages eight to eighty, had enrolled in the local freedom school.

In Laurel, Jay West at the *Laurel Leader-Call* made only one editorial reference to the civil rights workers during Freedom Summer, and that was on 26 June 1964. He advised President Johnson to halt the Freedom Summer project because, "The general climate is not conducive to calm, reasoned thinking at a time when it is most needed." Unlike many of the Mississippi daily newspapers, the *Laurel Leader-Call* made an attempt to cover local civil rights activity. When COFO workers began arriving in Laurel, a front-page headline on 20 June 1964 advised readers to practice "poise and forbearance," and the ensuing article reported that the Laurel Chamber of Commerce was requesting that people remain "calm and cool." On July 8, Laurel was in UPI news reports when the Laurel Police Department added four black officers to the force. The *Laurel Leader-Call* announced the decision in a supportive front-page article on 8 July 1964.

At the *Natchez Democrat*, the only mention of the summer workers was an editorial column on 9 June 1964 that advised readers to "completely ignore them," and editor James Lambert followed his own advice. The *Natchez Democrat* reported when summer volunteers arrived in Meridian, on the other side of the state, but not when they arrived in Natchez. Lambert offered scarce editorial leadership to his readers during Freedom Summer, other than to suggest noncompliance with the newly enacted Civil Rights Act and ostracism of the civil rights workers in the area.

On the Mississippi Coast at the Pascagoula *Chronicle*, editor Brown was a firm critic of the 1964 Civil Rights Act, and his idea regarding the civil rights workers on 24 June 1964 was that they should have stayed at home and "minded their own business." Civil rights activities from around the state reported by the wire services were published, though somewhat infrequently, in the *Chronicle*. The COFO office closest to Pascagoula was about five miles north in Moss Point, and the activity there was reported extensively by the *Chronicle*. A few weeks after the 1964 Civil Rights Act was signed into law, the grand jury in Pascagoula was asked to investigate voter registration. Jurors were told that blacks were often refused registration at the county courthouse. After mulling over the evidence, the jury concluded in an article on 19 July 1964 that "qualified Negro voters are never denied the right to vote in Jackson County." As Freedom Summer came to an end, a UPI story on 2 August 1964 reported that more than half a million blacks had been added to the voter registration rolls in the South in just a few months. In response, the *Chronicle* urged the white community on 5 August 1964 to vote in every local, statewide and national election.

At the *Starkville Daily News*, the front-page "Pencil Shavings" column of publisher Harris on 27 June 1964 referred to the summer workers as "nutniks." When actor Harry Belafonte made a financial donation to the COFO office in Greenwood, Harris wrote on 15 August 1964: "Hurrah, now these unkempt beatniks can buy their own soap. Cash, not conviction, is what brings the COFO workers into the state." Except for extensive coverage of the disappearance and murders of Chaney, Goodman, and Schwerner, only a few wire reports regarding Freedom Summer activity from around the state were published in the *Starkville Daily News*. Other than to editorially condemn the civil rights movement on all levels, the newspaper was silent.

Like Starkville, Tupelo had no COFO office during Freedom Summer, and the *Daily Journal* made no mention of the summer project in the editorial columns until 27 July 1964, when readers were reminded that the civil rights workers would be leaving the state soon. The community was urged to "show a little more patience." On 6 August 1964, editor Rutherford expressed his support for allowing "qualified" blacks to vote but encouraged them to attend school; a COFO campaign, he said, was not a substitute for a formal education. Rutherford complained on 21 August 1964 that COFO had done more damage than good in Mississippi during Freedom Summer.

At the *Vicksburg Evening Post*, the civil rights workers were accused on 14 June 1964 of "turning their backs on responsibility" by causing racial agitation. Except for coverage of the disappearance and murders of Chaney, Schwerner, and Goodman, wire service reports of civil rights activities around the state were rarely published in the *Vicksburg Evening Post*. The only local activity reported by the *Vicksburg Evening Post* was on 6 July 1964 after eight blacks were served, without incident, at the local Woolworth's lunch counter. When Martin Luther King, Jr., came to Mississippi in July for a four-day tour, his arrival in the state was reported by the *Vicksburg Evening Post*, and his departure was reported, but no coverage was offered of his stay, or speech, in Vicksburg.

Another ongoing story during and after Freedom Summer was an attack on the national news media by the Mississippi press. Emmerich at the McComb *Enterprise-Journal* suggested on 20 August 1964 that the national media often caused trouble with their reports, and the Pascagoula *Chronicle* implored angrily on 17 August 1964, "Spare us the CBS Crusade." Ellis at the *Clarksdale Press Register* voiced his outrage on 8 July 1964 over an incident at a local hotel where an attempt to integrate was "staged" for the news media by "an unknown, unnamed, undereducated lout from Columbia Broadcasting System." Ellis also protested "the sanctimonious sermon on these 'horrid Mississippians' by Walter Cronkite."

Two lawsuits against the national news media regarding civil rights activity in Mississippi were filed during Freedom Summer. Edwin Walker, the former major general in the United States Army who had been accused of instigating the riot at Ole Miss in 1962, sued the Associated Press for libel over reports of his involvement. In early June 1964, Walker was awarded nearly a million dollars by a Texas jury. A few weeks later, however, that award was reduced in a Texas District Court, and by the end of the summer, another appeal to the Fifth Circuit Court in New Orleans ended in a dismissal. In 1967, the United States Supreme Court reversed the libel judgment Walker had won, ruling in *Associated Press v. Walker* that he was a "public man in whose public conduct society and the press had a legitimate and substantial interest in." The Walker ruling and *New York Times v. Sullivan* (1964), which grew out of civil rights protest in Birmingham, remain two of the most influential libel decisions in press law.

Another lawsuit stemming from Freedom Summer was filed in Neshoba County, Mississippi, by Sheriff Lawrence Rainey, against NBC for the network's coverage of the disappearance and murders of Chaney, Schwerner, and Goodman, and Rainey's involvement in the case. That suit was also dismissed.

Overall, the editorial view of Freedom Summer by the Mississippi daily press reflected the same "us against them" mentality evident during the 1954 *Brown* decision and the racial integration of Ole Miss in 1962.

The "invasion" by outsiders reaffirmed a commitment to the preservation of the traditional South and a local version of the states' rights controversy—the right of each state, or rather the elite power structure, to manage their lives without interference. According to a Harris Poll following the 1964 presidential election, "Mississippi voters are dominated by the race question to the exclusion of almost any other political consideration."

Conclusion

An evaluation of the findings of this study through the recommendations of social responsibility made by the Hutchins Commission to the news media in 1947 can be formulated in two distinct ways. On one hand, the Mississippi daily press during the 1950s and 1960s failed to meet the standards of the Commission for "socially responsible" media. Mississippi daily newspapers, by the Commission's standards, failed "to provide a truthful, comprehensive, and intelligent account of the day's events in a context which gives them meaning" during the three crises. Most often, the "truth" of the reports was the truth as seen from the white, anti-civil rights perspective.

Mississippi daily newspapers, by the Commission's standards, failed "to provide a forum for the exchange of comment and criticism" during the three crises. For the most part, only editorials and letters that supported the white, anti-civil rights perspective were published. Only blacks who supported the precepts of the "closed society" were given a voice.

Mississippi daily newspapers, by the Commission's standards, failed "to project a representative picture of the constituent groups in society" during the three crises. Generally, the theme of the "happy Negroes" who did not want equality was the common representation of the black community in the white-owned Mississippi daily press.

Mississippi daily newspapers, by the Commission's standards, failed "to present and clarify the goals and values of the society," during the three crises. This was particularly true regarding the black community's goals and values, which were usually promoted as being the same as those of the white community.

And last but not the least, the Mississippi daily newspapers, by the Commission's standards, failed "to provide a full access to the day's intelligence" during the three crises. Gate-keeping of information by the white editors of the Mississippi daily press usually omitted any positive aspect of civil rights legislation. Equality for blacks was out of the question, especially if that equality challenged the "closed society."

On the other hand, the Mississippi press must be understood in terms of its primary readership, a white society that predominantly supported and desired a traditional South. Most whites in Mississippi understood and lived comfortably within the "closed society." Civil rights for blacks meant only upheaval to whites, especially the way civil rights were presented to them by their daily press.

Most white readers in Mississippi never considered the boost to their local economies that equal rights for blacks would bring, or the enrichment of both cultures that getting to know each other would bring. To most white Mississippians, and to most white editors of the Mississippi daily press, "socially responsible" editorship during those years meant the maintenance of Mississippi society as they knew it—racially segregated with blacks in subservient roles as second-class citizens. To most white Mississippians in the 1950s and 1960s, the "closed society" needed to remain that way.

References

Primary Sources: Unpublished Interviews

Weill, Susan. Unpublished cyberspace interview with Hodding Carter III. 4 October 1999.

———. Unpublished cyberspace interview with Hodding Carter III. 2 November 1999.

Secondary Sources

"Belting Down One for the Road." *Nation*, 6 October 1962: 190.

Booker, Simeon. *Black Man's America*. (Englewood Cliffs, New Jersey: Prentice-Hall, 1964).

Buford Boone, "Southern Newsmen and Local Pressure," in *Race and the News Media*, ed. Paul L. Fisher and Richard L. Lowenstein. (New York: Frederick A. Praeger, 1967): 53–62.

Boylan, James. "Birmingham Newspapers in Crisis," *Columbia Journalism Review*, 2 (Summer 1963): 30–42.

Bramlett, Sharon A. "Southern vs. Northern Newspaper Coverage of a Race Crisis—The

Lunch Counter Sit-In Movement, 1960–1964: An Assessment of Social Responsibility." Ph.D. diss., Indiana University, 1987.

Butts, Charles. "Mississippi: the Vacuum and the System." In *Black, White and Gray: 21 Points of View on the Race Question*, ed. Bradford Daniel, 103–114. (New York: Sheed and Ward, 1964).

Carter, Hodding III. "Comment on the Coverage in the Domestic Press," pp. 38–41, in *The Black American and the Press*. (Los Angeles: Ward and Ritchie, 1968).

Carter, Roy E. "Segregation and the News: A Regional Content Study," *Journalism Quarterly* 34 (1957): 3–18.

———. "Racial Identification Effects Upon the News Story Writer." *Journalism Quarterly* 36 (1959): 284–290.

Commission on Freedom of the Press (Hutchins Commission). *A Free and Responsible Press: A General Report on Mass Communication: Newspapers, Radio, Motion Pictures, Magazines and Books*. (Chicago: University of Chicago Press, 1947).

"Dilemma in Dixie." *Time*, February 1956, 76–81.

Dittmer, John. *Local People: The Struggle for Civil Rights in Mississippi*. (Chicago: University of Illinois Press, 1994).

"Dixie Flamethrowers." *Time*, March 1966, 64.

Fisher, Paul, and Ralph Lowenstein, eds. *Race and the News Media*. New York: Praeger, 1967.

Holloway, Harry. *The Politics of the Southern Negro*. (New York: Random House, 1969).

Hooker, Robert. "Race and the News Media in Mississippi, 1962–1964." Master's thesis, Vanderbilt University, 1971.

Hulteng, John L. *The Messenger's Motive: Ethical Problems of the Press*. (Englewood Cliffs: Prentice-Hall, Inc., 1976).

Johnston, Erle. *Mississippi's Defiant Years, 1953–1973: An Interpretive Documentary with Personal Experiences*. (Forest, Miss.: Lake Harbor Publishers, 1990).

Lippmann, Walter. *Public Opinion*. (New York: Harcourt, Brace, 1922).

Lively, Earl Jr. *The Invasion of Mississippi*. (Belmont, Mass.: American Opinion, 1963).

Loewen, James, and Charles Sallis, eds. *Mississippi: Conflict and Change*. (New York: Pantheon Books, 1974).

Lyle, Jack, ed. *The Black American and the Press*. (Los Angeles: Ward and Ritchie, 1968).

McAdam, Doug. *Freedom Summer*. (New York: Oxford University Press, 1988).

McMillen, Neil R. *The Citizens' Council: Organized Resistance to the Second Reconstruction, 1954–1964*. (Chicago: University of Illinois Press, 1971).

———. *Dark Journey: Black Mississippians in the Age of Jim Crow.* (Chicago: University of Illinois Press, 1990).

"Meredith File, The" Jackson *Clarion-Ledger*, 20 September 1997, 13A.

"Moderation in Dixie." *Time*, 19 March 1965, 71.

Payne, Charles M. *I've Got the Light of Freedom.* (Berkeley: University of California Press, 1995).

Peters, William. *The Southern Temper.* (Garden City, New York: Doubleday and Company, 1959).

Poston, Ted. "The American Negro and Newspaper Myths." In *Race and the News Media*, ed. Paul Fisher and Ralph Lowenstein, 63–72. (New York: Praeger, 1967).

Schlesinger, Arthur M., Jr. *A Thousand Days: John F. Kennedy in the White House.* (Greenwich, Connecticut: Fawcett Publications, 1967).

Silver, James W. *Mississippi: The Closed Society.* (New York: Harcourt, Brace and World, 1964).

Watters, Pat, and Reese Cleghorn. *Climbing Jacob's Ladder: The Arrival of Negroes in Southern Politics.* (New York: Harcourt, Brace and World, 1967).

Weill, Susan. "In a Madhouse's Din: Civil Rights Coverage by Mississippi's Daily Press, 1948–1968." Ph.D. dissertation. University of Southern Mississippi, 1998.

Williams, Roger. "Newspapers in the South." *Columbia Journalism Review* 6 (Summer 1967): 26–35.

Percy Greene and the *Jackson Advocate*

Caryl A. Cooper

Percy Greene aroused disparate reactions among colleagues during his turbulent career as editor of the *Jackson Advocate*, Mississippi's leading black newspaper during the state's strife-filled struggle for civil rights. From 1939 until his death in 1977, Greene charted an editorial path that earned him both high praise and passionate loathing. Accused of being a traitor to the black cause and a foil for the white man, he was revered and hated, celebrated and vilified.

In *Percy Greene and the Jackson Advocate* (1994), historian Julius Thompson asked Greene's friends to talk about the editor. Ruby E. Stutts-Lyells described Greene as a "prolific journalist" and a "bold and daring editor." James Rundle, who worked with Greene off and on, remembered the editor's relentless pursuit for black voting rights. "Time and time again . . . Greene put his life on the line fighting for black people. The battle for the vote, court battles, his friendship with President Truman all helped Southern blacks" (p. 45). Not everyone who knew Greene, however, had such fond recollections.

In *Local People* (1994), historian John Dittmer's book about the struggle for equality in Mississippi, civil rights worker R. L. T. Smith reflected on his relationship with Greene during the 1950s. "I worked with the man. He was a mail carrier when they hired me . . . I wish I knew something good about the man" (p. 74).

How did Greene, one of Mississippi's most influential black newspaper editors, become worthy of such praise and condemnation? The answer can be found in his political philosophy, in his choice of political allies, and in his editorials about the people and the events that shaped the civil rights movement. This chapter will demonstrate how Greene's philosophy and work cost him the respect and trust of Mississippi's black community during the civil rights movement from 1954 to 1965. To Mississippi blacks, Greene was on the wrong side of history. He closely followed the accommodationist philosophy of Booker T. Washington, became involved with some of Mississippi's staunchest segregationists, and used his *Jackson Advocate* to ridicule civil rights organizations and their leaders, such as the NAACP's Medgar Evers and Dr. Martin Luther King, Jr., of the Southern Christian Leadership Conference (SCLC).

In light of the political and socio-economic advances civil rights protesters initiated in Mississippi and the nation, Greene's conservatism, at best, is perplexing. Greene's editorial perspective can only be understood in the historical context of American race relations and the black press.

Historian Lauren Kessler explains in *The Dissident Press* (1984) that the overriding mission of the black press remained unchanged throughout the nineteenth and twentieth centuries—to instill a sense of racial pride, to educate, to vocalize the fight for democratic and economic freedom, and, when necessary, to mobilize and direct African-Americans to action. Due to slavery's restrictions, most early black newspapers originated in the North, where free blacks had the economic and educational resources to start newspapers. Black newspapers in the South did not emerge until after the Civil War. John R. Russworm and Samuel Cornish founded the nation's first black newspaper in New York in 1827.

In Henry L. Suggs' *The Black Press in the South, 1865–1979* (1983), historian Julius Thompson wrote that the first black newspapers to emerge in Mississippi were the *Colored Citizen* of Vicksburg, established in 1867; the *Canton Citizen*, founded in 1869, and the *Colored Citizen* of Jackson, founded in 1870. Seventeen publications emerged in Mississippi during Reconstruction from 1867 to 1899 (p. 178). The background of these early publishers varied; a few were ex-slaves, while others were born free or had escaped slavery. Despite their humble beginnings, the publishers worked to change the old order in the state by urging blacks to vote and elect public officials who were mindful of blacks' best interests.

In addition to politics, several economic and social issues faced the early black press as well as black leaders—land redistribution, education, economic aid, and social equality. Black editors lobbied for the government to give land to ex-slaves to compensate them for their unpaid labor, yet editors stopped short of recommending the confiscation of Southern land, except that owned by former Confederate leaders. They advocated equality of the races but devoted little space to the issue of interracial marriage. The Southern black press also supported voting rights, which included the voting rights of women, and advocated the establishment of public education.

Although Mississippi had its share of black newspapers, a poor advertising base and the economic impoverishment of blacks after the Civil War limited the growth of the state's black press. Moreover, inadequate educational opportunities kept readership of black newspapers low. Considering such conditions, the creation of seventeen black newspapers between 1869 and 1899 is impressive. Most periodicals, however, published for only one to two years. Only a few lasted more than five years.

Mississippi's social and political environment, particularly after 1875, also hindered the development of the black press. As historian James Silver notes in *The Closed Society* (1964), white Mississippians used propaganda to wrest control of state politics from blacks during Reconstruction. The early orthodoxy of white supremacy, mirrored in the state's white-owned newspapers, "contended that the Negro . . . would labor only under compulsion and was incapable of living without a master" (p. 12). Whites wanted to reinstate and maintain the "White Man's Government" with its "social and economic code," and to that end, they used ostracism and violence to achieve their goal. A riot in Meridian in 1871, an explosion in Vicksburg in 1874 that killed thirty-six blacks, and the presence of rifles and cannons at the polls in 1875 intimidated African-Americans into abandoning their democratic rights (p. 13–14).

The growth of the state's Jim Crow laws in 1885 also hampered the black press. The Mississippi Plan, which emerged from the revision of the state's 1890 constitution, instituted the white primary, which further curtailed black voting rights. Interestingly, Thompson (1983) writes that the only black editor present at the Constitutional Convention, Isaiah Montgomery of Mound Bayou, voted with the majority. Although Thompson fails to provide an explanation for Montgomery's position, the editor's accommodationist approach to race relations—a reluctance to tell the truth about social, economic and political conditions for fear of white reprisal—characterized the state's black press for the next ninety years.

From 1900 to 1950, the black press developed into a leading institution within black communities across the nation, if not in Mississippi. In addition to local and social news, black newspapers kept readers informed about the political, economic, and social philosophies of African-American leaders. During the early twentieth century, Booker T. Washington, a former slave and principal of Tuskegee Normal and Industrial Institute in Tuskegee, Alabama, emerged as a national leader after addressing an interracial crowd at the Atlanta Exposition in 1895. In his autobiography, *Up From Slavery* (1901), Washington wrote that he saw the Exposition as a unique opportunity to "cement the friendship of the races and bring about hearty cooperation between them" (p. 330). He advised blacks to start at the bottom of the socio-economic ladder by learning a trade, then to accumulate land or wealth rather than seeking political office. "In all things," Washington said in an implicit endorsement of segregation, "we can be as separate as fingers, yet one as the hand in all things to mutual progress" (p. 332). Washington advocated voting rights for propertied blacks, but he believed that these rights would be "accorded to the Negro by the Southern white people themselves, and that they will protect him in the exercise of those rights" (p. 339).

Washington recalled that African-Americans and black newspapers initially responded favorably to his ideas, but "after the first burst of enthusiasm began to die away, and the coloured people began reading the speech in cold type, some of them seemed to feel . . . that I had been too liberal in my remarks toward the Southern whites, and had not spoken out strongly enough for what they termed the 'rights of the race' " (p. 336). Historians note that Washington's accommodationist philosophy reflected the South's social climate. Arthur Tolson writes in *Booker T. Washington—Interpretative Essays*, that during the Washingtonian Era, 1895 through 1915, African-Americans in the South endured severe social controls from Southern whites, including murder, whippings, lynchings, and burnings;

more than 3,600 African-Americans were lynched. "Undoubtedly," writes Tolson, "such external circumstances had a tremendous impact upon the development of [his] philosophy" (p. 25).

Washington's accommodationist prescription for the race problem, however, was not the only political and economic philosophy to emerge after Reconstruction. Among those offering differing philosophies were Marcus Garvey (1887–1940) and Reverend Henry M. Turner (1834–1915), bishop of the African-American Episcopal Church and a Georgia state legislator. Both encouraged blacks to become economically independent of whites and return to Africa. Another black leader, Dr. W. E. B. Du Bois, advanced a philosophy that resonated with most of the nation's African-American population. Similar to Washington, Du Bois' personal history contributed to his social, economic, and political theories. Du Bois was a college-educated sociologist and renowned intellectual who came from an integrated background. Born in Massachusetts in 1868, he was educated in some of the world's finest institutions, Fisk University, Harvard University, and the University of Berlin. In *The Souls of Black Folk* (1903), Du Bois criticized Washington's "Atlanta Compromise" because it "practically accepts the alleged inferiority of the Negro races" and "asks that black people give up three things—first, political power, second, insistence on civil rights, third, higher education of Negro youth" (p. 52–53). Scholar John White writes in *Black Leadership in America* (1985) that three years later, in a meeting of black radicals, also known at the Niagara Movement, Du Bois issued his own remedy for "the problem of the color line." He advocated freedom of speech, manhood suffrage for all African-Americans, the eradication of the caste system, universal education supported by federal funds, equal employment opportunities, and constant protest to secure democratic rights. Although Washington used "his obstructionist tactics and influence to undermine the movement," White writes, the Niagara Movement laid the foundation for the creation of the NAACP in 1908, which Washington opposed (p. 46).

During World War I and World War II, black newspaper editors, especially those in the North, remained patriotic yet questioned African-Americans' participation in a war while blacks' democratic rights were being denied at home. But it was a different story south of the Mason-Dixon line, as Thompson explains in *The Black Press in Mississippi* (1993).

The period from 1900 to 1950 was a time of despair for black newspapers in the South, and for Mississippi in particular. In 1920, the Mississippi Legislature passed a law making it a misdemeanor to publish and distribute any publication advocating social equality or interracial marriage. White citizens issued death threats to publishers who failed to obey the law. In addition, the state's black press was hard hit by the Great Depression. Between 1910 and 1919, forty-six black newspapers were being published in the state. Between 1930 and 1939, only thirty-three publications remained (p. 11). Mississippi, an originator and relentless enforcer of Jim Crow laws, had curtailed the black newspapers' role as a forum for expressing views on segregation, lynching, and political rights. Between 1930 and 1950, approximately 30 lynchings took place, including that of Rev. T. A. Allen, who was killed for organizing sharecroppers in 1935. Black newspaper editors in the state took varied positions on these issues, but most failed to address the violence against African-Americans or the need for democratic rights.

Despite the dangerous and often hostile environment that surrounded black publishers in Mississippi, several prominent editors and newspapers emerged between 1900 and 1950. B. A. Wade began the *Southern Advocate* in Mound Bayou in 1933, and the *Delta Leader*, edited by Rev. H. H. Humes, began publication in Greenville in 1938. Due to the state's white supremacy system, which had little tolerance for those who criticized it, Mississippi's black newspaper editors avoided issues related to the attainment of civil liberties. The *Southern Advocate* did not have a strong editorial page and did not focus on international news. The *Delta Leader* carried local, state, regional, national, and some international news, and stories provided by the Associated Negro Press (ANP). The philosophical approach of both newspapers followed Washington's accommodationist philosophy. Greene took the same approach when he began publishing the *Jackson Advocate* in 1939.

Like most other black newspaper editors who began their careers between 1900 and 1950, Percy Greene was not a trained journalist. Historian Julius Thompson's *Percy Greene and the Jackson Advocate* (1994) provides insight into the editor's life. Born in Jackson in 1897, Greene came of age while living under Mississippi's oppressive apartheid system; sharecropping, lynching, and discrimination were a part of life. His high school and college education was patterned after the Washingtonian model: literature, agricultural, and industrial courses were standard fare. After receiving his high school diploma and some college training at Jackson College, he left Mississippi in 1915 during the Great Migration and traveled to Ohio, Illinois, and Iowa. During World War I, he served in Company B, 25th Infantry of the United States Army, where he served two tours of duty. He received an honorable discharge after living a short time in England and France. When Greene returned to Mississippi in 1920, the rules of the state's caste system remained firmly in place. Silver writes that "the segregation creed assumes the biological inferiority of the Negro, the sanction of the Bible and Christianity, the aptitude of the Negro for menial labor only, and racial separation as an absolute requirement for social stability" (p. 22). Although the creed also maintained that blacks should "earn their way to a higher and more responsible citizenry," hard work did not always guarantee success. In the early 1920s, Greene worked as a mail carrier and participated in a law apprenticeship program. Thompson (1994) writes that, after an altercation with a white man in 1926, state officials punished Greene by insisting that he had failed the bar examination. Discouraged and in need of a career, Greene turned to journalism and began editing the *Colored Veteran*, which served World War I's black veterans denied admission into the Foreign Legion and other veterans' organizations. The periodical, sponsored in part by the National Association of Negro War Veterans, was published in Greenwood from 1927 to 1928.

When Greene began publishing the *Jackson Advocate* in 1939, Mississippi had a large but economically and educationally impoverished African-American population. Black population in 1930 was slightly more than one million, with slightly more than 5,500 professionals, including clergy, teachers, physicians and lawyers. The remaining population largely consisted of sharecroppers and farmers. In *After Freedom*, her 1932 study of sharecropping in Sunflower County, anthropologist Hortense Powdermaker estimated that only a small percentage of black families in the Delta made a profit; most did not make enough money to eat properly. Thompson (1994) also explains that the benefits provided by the Works Progress Administration and the New Deal agencies barely made an impact in the state's black community (p. 13). Yet, as Thompson explains, a middle class emerged out of the impoverishment. Mississippi had approximately 1,300 black-owned businesses with net sales of more than $1.8 million. Jackson, the city with the highest population, had a Black Chamber of Commerce, established in 1932, a Progressive Business League, and a state branch of the National Negro Business League (p. 28–29).

Greene and his family were part of this small black middle class; both he and his wife, Frances Reed Greene, had attended college. The couple married in 1921, bought a home in 1931, and raised two daughters who attended public schools. After the *Colored Veteran* closed in 1928, Greene worked as a journalist for several other black newspapers, the *Negro Citizen* and the *Mississippi Enterprise*, both published in Jackson. With his wife's support and financial backing from childhood friend William A. Scott II and his brother Cornelius A. Scott, Greene founded the *Jackson Advocate*. The newspaper became a part of the Scott Newspaper Syndicate of Atlanta, Georgia, publisher of the *Atlanta Daily World*, Atlanta's leading black newspaper. Greene relied upon Washington's theory of racial cooperation to develop a mission statement for the *Advocate*. In editorials published on 14 August 1965 and 7 March 1970, he recalled that he wanted his newspaper to encourage "an atmosphere in which responsible Negro and white citizens of the state could work together for a solution of its problems, and gain for the Negro citizens of the state the right to vote and political participation."

But conditions allowed black activism to increase during the 1940s. Mississippi began to move away from a cotton economy. Technology in harvesting gradually reduced the need for laborers, which, in turn, may have decreased the need for whites to control blacks. In addition, a wartime economy spurred by government contracts increased industrial productivity and increased the move of the state's population from rural to urban centers. Scholars have hypothesized that these factors, along with the return of the state's 83,000 black World War II veterans, combined to create opportunities for activism with fewer reprisals.

Like most black newspaper editors, Greene supported African-American involvement in World War II. The war presented unique opportunities for the press, blacks, and U.S. race relations. In a 13 December 1941 editorial, Greene wrote that black newspapers should "spread such information considered necessary to create in the minds of the American Negro, a deep appreciation of the serious situation confronting the country." Again, like other black editors, Greene spoke out against segregation in the armed forces and the mistreatment black soldiers endured at military bases.

As one might expect, due to his philosophical attachment to Booker T. Washington, Greene disagreed with activist leaders such as W. E. B. Du Bois, and A. Philip Randolph. Greene opposed Randolph's proposal for blacks to march on Washington in 1941 to protest segregation. Similar to Washington, Greene did not approve of direct, militant action lest white Southerners feel coerced into changing the social and political system. Rather, Greene advocated extending voting rights to African-Americans, and he believed whites should work with blacks to do so. In a 30 April 1949 editorial, Greene told the *Advocate*'s readers that partnering with the upper classes of the black and white voting population was the only way to bring about social change. "We want to assure the white political leaders of the Democratic Party in Mississippi that our only purpose is to join with them in the spirit of the Constitution in Democracy in making Mississippi a better place for both its white and Negro citizens to live."

Greene's support of voting rights went beyond editorials. He was actively involved in encouraging blacks to register to vote. Prior to Franklin D. Roosevelt's presidency, Greene was a member of the Black and Tan division of the Republican Party. At that time, Mississippi Democrats routinely denied blacks admission to the party. Greene's conversion to the Democratic party began during Roosevelt's first administration. He felt that blacks could benefit from the president's New Deal policies. As a result, he began encouraging other blacks within the state to join the Democrats.

Party politics was not the only issue that motivated Greene to make black suffrage his major concern. *Smith v. Allwright*, the Supreme Court's 1944 decision that outlawed the white primary, also encouraged him to lead the fight for black voting rights. Two years later, in April 1946, Greene, along with fifty other black Mississippians, organized the Mississippi Negro Democrats Association (MNDA), and he became the organization's president. He also supported and worked with the National Progressive Voters League (NPVL), a group headed by the secretary of Jackson's NAACP, T. B. Wilson. In addition, he was active in numerous civic organizations and made numerous speaking engagement throughout the state.

By the end of the decade, Greene was a well-known journalist as well as a respected member of Mississippi's black society and the journalism profession. He received a "certificate of award" for courage in journalism from the *Chicago Defender* in 1946, a citation recognizing his work from Washington, D.C.'s Institute on Race Relations in 1947, and awards from the Mississippi Association of Colored Teachers and the *Pittsburgh Courier*. Mississippi's keepers of the status quo, however, regarded Greene with some suspicion. In a 17 June 1945 editorial, *Jackson Daily News* editor Frederick Sullens informed his readers, "If that Negro newspaper, the *Jackson Advocate* keeps on talking about Negro voting and participation in politics, there is going to be a lynching in Jackson and that Negro editor, Percy Greene, is going to be in the middle of it."

Greene's influential position in the postwar years placed him in a unique position to be a spokesperson for civil liberties as the civil rights era unfolded in Mississippi. Black newspapers had traditionally been a tool for education and motivation, and the *Jackson Advocate* had a healthy circulation of 5,500 in 1950. But as Thompson writes, Greene held fast to Washingtonian goals of black self-improvement, "with a focus on improving black businesses, farms, homes, living conditions, and health practices" (p. 42). He could move past these goals to promote black activism. Greene's Washingtonian principles, coupled with a lack of vision, led him to make decisions that would jeopardize his credibility and the future of the *Jackson Advocate*, rendering him an enemy to civil rights workers and a relic in his times.

The Supreme Court's landmark *Brown v. Board of Education* decision, handed down in May 1954, was meant to address the very sort of educational inequities as found in Mississippi. The Court's decision nullified *Plessy v. Ferguson*, the 1896 ruling that legalized Jim Crow laws, and by extension segregation in education. In *Brown* the justices ruled that segregation in public schools produced school systems that were unequal and unconstitutional. That was certainly the case in Mississippi, where no state in the nation spent less on education for blacks. As scholar Neil McMillen writes in *Dark Journey* (1989), the state's segregated educational system, established in 1870, was designed to limit blacks' political aspirations, render them economically powerless, and guarantee a low-wage labor force. Between 1940 and 1950, the state spent $122.93 per white pupil, compared to $32.55 per black pupil. Because their labor was required in cotton harvesting season, many blacks attended school less than seven months per year, while white students attended school for nine months (p. 73).

Facilities for black schools were extremely poor. Until 1950, 60 percent of black public schools were rural, elementary, one-teacher institutions. Even the Rosenwald Fund—private donations which contributed to the construction of 633 black schools throughout the state during the 1930s—barely made a difference. The number of black schools was also appalling. A survey taken in 1940 revealed that 25 of the state's 82 counties had no black secondary schools. Consistent with those findings, a 1950 survey of black schools in Sunflower County revealed that no black high schools existed. In addition, black public school teachers, although a large component of the Mississippi's black middle class, were underpaid. In 1945, black teachers made $426 per year while white teachers made $1,211 per year (p. 79–87). The Mississippi Legislature, in an attempt to influence the Supreme Court's decision, had enacted a public school equalization program in 1953 that called for equal salaries for black teachers and equal educational opportunities for black students but continued to require segregated schools.

Most of the nation's African-Americans reacted positively to the NAACP's victory, seeing it as essential for a good education and full citizenship. But African-American opinion was not unified in Mississippi. Thompson (1994) explains that Greene, along with black teachers and educators, was less receptive. As the foundation of the state's black middle class, educators had a vested interest in maintaining the status quo. Although they received lower salaries and worked in schools with poorer facilities than white teachers, black teachers had jobs, and with that came a certain amount of prestige. While they all welcomed the end of segregation, they questioned the positions black educators would hold in an integrated system. Consequently, as a protective measure, Greene advocated a separate but equally funded school system in his editorials in the weeks that followed the ruling.

Greene feared integration; he thought that it would ruin racial pride and would usher in a new kind of black leader. In an editorial published 28 August 1954, he suggested that blacks should seek "friendly relations with white people," who controlled the "political and economic strength" of society. At all costs, Greene suggested, Mississippi's dual public educational system needed to be preserved. His belief was fueled by a justifiable fear that the Mississippi legislature would introduce a bill to abolish all public education. Greene's worst fear materialized in September 1954, when lawmakers introduced a constitutional amendment allowing the abolition of public education if the Court's order could not be circumvented. The amendment, which was defeated by the Senate, would have authorized tuition grants for parents who wanted to send their children to private elementary and secondary schools.

After the *Brown* decision, Governor Hugh White, along with the Legal Educational Advisory Committee, decided that the best approach was to persuade black leaders that voluntary segregation was the answer. During the summer of 1954, the governor called a meeting of the state's black leaders in an effort to win endorsement of a plan to continue segregated schools voluntarily in return for higher teacher salaries and improved maintenance for black schools. The governor invited seven black educators and community leaders to the summit. The group included Greene; Rev. H. H. Humes, minister and editor of the *Delta Leader*; J. D. Boyd, president of Alcorn College; and J. H. White, president of Mississippi Vocational College. Dittmer (1994) writes that in the July 1 meeting, the men supported all-black schools and convinced the governor that the proposed plan to keep public schools segregated was sound. However, they also encouraged the governor to call a second meeting with additional black leaders. Greene and the others suggested that this second meeting, which should include representatives from the NAACP and other groups, would give the plan the credibility needed to attract black support.

The night before the July 30 meeting, Mississippi NAACP president and dentist Emmett J. Stringer met with those invited to the governor's meeting. At this "meeting the night before," the progressive faction overruled Greene and his accommodationist cronies. During the next day's meeting, in a united front, the black leaders resoundingly rejected the governor's plan. After the meeting, the leaders congratulated themselves on standing up to Mississippi's white power structure. Scholar John Dittmer (1994) writes that Aaron Henry, a Clarksdale druggist and later NAACP state president, recalled, "we shook hands, congratulating each other on what appeared to be a major triumph . . . I was really proud to be a Negro in Mississippi" (p. 38-40).

Although many black leaders were proud of their decision to support the Supreme Court's judgment, others began to backpedal. Dittmer (1994) writes that the president of Mississippi Vocational College, J. H. White, who served as the educational liaison between the governor and black educational institutions, wrote to the NAACP's Emmett Stringer and claimed that "the meeting we had at Jackson retarded the progress of the Negro" because "the white people of Mississippi are not ready . . . we cannot change over night discrimination and irregularities" (p. 44). Greene was also reluctant to support a fully desegregated school system. In 28 August and 4 September 1954 editorials, he supported the governor's plan for segregated but equally funded public schools. He also developed his own seven-point program demanding a long list of improvements:

> Equal public schools, including teacher salaries, books and courses offered . . . from the First through the Twelfth Grade . . . Alcorn College, Jackson College and Mississippi Vocational College be brought up to the highest standards . . . admission of Negro students to the University of Mississippi and Mississippi A & M College for professional studies and graduate work . . . permission of athletic competition between Negro and White High School and College teams . . . the election and or appointment of Negroes on all policy making Boards and Committees . . . elimination of all Jim Crow signs and segregation of all types of . . . public transportation . . . [and] the immediate removal of all restrictions against Negro voting in the state as a means to securing greater cooperation between Negro and White Citizens in developing and carrying out this program.

Mississippi whites adopted another approach to maintain segregation and the Southern way of life. In Indianola, Robert "Tut" Patterson organized the White Citizens' Council (WCC) in July 1954. White Citizens' Councils, one of many protective societies organized to maintain Southern traditions, sprang up throughout the region. The primary goal of the WCC was to deny African-Americans social and political equality. By October, the organization had 25,000 members from across the state, as well as support from the capital city newspapers, the *Daily News* and Jackson *Clarion-Ledger*. The organization, consisting of congressmen, judges, bankers, lawyers, physicians, business owners, and other civic leaders, developed a campaign of economic intimidation aimed at deterring blacks from organizing voter registration drives and petitioning local school systems to desegregate.

The WCC first targeted leaders of the NAACP, then the black middle class. State NAACP president Emmett Stringer was refused credit at a local bank, audited by the IRS, and his wife lost her teaching position. Stringer's patients told him that their employers instructed them not to patronize him. Dr. T. R. M. Howard, mayor of the all-black town of Mound Bayou, lost thousands of dollars in property assets, and his life was threatened. The black middle class was the next target. After the NAACP urged black parents to submit desegregation petitions to local school boards after the Court's implementation decree in 1955, the WCC took out a full-page advertisement in Yazoo City's local newspaper listing the names of the petitioners. Almost immediately all of the men and women listed in the ad lost their jobs. In response, some parents removed their names from the list; others, fearing further reprisals, left the state. Scholar John Dittmer notes that the WCC's tactics were successful; the NAACP "dropped Mississippi like a hot potato" and did not file another petition for eight years (p. 45–52).

Encouraged by the WCC's tactics and the perception that the NAACP had no real power, Mississippi's white citizens took intimidation a step further. In May 1955, NAACP member Rev. George W. Lee was assassinated for his work with voter registration. When called to investigate, the FBI performed only a cursory investigation. Also killed for encouraging Mississippi's black population to vote was Lamar Smith. The 66-year-old farmer and World War II veteran was shot in front of the courthouse at Brookhaven, a murder described as "the most blatant political execution in that bloody year" (p. 53–54). Similar to the Lee murder, the police made no arrest for Smith's death. In August, two white men lynched 14-year-old Emmett Till. The lynching, unlike earlier ones, received much national media attention, and arrests were made. As journalist Simeon Booker reflected in Hampton and Fayer's (1990) oral history of the civil rights movement, "it was the first time the daily—meaning white—media took an interest in something like this." Yet, even arrests did not assure that justice would be carried out. Despite overwhelming evidence to the contrary, an all-white jury found the defendants, Roy Bryant and J. W. Milam, not guilty.

The murders of Lee, Smith, and especially Till were covered by the national media. The *Jackson Advocate*, however, paid little attention to the events; Greene's editorials rarely addressed the murders of Lee and Smith, the tactics of the WCC, or the subsequent shutdown of voter registration. Beyond the observation that the murder failed to improve race relations, he said little about Till's lynching. Greene maintained his Washingtonian approach; the answer to racial problems in Mississippi rested in improved relations with whites. Moreover, he asserted that educational facilities should remain separate but equal because such a system created racial pride in black students. From 1955 through 1960, it seemed that change would come at a snail's pace in Mississippi.

Greene's conservative stance led him to make questionable political alliances. In 1956, to further support white segregationists' stand against integration, Greene became a paid agent of the Mississippi Sovereignty Commission (MSC), a secretive state agency created to spy and plot against those who supported integration. He became the mouthpiece for white anti-integrationists: He attacked desegregation, Dr. Martin Luther King, Jr., other important national figures, and vilified the motives and credibility of local civil rights leaders. With the assistance of the Commission, Greene, an African-American proponent of continued racial segregation, entered the national debate. A *U.S. News & World Report* article of 26 February 1956 gave Greene the opportunity to put his ideals before the nation. He criticized the desegregation efforts of the NAACP and stressed his opposition to integration. Greene also stressed his seven-point program he promoted in 1954. Historian Julius Thompson (1994) writes that in addition to viewing his comments as detrimental to the success of the movement, many African-Americans involved in the civil rights struggle in Mississippi saw this as a tremendous breach of trust (p. 77–78). But Greene did not look back; he became more entrenched with the Mississippi power structure.

Greene let the WCC use his newspaper as a vehicle to spread its anti-integration message. In November 1958, the WCC paid for the publication of a special free issue of the *Jackson Advocate*. Thompson (1994) explains that the issue was consistent with Greene's philosophy on race relations and commemorated the 63rd anniversary of Washington's famous "compromise" speech given in 1895. In 1959, in a trip underwritten by the MSC, Greene traveled to Washington D.C., to testify about the conditions of blacks in Mississippi to the Senate Subcommittee on Constitutional Rights of the Judiciary Committee. His comments and opinions on the state of race relations within the South were predictable. Thompson (1994) writes that Greene "had faith in the political value of black voting" (p. 79). Greene also stated that he did not favor and would not support any federal civil rights legislation. During the hearing, Greene was asked about his connection to the Mississippi Sovereignty Commission. Greene admitted taking more than $500 for travel and advertising. He also acknowledged that his opinions were consistent with anti-integrationist organizations opposed to the civil rights struggle and rationalized his position by asserting that "anybody—Sovereignty Commission, the man from down under, who[ever] wants to buy my paper and pay me for the service, I am going to sell it to them" (p. 79). He also stated that the Sovereignty Commission had paid "The National Association of Colored People of the South and me for the privilege of circulating a speech that I made on parallel progress, which was subsequently produced as an editorial in my paper, and not as an employee of the Sovereignty Commission" (p. 79).

The drive for civil liberties ground to a stand-still in Mississippi during the late 1950s due, in part, to the WCC's activities. Even as blacks in neighboring states organized and mobilized to end segregation, Greene supported none of it. He denounced Dr. Martin Luther King, Jr.'s philosophy of social change through non-violence, and criticized the value of the Montgomery Bus Boycott in 1956. In editorials published 5 January 1957 and 15 March 1958, Greene lashed out at King's efforts. "We have never been among those who widely applaud the efforts of Rev. King in the Montgomery matter, for the reason that his efforts there have succeeded in making matters worse for the masses of Montgomery Negroes, and as far as the abolition of bus segregation there from recent observations, and more recent reports there has been no change in the conditions there, a fact which makes Rev. King's, despite great national and international publicity, nothing more than a 'paper victory.'" Yet, on 13 November 1957 the Supreme Court ruled that Alabama's state and local laws requiring segregated accommodations were unconstitutional. The ruling motivated King, the SCLC, and other civil rights groups to try other non-violent strategies to end segregation.

Successful black protest campaigns did not stop Greene from criticizing the leaders of the movement. In a 16 April 1960 editorial, he sharply rebuked the NAACP's Medgar Evers, calling him a "zealot" who "is not able to see that the masses of Negroes in the state, and more and more responsible Negro leaders, understand that his organization thrives on tension and turmoil and easily accentuated emotions of Negroes." Greene also disapproved of religious groups that became involved in civil rights. In a 26 May 1962 editorial, he described the Black Muslims as an "organization whose activities are serving to delay and defer, rather than hasten [blacks'] full emancipation." In a 1 July 1961 editorial, he condemned Dr. Martin Luther King, Jr., for encouraging "anyone of 19-million Negroes to battle with anyone of 160-million white people." In addition, he failed to support the March on Washington in 1963 because, as he explained in a 24 August 1963 editorial, such demonstrations "prevent, rather than help, the development of public opinion, and public support, in the White community where the real power lies, in support of the Negro cause."

As Greene held firm to the racial status quo, black activism in Mississippi and the nation increased. Although the SCLC and the NAACP were the leading organizations implementing strategies, several other groups organized during the early 1960s and created their own plans. In 1960, college students formed the Student Non-Violent Coordinating Committee (SNCC) to fight segregation on their own terms. In addition, the Congress for Racial Equality (CORE) and the Urban League (UL) also adopted non-violent actions to end segregation. A coalition of civil rights groups in Mississippi combined resources in 1962 to form the Council of Federated Organizations (COFO) to coordinate voter registration efforts. These groups dominated the leadership of the movement, and out of necessity they often worked together.

Civil rights work undertaken by these groups received little sympathy from Greene. One such event, the Freedom Rides of 1961, was organized by CORE and used SNCC reinforcements. In 1946, the Supreme Court had ruled that segregation on interstate travel was unconstitutional. In 1961's *Boynton v. Virginia,* the court extended the unconstitutionality of segregation in interstate travel to the terminals. Southern states, however, still enforced Jim Crow regulations on buses and in terminals. On 4 May 1961, the Freedom Riders, two groups of students and activists from civic and religious organizations, boarded Greyhound buses in Washington, D.C., with New Orleans as the final destination. Their aim was to desegregate buses as well as bus terminals, and along the way they met fierce resistance from whites. Riders were beaten and their bus was burned in Alabama. Riders were summarily arrested when they arrived in Jackson.

Most Americans learned about the Freedom Riders and the violence which greeted them throughout the South in the news media. But Greene gave the Freedom Riders little sympathy or notice in his editorials. Moreover, Greene wrote that deliberately planned confrontations with the white power structure were futile. In a 26 August 1961 editorial, Greene stated that civil rights leaders were communist agitators that used "the sit-in, boycott, and other forms of public demonstrations, to cause the clashes between the Negro's hopes and aspirations, and the white power and authority."

But Greene would be more sympathetic with the efforts of James Meredith, who in 1962 became the first black student to enroll and attend the University of Mississippi. His admission to Ole Miss, however, did not come without resistance or violence. After being denied admission, Meredith, working with Medgar Evers and lawyers from the NAACP, filed a suit in 1961 alleging that he had been refused admission based on race. On 10 September 1962, the U.S. Supreme Court affirmed Meredith's right to be admitted. Mississippi's governor Ross Barnett vowed to block Meredith's admission. In addition, the state legislature passed a law barring admission to anyone convicted of a state crime. While trying to get admitted, Meredith was convicted in absentia of false voter registration. Despite Barnett's repeated vows to uphold the Southern racist tradition, he negotiated with the Justice Department to bring Meredith to the university. On 30 September 1962, Meredith went to Oxford, Mississippi. More than 2,000 pro-segregation protesters, however, attacked the federal marshals in a riot protesting the admission. Despite the violence (two people were killed and 160 injured), Meredith enrolled at 8 a.m. the next day.

Consistent with his support of equal education, Greene supported Meredith's admission into Ole Miss. In a 4 August 1962 editorial, he described the NAACP's suit as a chance to give "this state the opportunity to at once remove one of the major stumbling blocks to better race relations and equal educational opportunity for Negroes of the state." However, Greene failed to condemn the whites who rioted at Ole Miss to protest Meredith's admission. Instead, in a 12 October 1962 editorial, he warned blacks to watch their behavior because the advancements made by Meredith's admission into Ole Miss could lead to another post-Reconstruction era.

Meredith's admission into Ole Miss seemed to encourage more protests. Scholar Charles Payne writes in *I've Got the Light of Freedom* (1995) that just before Christmas 1962, Jackson activists launched a boycott against downtown Jackson businesses. The campaign, much of it initiated by NAACP youth, included marches, meetings, and picket lines. By early spring 1963, Jackson's police had arrested more than 600 protesters. Students from Jackson's Tougaloo College chose a downtown Woolworth's lunch counter for a sit-in on 28 May 1963. As expected, a group of whites beat several protesters. This demonstration, however, generated national attention, which in turn, helped pressure the city's mayor, Allen Thompson, to consider making several concessions, such as hiring more black policemen, taking down segregation signs, and opening public libraries to blacks. The concessions never materialized. Payne writes that, under pressure from anti-segregationists, Thompson withdrew the concessions (p. 286).

Although the boycott was successful in mobilizing Jackson's black community and garnering national publicity, the boycott also left Medgar Evers vulnerable. In *The Ghosts of Mississippi* (1995), author Maryanne Vollers writes that the Mississippi Sovereignty Commission used informants to collect information about Evers' activities. Greene provided some of this information. By the spring of 1963, Evers knew that his life was in danger. As a result, he began to take precautions to protect himself and his family. But on 12 June 1963, Evers was shot outside his home by Byron De La Beckwith. Although the *Advocate*'s editions immediately following Evers' death carried the story on its front page, Greene never editorialized about the man, the murder, or the trials of De La Beckwith.

Greene did not openly support Medgar Evers while the civil rights leader was alive. Although both worked to secure voting rights for Mississippi's black citizens, their strategy for achieving that goal differed. Greene viewed the NAACP's use of boycotts to gain voting rights as unproductive, since such actions prompted economic reprisals from whites. In a 16 April 1960 editorial, he criticized Evers' reported $10,000 salary. Greene wrote that Evers was drawing a healthy salary "even though every other Negro loses . . . if the white merchants start a counter boycott and start firing all their Negro employees." In place of boycotts, Greene proposed that blacks and whites in Mississippi work together, as he put it in a 12 June 1963 editorial, for "inter-racial progress."

Before his death, Evers had worked hard to increase black voter registration throughout the state. The momentum he helped create did not end with his death. COFO decided to use an old Reconstruction Era law that allowed people to vote provided they submit an affidavit asserting they were qualified to do so. Using this strategy, called the Freedom Vote, COFO decided to participate in the gubernatorial primary scheduled for 6 August 1963. A few days before the election, Joe Patterson, the state's attorney general, issued a statement indicating that those who tried to vote would be arrested. Despite his warning, there were few arrests. Mississippi's white power structure took another approach; they inspected the ballots and deemed them invalid. Despite the actions of whites in the state, COFO considered the Freedom Vote a success. The campaign's objective was to show the nation that black Mississippians wanted to vote. In addition, activists wanted to mock the legitimacy of the regular election by showing officials that voters wanted other representation. Payne writes that by the end of the campaign, COFO estimated that more that 80,000 votes were cast (p. 297).

While COFO considered the campaign successful, Greene considered the mock election an "exercise in futility." In a statement made to COFO's *Mississippi Free Press* on 7 December 1963, Greene alleged that "the Freedom Vote is just another foolish thing invented by those who seek to sensationalize the Negroes' civil rights drive, and play upon the less intelligent of the Negro masses." This time, however, Greene's comments and conduct did not go unchallenged. By 1963, Jackson had another local black newspaper that could dispute Greene's conservative philosophy.

In Mississippi during the civil rights movement, the *Jackson Advocate*, the state's leading newspaper, would not serve as a vehicle for disseminating the black protest message. The lack of access to existing media forced civil rights organizations to establish their own publications to meet the needs of the black protest movement. The *McComb Freedom's Journal*, the *Jackson Mississippi Freedom Democratic Party Newsletter*, and the *Vicksburg Citizen's Appeal* were created in the early 1960s. The leading newspaper to emerge from Mississippi's black protest movement was the *Mississippi Free Press*, which began publishing in 1961, and became the mouthpiece of COFO. According to a 16 December 1961 editorial, the journal's mission was to "at all times champion the cause of justice. It will fight injustice. It will take no backward steps." In Thompson (1993) civil rights activist John Salter described the *Mississippi Free Press* as "a blend of social news and civil rights, with the latter paramount, and because of this, the power structure condemned it vigorously" (p. 74). The newspaper's supporters included Medgar Evers, two white Mississippi lawyers, and Hazel Brannon Smith, editor of the *Lexington Advertiser*. The newspaper was printed on Smith's presses, an action which caused her innumerable problems.

Not only did the *Mississippi Free Press* espouse the ideals of the civil rights movement, the newspaper took Greene and his *Jackson Advocate* to task for its role in maintaining the status quo and serving as a mouthpiece for segregationists. Greene continued to work for the MSC during the late 1950s; his actions continued throughout the early 1960s. Thompson (1994) writes that during the 1960s the Sovereignty Commission paid Greene more than $3,500 for a variety of vaguely described services. Most entries were classed as "In return for subscriptions." In 1965, Greene received $750 for publishing a special supplement for the Commission. Thompson notes that the issue was designed to play down discrimination and portray blacks as a positive influence in the development of Mississippi's industrial complex (p. 74). It was the concern over the political impact of Greene's special issues that raised the ire of the *Mississippi Free Press*.

In November 1963, Greene published a special "Emancipation Proclamation" issue, which highlighted the accomplishments of Governor Barnett and the political and economic philosophy of Booker T. Washington. The MSC distributed these issues to members of Congress in an attempt to convince them that Mississippi's blacks were satisfied with the social and political environment in the state. Congressman Robert Kastenmeier, member of the House Judiciary Committee, which was holding hearings about the civil rights bill, alerted the *Mississippi Free Press* to the *Advocate*'s special edition. He worried that the *Advocate* might persuade some members of Congress into believing that conditions were not so bad for blacks in the state. On 7 December 1963 the *Mississippi Free Press* denounced Greene on its front page, claiming that the "Emancipation Proclamation" issue "reveals the paper's successful and total sell-out to Mississippi's white power structure." When the *Free Press* asked him about the content of the issue, Greene explained, "It was a pure public relations gesture. We sent them the issue to give our paper a wider currency and to evoke a larger source of advertisers. The Negro must learn the value of cultivating friendly relations with white people who command power and authority in order that they may help him reach his goals."

In the 14 December 1963 editorial, the *Free Press* continued to separate its political, social and economic philosophies from those advocated by Greene:

> We feel that our action is an example of the responsibility that each citizen must take when inaction results in the subtle damage of the civil rights struggle. The community has long known of the activity of this paper, yet has voiced no opinion. For reasons unknown, we have let this operation slide. We must face the question: What is being lost when we do not attempt to change those things which are destructive to the fight for truth in our state and nation.

In a 14 December 1963 editorial Greene tried to defend his newspaper by claiming that the *Free Press* wanted to "[put] my paper out of business because of my refusal to use the paper to promote and support everything" proposed by civil rights organizations. Greene claimed that the *Free Press* was run by communist, Northern whites involved in CORE. He also wrote that the *Free Press* had initiated a boycott of black and white local businesses that did not place advertising in the newspaper. Greene defended the *Advocate* based on its circulation and longevity. He reminded his audience that he had organized the Mississippi Negro Democrats Association, which helped increase black voter registration before the Supreme Court outlawed the white primary. In the same editorial, Greene accused the *Free Press* of initiating a campaign to destroy him and his newspaper. "I see the Emancipation Proclamation Centennial Edition as forcing the *Mississippi Free Press* out into the open with its avowed purpose of destroying the *Jackson Advocate*." The tension between the two newspapers remained steady throughout the 1960s. Greene repeatedly claimed that the *Free Press* was trying to put him out of business because he refused to promote the ideals of the civil rights movement.

The movement for civil rights escalated during the summer of 1964 when SNCC, CORE, and COFO stepped up their efforts to get the state's white power structure to eliminate barriers to black participation in the political process. The primary objective of the project was to register as many black people as possible for the vote. The other goal was to establish community centers as well as "freedom schools" to supplement the education of blacks in the state. The schools included black history and a special curriculum that encouraged the young to question Mississippi's racial caste system. The drive to increase the number of black voters in Mississippi should have pleased Greene. After all, he had consistently supported black voting rights since the 1940s. Greene, however, was not mollified by the Freedom Summer campaign. Rather than condemn local whites for murdering Michael Schwerner, James Chaney, and Andrew Goodman, Greene blamed outside agitators and demanded that the volunteers return to their home states to work on racial issues. The workers, Greene wrote in an 18 July 1964 editorial, should "leave the affairs of Mississippi to the white people and Negroes of the state."

The "agitators," however, helped push COFO's voting campaign into the national debate. The number of African-American voters in the South increased by approximately one-half million between 1960 through 1964. Despite COFO's efforts, Mississippi's Democratic Party continued to systematically exclude blacks, sending an all-white delegation to the Democratic National Convention. COFO planned to challenge the seat-ing of the regulars and bring the state's terrible voting rights record into the national debate. In April 1964, in conjunction with the Freedom Summer Project, the Mississippi Freedom Democratic Party (MFDP) sponsored its own statewide election of delegates for the Democratic National Convention in Atlantic City, New Jersey, using a selection process mimicking the national party. Aaron Henry was selected as the chair of the delegation. The project aimed to demonstrate to the country both the degree to which black Mississippians wanted to vote and how completely they had been excluded from the political process.

Although the MFDP was unsuccessful in unseating Mississippi's all-white delegation, Aaron Henry considered the campaign a success. But Greene was not impressed. In a 7 August 1965 editorial, he compared the organization to communists. "The chief aim of the Communist Party in the United States is not to solve the Negro problem, but to keep agitating and stirring the issue as long as possible in the hope of having Negroes become the revolutionary phalanx leading to the destruction of the United States and it's taken over by the Communists. We have always viewed the MFDP as the beginning of an effort to do so state by state. . . ."

In August 1965, President Lyndon Johnson signed the Voting Rights Act giving blacks the right to vote and to elect those who represented their interests. The law abolished the policies many Southern states used to prevent blacks from voting. The act suspended literacy tests, authorized federal examiners to replace local officials for voter registration, and stepped up federal oversight of elections. Greene heralded the Voting Rights Act, tempered, of course, by his Washingtonian views. In a 14 August 1965 editorial, Greene reflected on the original mission of the *Jackson Advocate* and surmised that the only reason the Negro should want the right to vote was "to be able to join with a better class on White folk . . . It is extremely unfortunate that the spokesmen for Negro civil rights organizations [have] created in the minds of Negro masses the fallacious idea that the obtaining of the right to vote and political participation means that Negroes will take over the affairs of the state . . . it is an idea in the long run that will lead to disaster."

While this chapter has chronicled one black editor during the civil rights movement in Mississippi between 1954 through 1965, the struggle for full democratic and economic participation in American society did not end with the passage of the Voting Rights Act. The late 1960s were turbulent years for both Mississippi and the nation. In 1966, Mississippian James Meredith, who began his "march against fear" in June, was gunned down by a sniper on the second day of his crusade. In response, Stokely Carmichael and others continued Meredith's work by leading another group of marchers through the state. In an interview during the march, Carmichael popularized the slogan "Black Power," two words that came to symbolize a new, more confrontational orientation for young African-Americans.

But as black Americans' struggle evolved, Greene's philosophical and political beliefs did not. Even as the black nationalist movement grew amid cries of "Black Power" and "Black is Beautiful," Greene continued to oppose the goals and leadership of the NAACP, SNCC, and the SCLC. Greene criticized Carmichael's call for "Black Power" because he believed that acting on such a slogan would result in mass oppression of African-American communities. Greene also criticized the activism of Meredith and SNCC leader Julian Bond. Although he was a staunch supporter of black voting rights, Greene never endorsed the state's black Democrats or COFO's voter registration drives. In addition, Greene continued to serve as an agent for the Mississippi Sovereignty Commission throughout the 1960s. He continued his pro-segregation editorials in the *Advocate*. Although he showed an interest in the Black Studies movement, Greene wrote what the members of the Committee wanted to read—he supported separate, but equally funded, schools.

Greene's refusal to endorse the fight for civil rights in Mississippi was a breach of trust with Jackson's black community. After honoring Greene as a type of celebrity during the 1940s and 1950s, Jackson's black community treated him like a social leper in the 1960s. Reflecting the view of civil rights activists, *Mississippi Free Press*' editorials on 7 and 14 December 1963, portrayed Greene as an enemy of the state's civil rights movement and described the *Jackson Advocate* as harmful to Jackson's black community. Quoting opinions from several Jackson citizens on 14 December 1963, the *Free Press* demonstrated Greene's low standing with fellow blacks. A retired Jackson businessman commented, "Percy Greene? Everybody knows he's sold out. I regard his paper just as I regard the White Citizens' Council paper." A Jackson barber concurred. "Well, all indications in the paper show that he's not for us. The *Advocate* is trying to influence people to say that we're satisfied—and we're NOT!" (In spite of the attacks, the *Jackson Advocate* outlived the *Mississippi Free Press*, which ceased publication in the 1970s.)

The 1970s were relatively quiet for Greene and his family. Greene was in his seventies, and his health began to fail. Both he and his wife were hospitalized early in the decade for a variety of ailments. But even as Greene's health failed, his social acceptability improved. In the 1970s, Greene became a principal speaker at Jackson's Masonic Lodge celebrations and attended several National Newspaper Publishers Association (NNPA) meetings. Moreover, the editor of the *Advocate* received invitations to affairs where he could rub shoulders with the nation's political elite. At such an event in September 1976, Greene suffered a heart attack while on a Mississippi riverboat cruise with President Gerald R. Ford. After receiving emergency treatment by the president's physicians, Greene was transferred to a hospital in New Orleans, and later, he returned to Jackson. He lived another seven months and died on 16 April 1977. Several months after his death, in July 1977, Greene received a posthumous honor for his service in the armed forces by President Jimmy Carter. Because he did not leave a will, the newspaper and all of his assets transferred to his wife.

In 1978, Frances Greene sold the newspaper to Charles W. Tisdale. The new editor worked hard to resuscitate the image and prestige of *Jackson Advocate*. According to historian Thompson (1994), despite initial opposition by Jackson's black businesses, Tisdale reported significant increases a year later in the newspaper's circulation and advertising sales. In 1978, the *Jackson Advocate* received a special merit award for its efforts to revitalize an important black media outlet during the Fourth Annual Project Media Awards Banquet. In 1979, the newspaper received an award for the "Best Business Section" and the "Best Woman's Page" produced by a black newspaper from the NNPA. The *Jackson Advocate* continues to publish today.

Although the *Advocate*'s image was successfully revamped, Percy Greene's legacy continued to be controversial. Scholar Neil McMillen (1972) interviewed Greene as a part of an oral history project sponsored by the University of Southern Mississippi. Greene held fast to his Washingtonian ideals. He continued to advocate "equal education and drop the word[s] 'separate but equal.' " He called for a "new idealism, new liberalism . . . not integration. . . . I want mutual understanding and cooperation," he said, "and a total abolition of the word 'integration' because the word has become provocative of conflict." He believed that civil rights leaders were duped by communist agitators to push for integration as a way to "tear up racial relations in this country."

It is difficult to explain Greene's actions, beliefs, and editorials. Viewed decades later, Greene's refusal to support the democratic rights of Mississippi's black citizens seems incredulous. Even when judging his actions within the context of his times, Greene's actions defy understanding. Here was a man with the tools and expertise to carry out the preeminent mission of the black press—to educate and mobilize African-Americans in the attainment of the democratic rights guaranteed by the Constitution. Yet, even as civil rights leaders made progress in challenging and dismantling segregation laws, Greene refused to change his position. Rather, he aligned himself with white segregationists and allowed his newspaper to be used to maintain the status quo. Why Greene took this approach remains a mystery; his editorials leave few answers for tough questions. Did Greene take a hard-line, pro-segregation stance because he feared for his life? That would be understandable, especially when one considers that White Citizens' Councils targeted many of Mississippi's black middle class for physical and economic reprisal, particularly during the 1950s. Or, did Greene sell his and the *Advocate*'s soul to the MSC so that, as he claimed in the late 1950s, he could accept advertising from whomever was willing to pay for it? Indeed, the newspaper received a significant percentage of its advertising from white-owned businesses, but the cost, the loss of respect from Jackson's, as well as the nation's, black community, and damage to the *Advocate*'s credibility, was a high price to pay.

Thompson (1994) offers one explanation for Greene's dogged refusal to support the civil rights movement—the psychological ravages of racism:

> So much [of] his spirit internalized much of the propaganda produced and distributed across the generations by the slaveholding aristocracy and its descendants, as well as by the supporters of the modern industrial and agricultural age, "King

Cotton's children." Greene's irrational values and self-hatred were the products of this propaganda leveled against the black community. Perhaps he wished to be white too, but knowing he could never reach this goal, he chose to idolize and imitate his heroes—the white elites of the South. (p. 84)

Greene was a product of the Jim Crow system. And, despite the system's obstacles and seemingly insurmountable challenges, Greene not only survived, but he prospered. After Mississippi's white power structure denied him the opportunity to become a lawyer, he became one of the state's most successful, controversial, and unforgettable newspaper editors.

References

Blumberg, Rhoda Lois. *Civil Rights: The 1960s Freedom Struggle.* (Boston: Twayne Publishers, 1984).

Branch, Taylor. *Parting the Waters: America in the King Years, 1954–63.* (New York: Simon & Schuster Inc., 1988).

Dittmer, John. *Local People: The Struggle for Civil Rights in Mississippi.* (Urbana: University of Illinois Press, 1994).

Du Bois, W. E. B. *The Souls of Black Folk.* (NY: Random House, Inc., 1996).

Finkle, Lee. *Forum For Protest: The Black Press during World War II.* (Canbury, NJ: Associated University Presses, 1975).

Hampton, Henry, and Steve Fayer. *Voices of Freedom: An Oral History of the Civil Rights Movement from the 1950s through the 1980s.* (New York: Bantam Books, 1990).

Kessler, Lauren. *The Dissident Press: Alternative Journalism in American History.* (Newbury Park, Sage Publications, 1984).

McAdam, Doug. *Freedom Summer.* (New York: Oxford University Press, 1988).

McMillen, Neil R. *Dark Journey: Black Mississippians in the Age of Jim Crow.* (Chicago: University of Illinois Press, 1989).

———. *The Citizens' Council: Organized Resistance to the Second Reconstruction, 1954–1964.* (Chicago: University of Illinois Press, 1971).

Payne, Charles M. *I've Got the Light of Freedom: The Organizing Tradition and the Mississippi Freedom Struggle.* (Los Angeles: University of California Press, 1995).

Silver, James. *Mississippi: The Closed Society.* (New York: Harcourt, Brace & World, 1964).

Thompson, Julius E. *Percy Greene and the Jackson Advocate.* (Jefferson: McFarland & Company, Inc., 1994).

———. *The Black Press In Mississippi, 1865–1985.* (Gainesville: University Press of Florida, 1993).

———. "Mississippi." Henry Lewis Suggs, ed., *The Black Press in the South, 1865–1979.* (Westport: Greenwood Press, 1983).

Tolson, Authur L. "Booker T. Washington's Philosophy and Oklahoma's African-American Towns," Tunde Adeleke, ed., *Booker T. Washington—Interpretative Essays.* (Lewiston, NY: the Edwin Mellen Press, 1998).

Vollers, Maryanne. *The Ghosts of Mississippi: The Murder of Medgar Evers, the Trials of Byron De La Beckwith, and the Haunting of the New South.* (New York: Little, Brown and Company, 1995).

Walker, Juliet E. K. "The Promised Land: The Chicago Defender and the Black Press in Illinois: 1862–1970." Henry Lewis Suggs, ed. *The Black Press in the Middle West.* (Westport: Greenwood Press, 1996).

Washburn, Patrick. *A Question of Sedition: The Federal Government's Investigation of the Black Press During World War II.* (New York: Oxford University Press, 1986).

Washington, Booker T. "Up From Slavery." Louis R. Harlan, ed. *The Booker T. Washington Papers: Volume I The Autobiographical Writings.* (Chicago, IL: University of Illinois Press, 1972).

White, John. *Black Leadership In America 1895–1986.* (NY: Longman, 1985).

Jimmy Ward and the Jackson *Daily News*

David R. Davies & Judy Smith

The *Columbia Journalism Review*, looking back on the civil rights era in summer 1967, concluded that the Mississippi capital's two daily newspapers had performed terribly in covering the social upheaval of desegregation. Jackson's *Clarion-Ledger* and the *Daily News*, the *Review* concluded, were "quite possibly the worst metropolitan newspapers in the United States." Similarly, a 1967 critique described both the *Clarion-Ledger* and the *Daily News* as ardent segregationist journals that had misrepresented the civil rights movement at every turn. "[T]he *Daily News* freely paints Negroes as baboons and apish clowns, sees communists in every anti-poverty program not controlled by the local white power structure, and 'exposes' Northern white liberalism as carpet-bagging subversion," a civil rights worker recalled in the Frederick W. Heinze papers. *Time* magazine concluded 22 December 1961 that the Jackson *Daily News* had published "unabashed prejudice" for years (p. 44).

Both the *Clarion-Ledger* and the *Daily News* had justifiably earned such denunciation for unfailingly defending segregation in Mississippi's years of turmoil. The two newspapers had vigilantly guarded "the racial, economic, political, and religious orthodoxy of the closed society," as University of Mississippi historian James Silver concluded in his 1964 work *The Closed Society* (p. 30). Both Jackson newspapers were owned by the Hederman family, and Silver was not alone in believing they served as opinion leaders in Mississippi. Indeed, the papers were integral in the maintenance of the "Closed Society," in which the tenets of white supremacy dominated the state and relegated blacks to second-class citizenship.

The Jackson *Daily News*, Jackson's afternoon journal, typified the Hederman papers and their segregationist approach to covering race relations. Its editor beginning in 1957 was Jimmy Ward, a firebrand who held forth in a front-page column, "Covering the Crossroads." The editor's column was a mixture of down-home humor, criticism of blacks, and bitter commentary on the civil rights movement. As this chapter will demonstrate, Ward consistently reflected Mississippi's racial orthodoxy in the state's years of turmoil. Both in editorials and columns for the *Daily News*, and through behind-the-scenes cooperation with segregationist public officials, Ward served as a staunch defender of the closed society. He and his newspaper played no small role in segregation's maintenance.

James Myron Ward began his association with the *Daily News* as a child, delivering the newspaper in his hometown of Montrose in Jasper County. Upon entering Jackson's Millsaps College in 1937, he fell in love with newspapering. While in college, Ward worked on the student newspaper, the *Purple & White*, and also worked part-time at the *Daily News* during the school year and full-time during the summer. When war broke out, Ward took leave from the newspaper business to enlist in the Army Air Corps. After cadet training, he became a B-25 combat pilot and was commissioned as a second lieutenant, flying in more than fifty combat missions. He was eventually promoted to captain, a title he held in the inactive reserve after his honorable discharge.

After leaving the army, Ward returned to his journalism career as a photographer and reporter for the *Daily News*. In September 1954, Major Frederick Sullens, the newspaper's longtime editor, named Ward the city editor. Three months later, Ward was promoted to managing editor, second in command at the newspaper. After Sullens' death in 1957, Ward took over the reign of editor from his idol. He held that title and continued his front-page column until illness forced his retirement on 7 January 1984.

The Hederman family, which owned both the *Daily News* and the *Clarion-Ledger*, had considerable newspaper holdings. The family owned the *Hattiesburg American* as well as a Jackson television station. Their tight control of the Jackson media market had prompted area businessmen to band together to form a rival newspaper, the Jackson *State-Times*, in 1955, but the newspaper died for lack of advertiser support seven years later. The *State-Times*' owners sold out to the Hedermans' company, the Mississippi Publishers Corporation, in 1962.

Through his early career, Ward was heavily influenced by his mentor, Sullens, a staunch segregationist well known for his resistance to change and for his defense of the segregationist status quo in Mississippi and in the South. "Jimmy Ward was perhaps the favorite of all the young journalists trained by Major Sullens," the *Daily News* commented on 24 November 1957 in writing of Sullens' death. "The admiration was mutual, for Mr. Ward practically idolized Major Sullens, whose very apt pupil he was." Like Sullens, Ward prided himself on speaking his mind. "Say what you think and don't go around apologizing for it," Sullens had once advised Ward. Throughout his career, Ward took that advice to heart. "I have no regrets," Ward declared in the *Daily News* of 8 January 1984 upon his retirement. "I could not erase anything I have written if I wanted to. God gave man the right to be wrong. What better way to learn than to make mistakes?"

Both Sullens and Ward believed passionately in segregation and that mixing of the races would destroy Southern society. On January 19, 1956, Sullens agreed with a Boston critic who had called Southerners racists. "We surely are," Sullens editorialized. "A racist, as we see the word, is a person who approves his own race and prefers the society of his own people. Being a racist merely means you want to preserve the bloodstream purity of your own race. The racist is rational, reasonable, and wholly normal when he demands the right to keep the company of his own kind. Yes, we are racists, and need not offer apology to anybody for so being." Like Sullens before him, Ward believed that segregation was essential to the maintenance of law and order in Mississippi. Integration, Ward wrote on 23 February 1958, would "breed strife and misery." White supremacy, for both Ward and Sullens, was a given.

Both Sullens and Ward abhorred the Supreme Court's 1954 school desegregation decision in *Brown v. Board of Education*. Their segregationist beliefs were consistently reflected on the *Daily News* editorial page throughout the 1950s. "The (Supreme) court is obviously out to destroy the South's heritage at any cost," the *Daily News* editorialized on 5 December 1955. The *Daily News* dismissed the court's so-called Black Monday decision as "judicial jackassery." On 11 September 1957, the *Daily News* concluded that the ruling was "a ruthless invasion of the God-given right of human beings to choose their own associations. It put the stamp of approval not only on integration but likewise on social equality, miscegenation, mixed marriages, bastardy, and mongrelization of the human race."

The *Daily News* believed that Southerners stood the best chance of fighting the *Brown* decision by presenting a united front. "The South is being assailed today by sinister forces," Sullens wrote on 19 January 1956. "It is being maligned, abused and grossly slandered by the NAACP and White Negrophiles who want to use the Negro vote for their own purposes. This is no time for haggling, vain disputations, or legal technicalities." Southerners, Sullens argued, should respond to Brown with bravery and courage; it was no time for neutrality.

The *Daily News* would prove anything but neutral in the coming years, as Mississippi geared up to fight any efforts at integration in the state. From the time of the founding of the Mississippi Sovereignty Commission in 1956, the *Daily News* closely cooperated with the agency, whose purpose was to resist any attempts to desegregate the state. As the Jackson *Clarion-Ledger* documented in a 28 January 1990 retrospective on the agency's dealings with the press, "The *Clarion-Ledger* and *Jackson Daily News* regularly killed stories and ran segregationist propaganda at the request of the state Sovereignty Commission in the '50s and '60s." The public release of Sovereignty Commission files in the 1990s revealed a series of memoranda between Ward and Commission officials. Commission representatives freely suggested ideas for articles and editorials to Ward, at times even supplying agency-written stories and editorials for the pages of the *Daily News*. Erle Johnston, the Commission's director in its earliest years and its executive director from 1963 to 1968, was on friendly terms with journalists across Mississippi, not just Ward. Johnston owned the *Scott County Times* in Forest from 1941 to 1983 and served as president of the Mississippi Press Association in 1949–50.

Johnston supplied a steady stream of story suggestions to Ward. On

11 October 1965, for example, Johnston sent Ward a memo suggesting that the editor send a reporter to cover racial discrimination in Vermont, a state which had sent a number of civil rights workers to Mississippi. Johnston reminded Ward that a legislator from Vermont had "meddled in Neshoba County and succeeded in getting arrested so he would have a story to tell." Johnston told Ward that the *Vermont Free Press* had recently reported NAACP complaints of housing and social discrimination against Vermont blacks. "It occurred to me that the influence of the VIM (Vermont in Mississippi) project in Mississippi would be considerably weakened if publicity was given to discrimination in Vermont," Johnston commented. "If you could assign a member of your staff to go to Burlington and assess the situation there, it would be a big help to us in Mississippi." Johnston offered to share expenses of sending the reporter to the Northeast.

Sovereignty Commission files reveal numerous similar interactions between Ward and Johnston, and between Ward and the Citizens' Councils, the white groups formed to fight integration through economic retaliation and other legal measures against blacks. In a memo dated 21 February 1962, Robert B. Patterson of the Citizens' Council suggested that Ward and his reporters should refuse to cover the regional NAACP meeting in Jackson later in the month. "On Martin Luther King's recent visit to Mississippi, he received very little newspaper publicity. This is exactly what he did not expect and it dampened his visit somewhat," Patterson wrote. ". . . [It] seems to me that if Mississippi newspapers would adopt the same policy when the regional meeting of the NAACP takes place in Jackson, Mississippi in the near future, it would thwart the aims of that nefarious organization." Johnston freely made suggestions that Ward drop references in his columns to events for which the Commission sought coverage or which seemed to demand editorial comment. "It occurred to me," Johnston wrote to Ward in a typical memorandum of 2 August 1963, "that this might be good information for a typical Ward editorial."

Sovereignty Commission files document Johnston's successes in placing articles in the *Daily News* and elsewhere. In 1965 Johnston wrote an editorial rebutting accusations of brutality against the Jackson police, then paid a small press service, the U.S. Press Association, to include the piece in its editorial package distributed to newspapers across the country.

Twenty-seven newspapers, Johnston exulted in memoranda of 7 January 1966, picked up the piece and printed it as their own editorial opinion. This included Mississippi newspapers such as the segregationist *Holmes County Herald* as well as small out-of-state newspapers such as the *Tribune* of Lemmon, South Dakota. Ward took note of the South Dakota editorial on the *Daily News*' editorial page of 6 January 1966, commenting that the South Dakota editor "seemed to have grasped the situation well." Whether Ward knew that the editorial was planted by Johnston cannot be determined by the Commission files, but he probably did, as he would have been unlikely to happen across an editorial from an obscure out-of-state publication without the assistance of the Commission's clipping service. Either way, Johnston was delighted at the success of his efforts. "I think we really got our money's worth," Johnston wrote.

Johnston documented another success in a memorandum to the file on 16 June 1964:

> When it was announced that Eugene Carson Blake had called a press conference in Jackson to discuss plans for the National Council of Churches' program in Mississippi, we contacted Jimmy Ward, Editor of the Jackson *Daily News*. We offered Mr. Ward information in our files concerning Eugene Carson Blake and how he has aided communist causes. This information was published in the Jackson *Daily News* issue one day prior to Blake's press conference.

Indeed, the *Daily News* had published a piece on 12 June 1964 under the headline "Leftist Preacher Rallies Agitators." The article, which appeared without a byline, alleged that Blake, chairman of the council's commission on religion and race, "has been a leader in a campaign to change the church and social order of the United States." His supposed link to the communists was that he had once led a U.S. tour for a group of Russian churchmen said to have party ties. The lengthy article was a testament not only to the Commission's influence at the *Daily News* but also to the newspaper's eagerness to comply with agency requests.

As civil rights activists such as Blake stepped up their efforts to crack the closed society, Ward stood firm as a guardian of segregation. In his daily front-page "Covering the Crossroads" column, he ridiculed both blacks and the civil rights workers who attempted to organize them. His abhorrence of the civil rights workers would be obvious through the arrival of the Freedom Riders in Jackson in 1961, the admission of James Meredith in 1962, the Jackson movement of 1963, and Freedom Summer of 1964.

When the Freedom Riders arrived in Jackson, Ward began a campaign of ridicule that would last for weeks. The rides had been organized by the Congress of Racial Equality to integrate buses and bus stations, which had remained segregated in some areas of the South despite a Supreme Court ruling banning segregation in all facilities used for interstate travel. An integrated group of freedom riders boarded buses in Washington, D.C., in early May 1961, finally arriving in Jackson on 24 May 1961. Upon their arrival, Ward dismissed the civil rights activists as "human freaks." The next day, the editor derided the riders as "idiotic agitating nitwits" and "abnormal mammals" who, in their effort to desegregate bus station restrooms and cafeterias, had come to Jackson for the "dubious honor of standing hip-to-hip before a bus station urinal with each other." He called on the students to return to the North to solve their own region's race problems, such as the high number of rapes in that "model city for race mixing," Washington, D.C., and the high juvenile delinquency rate in New York City.

The *Daily News*' news pages reflected Ward's view of the riders as outside agitators. Those who favored integration, or "race-mixing," were dubbed "mixers" in the newspaper's headlines. Beyond the headlines, however, Associated Press and United Press International's accounts of freedom rides outside Mississippi were balanced as printed in the *Daily News*, containing even the "mixers' " version of events. When the freedom riders were savagely attacked in Montgomery, Alabama, the *Daily News*' wire article on 16 May 1961, was headlined "Mixers Attacked in Montgomery," and a smaller headline noted that a white mob had beaten the integrationists. Similarly, a 21 May 1961 wire service retrospective on the *Brown* decision bore the headline, "Seven Years Under Black Monday Rule," but the article below it was balanced, containing views of integrationists as well as segregationists. *Daily News* editors clearly did not have the time or the personnel to edit the reams of wire copy that routinely flowed into the newsroom.

But staff-written articles about the rides were more one-sided, speculative, and opinionated. A locally written article on 21 May 1961 on the freedom riders in Alabama quoted no sources by name but said "Montgomery hotel-lobby experts" were blaming out-of-state demonstrators for the trouble. The "average man on the street" was said to be surprised at the recent turn of events, which included a mob attacking the riders in Birmingham and setting fire to their bus in Anniston. "[W]hen Anniston and Birmingham reacted so positively last Sunday, it should have been sufficient to let anybody know that aggressive violations of Alabama law would evoke reactions if continued, local residents insist," the *Daily News* reported.

As the riders neared Mississippi, the *Daily News*' coverage on 22 May 1961 focused on state leaders' preparations for the riders. The views of civil rights workers were not sought, but the opinions of Citizens' Council leaders were. Citizens' Council administrator William J. Simmons characterized the bus-riding students as "invading integrationists" and asked rhetorically whether the federal government, which had finally escorted the freedom riders through Alabama, would show the same solicitude for a Council expedition to the "heart of Harlem" to break Northern laws and customs. Furthermore, Mississippi Governor Ross Barnett offered moral support to Alabama Governor John Patterson over the latter's experience with the riders and prepared for their arrival in Mississippi.

Writing on 23 May 1961, editor Ward approvingly noted the state's preparations for the impending arrival of the riders. While he warned locals to let the police deal with the integrationists, he paradoxically continued to attack the riders in inflammatory language. And while Ward said calm people regretted the "unfortunate mob action" in Alabama, "On the other hand there is no weeping in the street down here because one of the invading screwballs got his hair parted." Arriving in Jackson, the freedom riders were quickly arrested without incident. "Mixers Reach Jackson With No Violence," the *Daily News* announced on 24 May 1961, and an accompanying front-page editorial lauded Barnett for his law-and-order stand. The editorial questioned whether the freedom riders properly belonged in the local jail, the mental hospital, or the zoo.

As arrests mounted the following day, still with no violence, Ward congratulated the Jackson community in a front-page, signed editorial for maintaining Southern hospitality during adversity. The "mixers," Ward said, had made Mississippi look good. "We wish for these vulgar, restroom-loving quacks a pleasant journey home. Thanks to them for favors done in their illegal, scummy mission." As the number of arrests mounted, the *Daily News* of 26 May 1961 continued to poke fun at the riders by one turn, to excoriate them at another. On the same day Ward derided the "silly cranky visitors" as welfare cheaters and an editorial accused them of failing to bathe, the editor attacked the riders for uttering unspecified lies about Mississippi. "Social gangsters in our midst have spent years slandering and libeling all of us. It will take a long time to erase their filthy-minded lies."

The riders filled the local jail through the last week of May 1961, as the *Daily News* carried articles about the first rumblings of another Mississippi civil rights milestone, the application of James Meredith to enter the all-white University of Mississippi. Meredith, after months of wrangling with Ole Miss officials, sued for admission to the university on 31 May 1961. By September 1962, response to Meredith's application for admission was reaching a fever pitch after more than a year of legal maneuvering, appeals, and hearings. Justice Hugo Black had ordered Meredith's admission, and Governor Barnett had announced a statewide television speech to address the crisis. The *Daily News'* front page of 12 September 1962 announced that a cross had been burned outside the veterans' apartments where Meredith would soon be living. The accompanying picture of the blazing cross, the first of several to be burned at Oxford in coming weeks, carried the caption, "Greeting for Negro."

The *Daily News'* coverage of the Meredith crisis lacked the humorous edge of the accounts of the freedom rides. Meredith posed much more of a threat to the closed society than did the bus-riding students, who had challenged a form of segregation that did not touch most Mississippians' daily lives—interstate bus transportation—and who could be removed from public view swiftly with effective police work. Meredith's attack on segregation at the university, on the other hand, presented a greater threat to Mississippi's way of life, and its preservation was threatened by the federal government's persistence on his behalf. The higher stakes stiffened the *Daily News*' resistance.

The newspaper outlined the stakes in a front-page editorial after the cross-burning. Headlined "Blueprint for Destruction" in editions of 13 September 1962, the editorial noted that violence was increasing in New York City, a clear result of the "race mixing" so prominent there. Mississippians faced a choice between following New York's example of desegregation, which "leads straight to decay and corruption," or refusing to follow the path to oblivion. The editorial did not mention the Meredith crisis, but said it was important for Mississippians to consider such crucial choices "at this point in Mississippi history." The editorial foreshadowed the governor's themes that night in his televised response to the Supreme Court's decision to allow Meredith to enter Ole Miss. Saying no Caucasian race had yet survived social integration, he declared, "We will not drink from the cup of genocide." He repeated his pledge that no school would be integrated in Mississippi while he was governor.

The 14 September 1962 *Daily News* provided blanket coverage of Barnett's address as well as warm support for the governor's stand. "Mississippi Mix? Ross Says 'Never!'" headlined the primary article, accompanied by the full text of the governor's remarks and an editorial titled "We Support Gov. Barnett." The editorial said the governor's position is "one that is solidly endorsed by all right-thinking Mississippians." To underscore the point, a photograph showed a harried secretary sorting through the piles of supportive telegrams that had poured into the governor's office.

In the days after the speech, the *Daily News* marshaled support for Barnett's stand. "Let the Crackpots Scream," a *Daily News* editorial advised on 15 September 1962, saying the state would never please the "wild-eyed social bandits who have used this venom to turn many of the nation's cities into sidewalks of jungle terror." News articles in the combined Sunday edition of the *Daily News* and *Clarion-Ledger* on 16 September 1962 offered further support for the governor. A front-page article labeled "bulletin" reported rumors that Ku Klux Klansmen were gathering in Tuscaloosa, Alabama, in preparation to descend upon Oxford or Jackson. Another front-page article, lacking any named sources, exhorted state officials to "stand firm" with Barnett or face retribution by the legislature.

Even the newspapers' society reporter got into the act; Florence Sillers Ogden's "Dis An' Dat" column lavished praise on Barnett. The *Daily News*' support of Barnett held firm in the following weeks.

On its editorial page the *Daily News* excoriated out-of-state media for criticizing Barnett, praised Southern newspapers who supported him, urged citizens to be careful in dealing with reporters visiting the state, lauded Barnett in a lengthy profile, and continued to warn that desegregation would ruin Mississippi as it had defiled the North. Showing a rare crack in his humorless stance toward the Meredith issue, Ward suggested on 24 September 1962 that the government should sidestep the entire issue and declare every person in the state a Negro, "and the Magnolia State will become the happiest, biggest Harlem the world has ever known" (19, 21, 24 September 1962).

The Jackson newspapers' close relationship with Barnett was apparent from their favorable coverage of the governor and their news articles echoing the governor's themes. Moreover, the death notice on 20 September 1962 of longtime *Clarion-Ledger* city editor Gene Wirth in the midst of the Ole Miss crisis called Wirth a "confidant and close adviser" of the governor who "during the past days of crisis had spent many long and late hours conferring with the chief executive and other state officials." Barnett was an honorary pallbearer at Wirth's funeral.

The week prior to Meredith's admission, the *Daily News* followed closely the impending "invasion" of federal forces. The newspaper's articles and editorials argued paradoxically that federal troops and marshals were not needed in peaceful Mississippi and that Mississippians stood prepared to fight to the death to defend segregation. The newspaper's resolve against violence had faded. As the *Daily News* reported on 26 September 1962 that Lieutenant Governor Paul B. Johnson, Jr., had turned Meredith away from the Ole Miss campus, a front-page article warned that Mississippians would win the integration battle "regardless of the cost in human life." An accompanying article, datelined Birmingham, Alabama, noted that thousands of members of the States Rights Party were willing to take up arms on Barnett's behalf. Mississippi's United States senators said in an article on the same page that the use of troops in Mississippi would be illegal.

The next day, Ward's front-page column said the public should be congratulated for remaining calm, as no violence had been reported. "There is no cause whatsoever for Federal troops to [be] sent into Mississippi. With everyone acting peacefully, why would troops be sent unless it would be a military grab of power?" On the same page, an article described a gathering of 500 police officers in Oxford, "watchfully alert against a possible invasion of fifty to 100 U.S. marshals especially trained as riot-busters."

Two days before Meredith's arrival at Ole Miss on Sunday, 30 September 1962, the *Daily News* provided its readers a musical anthem of the state's determination. Words and music to the "The Never, No Never Song" ran in place of the usual cartoon on the editorial page of 28 September 1962. An editorial said the song expertly put the state's attitude to music and suggested that readers clip it for a possible mass rendition at the Ole Miss-University of Kentucky football game the following day. The song, an ode to segregation, declared that, at Ole Miss, "Never, never, never, shall our emblem go from Colonel Reb to Ole Black Joe."

After the riot that killed two and injured dozens the night before Meredith's admission, the *Daily News* on 1 October 1962 blamed federal marshals and the national government for the violence. The headlines expressed the newspaper's position completely: "Negro Troops Set Off Oxford Battle," "Marshals Fire Gas Without Warning," "Ross Blames 'Trigger-Happy' U.S. Officers." The newspaper's account was consistent with the support for Barnett and vilification of federal authorities that had marked the coverage leading up to the violence.

Following Meredith's admission, Ward in his column barraged the veteran with ridicule for daring to desegregate Ole Miss. He frequently made jokes, as on 13 November 1962, about "the most famous scholar in the world" or "the famous one." On 2 November 1962, Ward claimed that he had heard a rumor that Ole Miss head football coach John Vaught would seek Meredith's assistance as the Rebel squad took on Louisiana State University. "Vaught will use Meredith to take the ball and he'll be escorted by troops with bayonets pointed at the Tigers with a sign saying, 'Stop this boy and you're in contempt of court.'" Ward introduced a new cheer for the Rebels. "Roses are red, Violets are blue, Let's take Meredith to LSU."

Oddly, the story of Harry Murphy, a light-skinned black from New

York who claimed to have "passed" during his days as a Navy student at Ole Miss in the mid-1940s, received little notice in the *Daily News*. Murphy's attendance at Ole Miss beat Meredith to the honor of desegregating the university by almost two decades, but the newspaper buried a short account of Murphy's story on page eight of its 25 September 1962 issue and left the writing to the wire services.

If the *Daily News*' coverage of civil rights news was blatantly segregationist, its coverage of blacks in other arenas showed a similar segregationist bent that was, at least, more subtle. By and large, the *Daily News* simply ignored the black community. Blacks were seldom seen or heard in the news columns unless they committed a crime. The *Daily News*, which consistently ran page-one articles about honors given local white schoolchildren at area junior and senior high schools, did not honor black schoolchildren with similar coverage in these spreads. Society pages pictured pages upon pages of white brides, but no blacks.

Occasionally blacks made it into the newspaper, perhaps if they died violently or if public money was being appropriated for black schools. It helped, too, if a black had some connection with the newspaper. The manager of the *Clarion-Ledger* Colored Circulation Department, a 24-year veteran of the newspaper, was honored with a three-paragraph article on 2 September 1962, albeit in the classified section, on the occasion of his departure to California for another job. But participation in any violent act was a surer way for a black to win entry into the *Daily News* pages. Blacks who were accused of committing violent crimes, no matter how far away from Mississippi, could wind up on the front page. The stabbing of a white commuter on a New York City subway train, for example, merited a front-page story in the *Daily News* of 5 June 1964. When a group of blacks attacked two white couples celebrating a wedding anniversary, the newspaper responded with not only a front-page article on 15 June 1964 but also a three-column photograph of the victims.

Blacks frequently made it into the *Daily News*, however, as objects of ridicule in Ward's column. The editor filled his daily writings with jokes and stories about blacks, some with political points and some without, but all degrading. Ward wrote on 6 June 1961 of a black minister who got into trouble with his congregation and left with this parting comment: "Owin to de bad feelings what exists between mahself and sutton pussons in dis congreation, today's services terminate my pastorate in dis church. I will not say 'au revoir' because none of yo'all knows what dat means; I will not say farewell because dat am a term used when friends take leave of each other. But as I prominades down de aisle toads de doah, I desier to call attention of ever nigger in the congration to the spring of mistletoe which am attached to the lower end of mah coattail."

On 10 March 1962, Ward wrote about the efforts of the black community to get a black into the space program, but it said that situation would cause many problems for the black sent into space. "The pilot seat is at the back of the capsule. No Negro wants to sit at the back of anything. The federal government would have to station troops and bayonets in space to escort the Negroes through white clouds and since rockets fly so fast, wouldn't their squirrel tails be ripped from the capsules' big antennae." Despite those shortcomings, Ward said whites should expect blacks in space. "Clear the skies folks, for some enforced brotherhood on the moon," he wrote.

In 1963, the assassination of Medgar Evers, NAACP field secretary, gave the *Daily News* a rare chance for the newspaper to show empathy, even in a restrained way, to a black man. In the first story describing the shooting of Evers outside his home the night of June 11, Ward's column the following day called the killing a "dastardly act of inhuman behavior," virtually identical language to that used by Barnett. But the newspaper described the killing more in terms of its damage to Jackson's reputation for peaceful race relations than as a human tragedy. An editorial on 13 June 1963 blamed the bloodshed on professional agitators, usually synonymous for civil rights workers, and lamented the damage to Jackson's image. An accompanying cartoon depicted a book representing "Jackson's Record of Racial Harmony" as blemished by Evers' assassination. (In a famous headline, the *Clarion-Ledger* emphasized the out-of-state ties of murder suspect Byron De La Beckwith when he was arrested. "Californian is Charged With Murder of Evers," read the newspaper's front-page headline 24 June 1963, although Beckwith, though born in California, had lived in Mississippi since he was a child.)

The year 1964 had a wealth of civil rights news for the *Daily News* to cover, all of it controversial. The new civil rights bill was wending its way through Congress, much to Southerners' chagrin. Another black student,

Cleveland Donald, Jr., was applying to the University of Mississippi. And most controversially, hundreds of Northern college students were in Mississippi under a program organized by the Student Non-Violent Coordinating Committee and allied civil rights groups. The students, most from the North, planned to register black voters and to set up an elaborate network of "freedom schools" to offset the poor educational system afforded Mississippi blacks. The schools included not only the traditional subjects of reading, writing, and arithmetic, but also black history and a "citizenship curriculum" that encouraged young Mississippi blacks to challenge the racial and social status quo in their home state.

In contrast to its aggressive outspokenness in facing the Freedom Ride activities and Meredith's admission to Ole Miss, the *Daily News* was relatively silent regarding the activities of Freedom Summer. As the first students were arriving in Mississippi in early summer, the *Daily News* editorialized on 13 June 1964 that Mississippians should ignore the unwanted visitors. "As outside meddlers come into Mississippi in the coming weeks, the wise thing for all private citizens, old and young, to do is to refrain from any action on their part and let the proper officials handle the situation," the editorial stated. "The general public can wield a powerful influence for good and help send these malcontents back home by completely ignoring them. . . . Let's all ignore them." In the following months, Ward took his own advice and largely kept references to the summer project off the editorial page and out of his column.

With a few exceptions, Ward's references to the summer project were limited to humorous references to the civil rights workers' alleged uncleanliness. "The stringy hair and beards makes these characters look awfully alien to a bar of soap," Ward quipped on 24 July 1964. "Maybe somebody ought to get up a fund and buy them some detergent and deliver same to the various 'freedom houses' scattered about the state." The so-called beatniks' theme song, Ward wrote on 21 August 1964, was "Give me liberty or give me Lifebuoy." Ward put aside silliness, however, in welcoming allegations by Mississippi Senator James O. Eastland in July that communist influences were behind the civil rights activism in the state. He wrote on 23 July 1964 that Eastland had performed a lasting service to the community by exposing the alleged ties. Bob Howie, the *Daily News*' editorial cartoonist, reinforced Ward's point the following day with a drawing of civil rights "agitators" inciting racial disorder at Moscow's direction.

The *Daily News* often characterized the incoming students as invaders. At first, the newspaper closely followed the story when civil rights workers Michael Schwerner, Andrew Goodman, and James Chaney were reported missing. But coverage quickly slacked off until bodies of the three were found almost two months later on August 4. Then and afterward, the newspaper closely followed the search for their killers but refused to comment on its editorial page about the murders. The newspaper found space to editorialize on the nuclear age, sleeping habits, dairy herds, and Alaskan resources in late summer 1964, but it said nothing about what was one of the largest national news stories of the year.

While Ward did not comment directly on the disappearance of the workers, he did note that the influx of Federal Bureau of Investigation investigators would do well to return home to fight crime in the North. "It is good judgment, we believe," Ward wrote in his column of 10 July 1964, "to have many FBI agents live in peace and comfort in Mississippi." In an 8 July 1964 editorial titled "Where Feds are Needed," Ward detailed a recent murder in Washington, D.C., that he said required federal attention. "Paging Allen Dulles! Paging Leroy Collins! Paging J. Edgar Hoover!" the editorial began, listing the law enforcement officials visiting Mississippi. "The services of these three top Civil Rights enforcement emissaries busy in Mississippi affairs are needed in Washington to attend the senseless and unchecked murders." A 23 July 1964 editorial reprinted FBI crime statistics showing Mississippi's low crime rate and urged readers to clip the column and send it to friends "subjected to the barrage of slanted and distorted reports on Mississippi and its law-abiding citizens."

Ward's editorial page lamented the "evil consequences" of the civil rights bill working its way through Congress in early summer. The bill, Ward argued, signaled the end of constitutional guarantees and the beginning of totalitarianism. "The blackness of thorough and crushing domination of every business and professional activity in these United States, reaching into every home and every individual's life," the editorial of 25 June 1964 argued, "will descend with the inescapability of a never-ending nightmare." Howie's editorial cartoon of 20 June 1964 showed a beret-wearing, goateed beatnik filling in a grave marked "Rights of the Individual." After the Civil Rights Act was signed into law, the *Daily News* editorialized 17 July 1964 that the measure would curtail economic expansion. On 28 July 1964, a *Daily News* editorial linked the new law to recent rioting in Oakland, California, claiming the rioting proved that such liberal measures had failed.

In August, the *Daily News* took note of the peaceful token desegregation of Jackson's schools in the new school term. Desegregation would eventually bring unchecked violence to schools, an editorial predicted 21 August 1964, and henceforth school discipline would take precedent over education. "The lack of incidents should be taken as a manifestation of good behavior rather than approval of the forced desegregation," Ward wrote. "Time has taken its toll and Jackson falls unwillingly as a bastion of segregation. As the event came to pass, this city becomes a little bit pregnant with integration but the condition came about not voluntarily but with Federalized rape."

During Freedom Summer and indeed throughout the civil rights era, Ward vigorously defended Mississippi against outsiders, taking regular aim at groups and individuals he deemed a threat to Mississippi. Chief among his targets were CORE, Martin Luther King, Jr., and the NAACP, both the national and state organizations. The "Chronically insane NAACP," as Ward dismissed the group on 23 August 1962, elicited the most venom. Ward decried the organization as a hotbed of agitators intent upon spreading hate among otherwise-contented Mississippi blacks. He repeatedly charged that CORE and the NAACP were only interested in raising money in Mississippi, not in helping the black population. "CORE, braintrustors of strife, hate and violence doesn't hold its board of directors meetings in latrines," Ward wrote on 30 May 1961. "They and NAACP have plush offices. They send their hypnotized volunteers into the South to get their heads bashed in so they can recall this for foot-stomping and plate passing rallies in order to collect moola for their big salaries. This sort of slave traffic deserves the fullest attention by Federal authorities." Writing on 23 February 1962, Ward called the NAACP "a bunch of racial agitators" and said that "there are delightful signs that the nation is awakening from its extended state of hypnosis or quasi-insanity aroused by racial passions and propaganda."

Ward's primary weapon against the NAACP and its leaders was ridicule. With tongue in cheek, Ward alleged on 21 September 1961 that the NAACP might seek a federal injunction against the Mississippi oil industry because "it seems Mother Nature made oil 'black' in the bowels of the earth down heah and the race-mixers demand the stuff be half white and half black." When Mississippi was hit with a rare snow storm, Ward announced, "There is a rally today at 6:30 on Lynch Street. The NAACP is expected to meet and gather its flock to protest the fact that the snow that fell on Mississippi is white, nothing but white." Ward returned to this theme often. "Did you hear about the new NAACP doll?" Ward asked on 3 June 1963. "Yep, you wind it up and it screams 'police brutality.' " King had sued to get *Black Beauty* removed from libraries in New York, Ward joked on 12 April 1963, "until the censors discovered it was about a horse."

Ward often returned to the allegation that NAACP leaders and activists were out to enrich themselves at the expense of the black population. After 500 blacks were rescued by volunteer workers and disaster agencies when rainstorms caused flooding in Jackson, Ward commented on 20 December 1961, "Haven't seen a single representative of the NAACP or the CORE represented in this emergency work." When the NAACP held a fund-raising rally in Jackson, Ward said on 29 March 1961, "the plate was passed and no one knows—probably never will know—exactly how much money was raised." On 22 December 1961, Ward complained that "not a thin dime" had been contributed to flood relief along the Pearl River by CORE or the NAACP. "Yet," he continued, "when it comes to those foot-stomping parties and plate passing sessions, it's the NAACP and the CORE that smuggles Jackson green stuff into their pockets and they slip out of town."

King—nicknamed "Dr. Extremist Agitator Martin Luther King"—was a popular target for Ward's criticism. Ward depicted him as a selfish leader who preached hate for white people only to line his pockets. Ward derided the civil rights leader as "the czar of all Negro agitators in the land," "the world's most famous rabble-rouser and race agitator," or "the professional Negro." "There's a new doll on the market," Ward joked on 19 November 1964. "It's a Martin Luther King Jr. doll. Wind it up and it spews out lies." This was a frequent theme; Ward argued that King brought hate to every community. "When Dr. Martin Luther King hits a town," Ward wrote on 17 May 1963," he leaves in his wake bricks, glass and burned out buildings as well as bloodshed and a great amount of hatred." After the civil rights leader organized protests in Alabama, Ward reported on 4 May 1963, "Over in Birmingham, Dr. Martin Luther King encouraged school children to play hooky to get out into the street and raise hell with police. Dr. King's idea of the three Rs: readin' 'ritin' and riotin'."

Ward believed that King's advocacy of civil disobedience to unjust laws constituted a mockery of what he considered to be law and order. "Society would find itself in a complete state of collapse in little time if such were the case community wide," the *Daily News* editorialized on 22 July 1964. "Of course, this may be the ultimate objective of the non-violent movement now being espoused so fervently by the trouble-making agitators now engaged in aggravating violence." Here as elsewhere, however, Ward's defense of law and order and criticism of lawlessness stringently followed racial lines; he was critical only of black lawlessness, not white. Moreover, his enthusiasm for the law was limited primarily to the elaborate legal framework that enforced segregation in Mississippi, laws which he held should be inviolate. On the other hand, he believed that federal statutes and court rulings that challenged Mississippi segregation were unjust. In reality, then, Ward favored not so much law as order, specifically *racial* order, which he interpreted as acceptance of segregation.

At the same time Ward excoriated civil rights leaders such as King, he lionized state leaders, particularly Barnett, offering frequent praise for their segregationist stands. Ward's support of Barnett never wavered. "There is not a single person of statewide influence in political affairs who has not endorsed the strong position of courage taken by Governor Ross Barnett," Ward wrote on 24 September 1962. Ward presented Barnett as a hero and role model for Mississippians. "Gov. Ross Barnett, like Daniel, walks into the lion's den as he makes those speech making trips to those Eastern institutions of learning," Ward wrote on 3 October 1963 of the governor's speaking trips in the Northeast. "Those students look and act like Ol' Ross is the devil with a forked tale and is invading their angelic quarters." As Wilson F. (Bill) Minor, Mississippi correspondent for the New Orleans *Times-Picayune* in these years, recalled of Ward, "He always supported whatever the governor and police did." Minor recalled Ward as segregation's most consistent supporter. "He was siding with the segregation forces," Minor said. "That was what the Jackson *Daily News* preached. . . . I think he had a vision that he had to keep traditions going, which were started by Sullens. He felt he had to maintain that status quo of the time."

The *Daily News* and Ward's column presented Mississippi as a happy, peaceful state with few or no problems. "Despite tense situations, the relations between the races in Mississippi continues excellent and without friction," Ward wrote on 13 October 1962. "This is commended and is as would be expected. Mississippians actually love and appreciate the Negroes." Ward's Mississippi was peaceful and moral, in stark contrast to a violent and fractious North. "Officials in Philadelphia and Baltimore now claim that rioting in the North has been touched off deliberately due to a conspiracy among agitators," Ward wrote on 8 September 1964. "So this is news? Sounds like too many persons have been too busy criticizing Mississippi to be aware of what has been going on under their eyebrows." Writing on 22 September 1963, Ward stated that "a whole flock of New York reporters are back in the South to cover the 'racial' troubles. Wonder who covered Harlem while those fellows were in the Deep South. Wonder why those big city newspapers don't carry a boxscore on their front pages each day announcing the number of rapes the night before."

Ward, echoing a common complaint among Southern journalists who defended segregation, complained that the Northern press emphasized the South's problems while ignoring Northern disturbances. "The race situation seems to be getting badly out of hand in New York, but you wouldn't know that because only Southern photos seem to make global news," Ward wrote on 15 July 1963.

Ward and the *Daily News* publisher, the Hederman family, were "very much in tune on the racial issue," said W. C. "Dub" Shoemaker, a reporter for the *Daily News* in 1949–50 and from 1954 to 1965. But management generally did not pressure reporters to cover stories one way or the other. "They generally left us alone in coverage," Shoemaker recalled, as long as reporters followed the unwritten rule that no courtesy titles—Mr., Miss, or the like—could be used in front of a black person's name. Reporters who followed that rule faced only routine questions from their editors. Shoemaker could recall only one exception, a Shoemaker profile of a training camp for civil rights workers and its founder. "He didn't tell me to change it," Shoemaker recalled of Ward, "but he said, 'You're awfully friendly to him.' We let it run." By and large, however, Ward did not see the newspaper before it went to press, Shoemaker said. Instead, he left day-to-day editorial decisions to the mid-level editors who supervised city, state, and wire news.

Daily News reporters, Shoemaker recalled, were on good terms not only with Mississippi authorities but with the leadership of the civil rights organizations, even as Ward was excoriating civil rights workers in his columns and on the editorial page. "We as reporters had generally a pretty good relationship with the people who made the news on both sides of the racial issue," Shoemaker said. "They didn't tell us any secrets, but we were welcome to their [events]. They needed us." Shoemaker, for example, was friendly to Medgar Evers, the NAACP field secretary in Jackson, and even played penny poker with him a time or two. The two did not visit each other's homes, of course, as that would have been taboo in segregationist Mississippi of the early 1960s. But both Evers and other civil rights leaders were accommodating to *Daily News* reporters. "We got along all right," Shoemaker said. Such accommodation was consistent with the civil rights workers' efforts, particularly in Freedom Summer in 1964 and afterward, to get both state and national publicity for their activities.

His outspokenness aside, Ward got along very well with his reporters. In the newsroom, Ward had long enjoyed the reputation as a warm and fun individual who was both a good writer and a sound reporter.

"He was personally a very nice guy, fun to know, fun to go to his house, fun to visit with," Shoemaker recalled, and he had many friends in the relatively small town of Jackson. A longtime feature writer before joining the editorial ranks, Ward had never been known for extreme opinions. But as he became more outspoken in his segregationist views, "He got very opinionated in his writing," Shoemaker recalled. His hard-line editorial opinions drew him closer to some friends and estranged him from others. The editor's opinions eventually came to be regarded as extreme even within the *Daily News* newsroom, where reporters such as Shoemaker tried to stay neutral on racial matters in the interest of good reporting. Though he did not agree with Ward on the race issue, Shoemaker said, he was able to maintain a good relationship with both the editor and the

Hedermans, whom he described as good employers who treated him well. "They were people of strong opinions," Shoemaker said, "but they were fair to me."

The Jackson *Daily News*' brand of segregationist journalism in the 1960s attracted the notice of the newspaper's journalistic peers across the country. Surveying newspaper coverage of the civil rights movement for the *Columbia Journalism Review* of Summer 1967, journalist Roger Williams concluded that Ward and his newspaper had contributed to the poor image of Mississippi as well as its resistance to move out of the past. "Southern newspapers have failed to prepare the people of the South for the greater changes, economic as well as social, that have buffeted them," Williams concluded. *Newsweek* magazine, in noting "the inflammatory statements" of Jackson's daily press, was similarly derisive of the *Daily News* on 15 October 1962 (p. 100). "The *Clarion-Ledger* and its sister newspaper, the Jackson *Daily News*," a writer for the magazine declared, "seemed to erect a 'Magnolia Curtain' between the people of Mississippi and the truth." Ralph McGill, the well-regarded editor of the *Atlanta Constitution*, believed that the violence in Mississippi in recent years was primarily the result of newspapers' failure to lead.

Civil rights workers had an equally bleak view of the Jackson press. John R. Salter, Jr., who helped lead Jackson protests while a professor at Tougaloo College in the early 1960s, dismissed the newspapers in his personal writings as "the crude and venal Hederman press." The Student Non-Violent Coordinating Committee attempted to counter the Jackson newspapers' influence through its own newspaper, the *Student Voice*, which was distributed both to the student workers and to Northern supporters. In 1964, the newspaper published 40,000 copies weekly at the SNCC office in Atlanta, which also produced brochures, posters, leaflets, and flyers. The student workers saw the *Voice* as a vehicle to distribute information about the civil rights movement that had been omitted from Southern newspapers such as the *Daily News*.

Upon Ward's retirement in 1984, the *Daily News*, which had long since shed its segregationist image, lauded the editor's outspokenness. The *Daily News*' editorial page of 6 January 1984 took note of Ward's defense of segregation in previous decades but withheld judgment. "Jimmy Ward's place in Mississippi history we leave to Mississippi historians," the editorial declared. "To them he will be another figure in Mississippi's turbulent past. To those who had the pleasure and great honor of knowing him, of working with him from day to day, he will always be someone special, more human than the pages of any historian."

Ward died just two months after his retirement, a victim of cancer at age 65. Both houses of the Mississippi Legislature approved resolutions commending the editor's life and career. The resolution praised Ward as "a powerful voice of influence in this state through editorials and columns."

Ward and the *Daily News*' coverage of the civil rights movement mirrored the orthodoxy of the closed society. Blacks, so rejected by society, were rejected and maligned by the newspaper. Civil rights workers, so threatening to Mississippi, were scorned. The newspaper echoed the Citizens' Council and Mississippi's politicians, excoriating outsiders as agitators. The *Daily News* sustained the closed society and, by extension, the violence that enforced it. The newspaper did not openly invite disorder, although it came close to it in the Ole Miss crisis. But its news coverage and enthusiastic support of political leadership that compared integration to genocide constituted a more implicit invitation. Ward and the segregationist press played a key role in upholding the tenets of segregation even as its legal foundations were crumbling.

"Jimmy was a crusader," recalled former *Clarion-Ledger* executive editor Purser Hewitt. "He believed very fiercely and strongly in what he stood for. No compromises." Ward's passionate belief in segregation and white supremacy prompted print campaigns to discourage the civil rights movement and to encourage its opponents. His front-page column touched the lives of many Mississippians, who trusted his judgment. Ward could have used his influence to help Mississippi through one of the state's most difficult periods, but it was simply not in his nature; he believed too strongly in the ways of the Old South.

Ward's depictions of blacks were cruel, and many blacks were angered and hurt by his columns. Minor interviewed the parents of black protesters arrested in the Jackson movement in the early 1960s, and some mentioned the pain that Ward's writings had caused them. "When I talked to some of those parents, they told me that Jimmy's words did more to hurt them than anything else," Minor said. "They said they could take the restraint of the state, but his words hurt them more than anything else. He was brutal in his comments, and he even referred to those blacks as 'chimpanzees parading down Main Street' as they fought for the right to vote." Myrlie Evers-Williams, who decades after her husband Medgar Evers' death became the chairwoman of the NAACP, recalled in an 18 June 2000 interview with the *Clarion-Ledger* that newspaper coverage was both hurtful and dehumanizing to Mississippi blacks. "It certainly did play a part in making a minority race feel worthless," she said.

The *Daily News*' 8 January 1984 account of Ward's retirement took note of the considerable criticism of the editor's stands during the civil rights movement. "I thought he was 100 percent wrong," said the *Lexington Advertiser*'s Hazel Brannon Smith, who said many of Ward's editorial stands were "inexcusable." Medgar Evers' younger brother, Charles Evers, said Ward had written what whites wanted to hear. "He did what was popular at the time." William E. Spell, Jr., a *Daily News* reporter in the 1950s, said Ward's social stands were typical in civil rights-era Mississippi. "The whole state was racist," Spell said. "I think Ward reflected the attitude of the state. At the same time, I don't think that Ward ever wanted to see any individual mistreated or suffer."

Ward indeed may not have wanted to see anyone suffer, but it would have been difficult to discern it from his columns and editorials. His virulent segregationist views, as this volume shows, were not altogether typical in Mississippi; rather, they reflected the extremist segregationist positions of the worst elements of the Citizens' Councils and the Sovereignty Commission. Ward went much farther in his columns that was the norm in Mississippi journalism. His column was popular; of that there is little doubt. But Ward's popularity within the newsroom and with the public did not translate into good journalism. The *Columbia Journalism Review* recognized that fact in 1967, well aware of the *Daily News*' segregationist bias if not its behind-the-scenes collaboration with sources. It was not until the opening of the Sovereignty Commission files a quarter century later that the depths of Ward's and the *Daily News*' journalistic lapses were apparent.

By reflecting the closed society with such vehemence, the *Daily News* and Jimmy Ward contributed to its maintenance in long-suffering, racially backward Mississippi in the early 1960s. "Editor Ward stands aggressive guard against any threatened breach in the color line," *Time* magazine lamented in a profile of the *Daily News* editor on 22 December 1961:

> And his paper is one of the prime reasons why Mississippi remains the South's most stubborn center of segregation. . . . Former Editor Fred Sullens was a sulphurous segregationist who predicted that even Negroes would come to "curse" the U.S. Supreme Court's 1954 school integration decision. . . . When Sullens died four years ago, the editor's chair passed to onetime *News* carrier boy Jimmy Ward, and the *News*'s racist drum missed not a beat.
>
> Against its steady tattoo, the voice of moderation can scarcely be heard. Even if it were more audible, it is not likely that many would listen. In Mississippi the rednecks like what Jimmy Ward says. And he and the *News* will go right on saying it.

References

Dittmer, John. *Local People: The Struggle for Civil Rights in Mississippi.* (Urbana and Chicago: University of Illinois Press, 1994).

Minor, Wilson (Bill). Telephone interview. 8 April 1998.

Mississippi Oral History Program of the University of Southern Mississippi. An Oral History with Mr. Norman Bradley (Vol. 194, 1982).

Williams, Roger M. "A Regional Report: Newspapers of the South." *Columbia Journalism Review* (Summer 1967): 26–35.

J. Oliver Emmerich and the McComb *Enterprise-Journal*

David R. Davies

J. Oliver Emmerich knew that trouble lay ahead. In the tense spring that preceded Mississippi's long, hot summer of 1964, Emmerich, editor of the McComb *Enterprise-Journal*, predicted that the impending arrival of out-of-state civil rights workers could easily provoke a violent white backlash in his conservative southwest Mississippi town. Mindful of McComb's turbulent racial history, Emmerich wrote a series of signed, front-page editorials outlining community preparations for the "invasion" and pleading with McComb citizens to act responsibly. "Our conclusion is that we should all try to relax," Emmerich wrote on 29 May 1964. ". . . May we on Sept. 1 look back on the summer of 1964 and be able to truthfully say, 'We met a crisis with maturity. We did not panic. We exercised restraint. We upheld the dignity of the law. We met a challenge intelligently.'"

McComb did not respond as Emmerich had hoped. Between the spring and fall, there were twenty-five incidents of arson, as well as beatings, burnings, and widespread intimidation of McComb area blacks, and whites who were sympathetic to them. Sixteen homes and churches in the black community were dynamited, including the residence at 702 Wall Street where black and white workers of the Council of Federated Organizations (COFO) lived and organized black voter registration drives. McComb's violence drew the attention of the national news media,

Mississippi Governor Paul B. Johnson, Jr., and even President Lyndon Johnson, who promised quick action after meeting with three bombing victims.

But if McComb's upheaval was almost predictable, the sudden end to the violence was not. In early fall, business leaders, including Emmerich, got together first to raise reward money to catch the bombers, then to appeal for an end to the bombings in McComb. The bombers, all of them white, were arrested, and the *Enterprise-Journal* published a "statement of principles" on 17 November 1964 signed by hundreds of McComb citizens. The principles urged a return to law and order, an end to harassment arrests, compliance with the Civil Rights Act of 1964, and greater communication between the races. Finally, the violence ended in McComb, partly a credit to editor Emmerich and his *Enterprise-Journal*.

Emmerich was neither an arch-conservative on the race issue nor a flaming liberal, but an avowed segregationist softened by a belief in fair journalism. The ultimate businessman, Emmerich believed in doing what was good for business and what was good for his community, principles that lay at the base of growing business support for acceptance of civil rights laws across the South in the 1960s. By no means had McComb solved its racial problems by the end of 1964, but like other communities then and later, it at least had begun to face them without violence. McComb's story, then, is the story of the end of one community's resistance to desegregation, and how that evolution was reflected in the *Enterprise-Journal*, a medium that was the eyes and ears of white McComb.

A town of 12,000 people in 1964, McComb is just north of the Louisiana state line, seven miles north of Magnolia, the seat of Pike County. From personal experience, civil rights workers considered rural southwest Mississippi one of the strongholds of segregationist sentiment. Freedom riders had been beaten upon their arrival in McComb in May 1961. Cleveland Sellers recalled in *The River of No Return* (1973) that he and fellow civil rights workers regarded southwest Mississippi as "the ninth circle of hell" and believed that area whites were willing to kill to defend segregation (pp. 47–50). Activists, in reports compiled for release to the media, called McComb a "hard core area."

Indeed, McComb lived up to its reputation for violence when Bob Moses of the Student Non-Violent Coordinating Committee (SNCC) arrived there in August 1961 to spearhead a black voter registration drive. His first month in town, Moses was beaten on a McComb street when he tried to take two blacks to register to vote. A shotgun blast was directed at a car of civil rights workers. In September, a voter registrar in Tylertown pulled a pistol on two blacks attempting to register and pistol-whipped a SNCC worker. Then Herbert Lee, a black man active in the voter registration campaign, was shot and killed in Amite County by a state legislator, E. H. Hurst. More than 100 black high school students in McComb walked out of classes and staged a protest of Lee's shooting; all were arrested. Moses, as John Dittmer wrote in *Local People* (1994), found opposition in southwest Mississippi so severe that he moved on elsewhere, later directing SNCC's voter registration project in Greenwood. Despite SNCC's activism in 1961, Dittmer writes, "McComb remained the same Jim Crow town it had always been" (p. 114).

Because of its intransigence, however, McComb and Pike County remained a priority for civil rights workers. SNCC staffers made it a point to include McComb in the organization's plans for the Freedom Summer project. The plan was for hundreds of Northern college students to descend upon Mississippi—considered America's most segregated state—to run "freedom schools," including one in McComb. The schools would teach citizenship to blacks and prepare them to fulfill Mississippi's rigorous voter registration requirements. Mississippi, characterized by James Silver as "The Closed Society" in his 1964 book of the same name, held fast to racial orthodoxy and widespread pressure for conformity. The state prepared for an expected "long, hot summer" as if for an "invasion," two phrases used repeatedly in Mississippi newspaper articles about preparations for the summer.

Emmerich had reason to be tense; he had experienced McComb's racial turmoil firsthand. As the publisher described in his book *Two Faces of Janus* (1973), a stranger had punched him in the face in front of a McComb drugstore in 1961 in the wake of the newspaper's coverage of freedom riders' arrival in the city. Emmerich had pleaded for law and order after harassment arrests and violence had greeted the riders. In 1962, a circulation boycott had followed Emmerich's editorial assertion that Governor Ross Barnett, in fighting James Meredith's admission to the University of

Mississippi, was damaging the state's national image and ignoring constitutional government (pp. 127–128).

In 1964, Emmerich was 67 years old and had been a newspaper editor and publisher for 41 years. Born in New Orleans, Emmerich had grown up in McComb after his family moved there when he was four. In Mississippi he was steeped in what he called the "cotton-patch" mentality of the South. This philosophy, as Emmerich described it in his autobiography, demanded conformity, resistance to change, racial prejudice, and a rationalization of Southern traditions. Emmerich studied agriculture at Mississippi A & M College (now Mississippi State University), was graduated in 1918, and worked as a county farm agent for several years after college. In 1923 he bought the McComb *Enterprise*. Two decades later he bought the rival McComb *Journal* and merged the two newspapers to form the McComb *Enterprise-Journal*.

Emmerich was a firm believer in states' rights in the 1940s and 1950s and was one of the Mississippi delegates who walked out of the Democratic Convention in 1948 in protest of Harry Truman's civil rights policies and his renomination. But Emmerich opposed lynching and supported voting for blacks, and he wrote in his autobiography that he came to regret his states'-rights stand (pp. 87–89).

In McComb and in Mississippi, Emmerich had earned a reputation as a "moderate" because of his stands by the early 1960s. Silver in *The Closed Society* gave him that label, as did his fellow journalist Erle Johnston, publisher of the *Scott County Times* and director of the Mississippi Sovereignty Commission from 1963 to 1968. To be a "moderate" in 1960s Mississippi was to vary from the racial orthodoxy of the closed society, and Emmerich certainly did that by favoring black voting rights. But "moderate" was and is an imprecise label, as editors and others pinned with the label by their Mississippi neighbors held widely varying views. Charles Dunagin, who worked as Emmerich's managing editor at the *Enterprise-Journal* beginning in 1963, recalled in an interview that Emmerich did not believe that desegregation was the solution to racial injustices. "[Y]ou cannot say simply that integration would eliminate them and that segregation encourages them," the editor declared in an interview with the Philadelphia *Sunday Bulletin* on 17 May 1964. Moreover, Emmerich opposed the Civil Rights Act of 1964 and editorialized on 7 May 1964 that by requiring businessmen to serve patrons of other races the bill might violate the Constitution's Thirteenth Amendment prohibition against involuntary servitude.

Still, Emmerich would prove willing to speak out, and that was more than many editors in Mississippi were willing to do in these years. The majority of the Mississippi press in the early 1960s, according to Silver, vigilantly guarded "the racial, economic, political, and religious orthodoxy of the closed society" (p. 30). Silver believed that the Hederman family—which owned the Jackson *Clarion-Ledger* and the *Daily News* as well as the Hattiesburg *American*—dominated Mississippi thought. In its summer 1967 issue, the *Columbia Journalism Review* noted that the *Clarion-Ledger* and *Daily News* had recently eliminated some of their most outrageous anti-black sentiments but remained "quite possibly the worst metropolitan papers in the United States" (p. 26). The Hedermans' tight control of the Jackson media market in the 1950s had prompted the founding of a rival newspaper, the Jackson *State-Times*, for which Emmerich had written editorials from McComb. The newspaper closed in 1962 after publishing for just seven years.

In 1964, Emmerich was the editor and publisher of the *Enterprise-Journal*. His writing for the newspaper was limited primarily to editorials and to his daily, front-page column, "Highlights in the Headlines," a chatty column with a hometown flavor that often included jokes and tidbits of town gossip as well as commentary on issues of the day.

Dunagin was the *Enterprise-Journal*'s managing editor, and he also covered news for the newspaper along with one other reporter, Charles B. Gordon. Dunagin occasionally contributed a signed editorial column on the editorial page, as did John Emmerich, Jr., Emmerich's son and a writer for the Baltimore *Sun*. Dunagin and Gordon wrote all of the *Enterprise-Journal*'s news articles about the summer of 1964.

Typical of Mississippi newspapers of the period, the *Enterprise-Journal* always included a racial identification any time African-Americans were mentioned in the newspaper. Blacks were identified in headlines and in news copy as "Negroes," whether their race had anything to do with the news or not. Those who favored integration, or "race-mixing," to use the term of the era, such as the Senate Democrats backing the civil rights bill of 1964, were dubbed "mixers" in headlines. By and large, blacks were not mentioned unless they committed a crime or died in an accident, although the *Enterprise-Journal* sometimes pictured black athletes and printed articles about blacks who had won civic awards. Thirty years later, Dunagin recalled with regret that the newspaper had made little effort to cover the black community in these years, although the newspaper did print black-related news supplied to the newspaper.

Beginning in mid-May 1964, Emmerich's writings in the *Enterprise-Journal* began to urge state and local preparations for the impending arrival of the COFO workers. Emmerich's editorials and columns consistently opposed violence but otherwise reflected the racial mores of white Mississippians. Acknowledging that the community was indeed threatened by the invasion that had "but one purpose—to provoke our own people to violence," Emmerich nonetheless urged calm on 13 May 1964. He said Mississippi no doubt had a policy for dealing with the "invasion" and that the state should tell residents about it. The next day, Emmerich reported that he had talked with Governor Johnson and learned the governor's official policy, which was to ignore harmless demonstrations and to arrest people who took the law into their own hands. Emmerich said in his column that Mississippians should take comfort in the fact that the state was "confronting this invasion threat with the determination to avoid violence." An accompanying page-one article written by Emmerich explained the governor's policy and state preparations.

The Association for the Preservation of White Race (APWR) and the Ku Klux Klan were also making preparations; both had meetings in mid-May. Civil rights workers writing in the SNCC newspaper, the *Student Voice*, worried on 15 July 1964 that the two groups—more extremist than the Citizens' Councils, which were losing in influence—were conducting organizational drives in Mississippi to take advantage of widespread opposition to the voter drives. Both the KKK and APWR meetings were covered in the *Enterprise-Journal* so matter-of-factly as to underscore the widespread acceptance of white supremacy groups in McComb at the beginning of the summer. The newspaper reported on 15 May 1964 that speakers at the previous day's APWR meeting, held at the Summit Town Hall, included Pike County Sheriff R. R. Warren, Shelby Brewer of Brookhaven, chairman of the Lincoln County chapter of the organization, and Emmerich. Both Brewer and Warren spoke out against the threat of violence, with Brewer declaring that "boycotts can replace bullets in Pike County this summer." Emmerich, according to the *Enterprise-Journal* account, discussed his recent conversations with Governor Johnson and explained his editorial position that the civil rights bill might violate the Thirteenth Amendment's prohibition against involuntary servitude.

The same day, the *Enterprise-Journal* ran a short, front-page article about a Klan meeting to be held the following Saturday night at the Pike county fairgrounds. A three-column-wide advertisement on page three promoted the rally. The *Enterprise-Journal*'s 18 May 1964 account of the rally, headlined "Reds Blasted, Wallace Boosted at Klan Rally," noted that more than 800 people attended the gathering, identified as the first large-scale Klan rally in recent history in Pike County. Two local ministers and a city selectman spoke at the rally, as did Robert M. Shelton, Imperial Wizard of the United Klans of America. "The soft-voiced speaker," the *Enterprise-Journal* wrote of Shelton's eighty-minute talk, "held his crowd pretty well spellbound despite the length of his low-key speech."

On Monday, 25 May 1964, Emmerich began a five-day series of front-page editorials to prepare McComb for the coming "invasion." The editorials urged McComb citizens to relax, pointed out Governor Johnson's plans to control the situation, noted local preparations, and warned McComb residents not to panic. Hysteria and mob action would only invite the federal government to send troops to McComb, which is precisely the action the college students wanted, Emmerich declared. Federal intervention, for Emmerich and for other Mississippians, was to be avoided at all costs. McComb citizens, Emmerich wrote on 29 May 1964, should let city, county, and state officials handle the "invasion."

> Our choice is quite simple. We can be smart or we can be outsmarted.
>
> Our people could become emotional and panic. We could even resort to mob action and with extreme hysteria find federal troops in our community.
>
> If this should happen it would prove that we were not smart but rather that we were out-smarted.
>
> It is necessary that Negro people, as well as white people, relax under the pledge of protection under the law. . . .

> Our conclusion is that we should all try to relax. Let the law enforcement officers handle the situation for us. They are willing. They stand committed. They insist that they are prepared. What more could we ask?
>
> May we on Sept. 1 look back on the summer of 1964 and be able to say, "We met a crisis with maturity. We did not panic. We exercised restraint. We upheld the dignity of the law. We met a challenge intelligently."

McComb was clearly on edge. On 2 June 1964, Dunagin reported in his column that a policeman had questioned Dizzy Dean, the former baseball player who was a Wiggins resident. Dean, who was white, had stopped in McComb for a soft drink with two black maids. Dean told the policeman who he was, and the policeman moved on. The next week, Dunagin reported 8 June 1964 that locals had reported suspicious groups of blacks and whites mingling at a bus stop. Police arrived to find not agitators but fresh Army inductees waiting on a bus to camp.

Violent incidents seemed to escalate in the days that followed. On June 9, the newspaper reported that three whites from out of town who were asking questions about McComb racial matters were stopped and beaten outside of town. Then Wilbert Lewis, a 46-year-old black auto mechanic, was jumped by four white men who took him out of town, lowered his pants, and beat him with a leather strap while asking him questions about NAACP activities. "They would ask questions and then hit me," Lewis explained in a lengthy *Enterprise-Journal* account on 19 June 1964. The article totaled twenty-nine paragraphs—an unusually detailed account for a description of an attack on a black man in a Deep South newspaper—and Lewis's verbatim description of the account comprised more than half of the article. Clearly, Emmerich and his staff had a genuine commitment to covering the news, even if it sometimes contradicted the tenets of the closed society.

McComb's summer of bombings began the night of June 22. Explosions shook three black homes, including that of Curtis C. Bryant, president of the Pike County NAACP chapter, whose barber shop had been damaged by an explosion several months before. The *Enterprise-Journal*'s account published the following day noted Bryant's NAACP connections and quoted speculation that another bombing victim, Corrine Andrews, may have been targeted by mistake, as she was not involved in the civil rights movement. This was a pattern the *Enterprise-Journal* was to repeat throughout the summer—to report the bombings fully but also to note the presence or absence of the victims' ties to the civil rights activism. The implication was that bombing victims with movement ties had been bombed because of their activism; others were innocent victims.

The following week, a Molotov cocktail was thrown at Dunagin's house. An envelope attached to the bottle, which did not explode, contained a message. "Dunagan [*sic*] keep anti civil rights action off the front page or move[.] Work with us or against us and take the hard way Take heed KKK." The *Enterprise-Journal* covered the incident on 29 June 1964. In response Dunagin pulled a shotgun out of his closet, he recalled in an interview, and spread the word around McComb that he was prepared to use it.

The backlash in southwest Mississippi worried Moses, who called a news conference in Jackson to comment on the bombings. A wire service dispatch, carried in the *Enterprise-Journal* of 1 July 1964, quoted Moses as saying he did not plan to send additional student volunteers to McComb anytime soon. He said he had heard that people in southwest Mississippi were arming with automatic weapons and hand grenades. He noted "a pattern of terror and vigilantism in the whole southwest and in the area northeast of Jackson." A campaign of violence, he said, had begun in the previous fall. "Large scale cross-burnings and killings began in December," he said. "The problem we face is what we can do to bring about an end of terror to local Negroes."

Moses' fears proved founded. A week later a bomb exploded at the COFO house at 702 Wall Street, slightly injuring two workers. City police patrols were passing the house every hour yet saw no trace of the bombers. The *Enterprise-Journal*'s account of 8 July 1964 noted that the group staying at the house was racially "mixed." Emmerich's front-page column the following day said that McComb residents deplored the bombings. He suggested that the civil rights workers meet with the mayor. "An entire community should not be condemned" as a result of the bombings, he wrote. "One individual or a half dozen individuals could be solely responsible. And these individuals could be from outside the limits of the community."

The bombing did not prevent the opening of the McComb freedom school a week later. The school's opening had already been delayed once as a safety precaution after three civil rights workers, later found shot to death and buried in an earthen dam, disappeared in Neshoba County. Freedom School director Ralph Featherstone, a 25-year-old speech teacher from Washington, D.C., found the local students to be enthusiastic. "They'd heard about the school and they felt left out because we didn't arrive on time," he declared in the *Student Voice* of 5 August 1964. Classes met in the backyard of 702 Wall Street for a week, but then the blistering heat forced a move to a nearby church. Attendance by summer's end was 110, reported the *Student Voice*, with many of the students the younger brothers and sisters of students arrested in the high school walkout three years earlier. Among the students' activities was a newspaper, which SNCC volunteer Ira Landess, an experienced teacher before joining the movement, reported to be a resounding success. Landess, in a 25 July 1964 report of his activities in the Harry J. Bowie papers at the Wisconsin Historical Society, found the Freedom School experience to be reinvigorating.

> In my three years of teaching this work here has provided the most interesting, pleasurable, stimulating situation. I find most of the kids to be academically knowledgeable in the field of English, both in their written work and in their verbal activities. They are a select group, it is true (they have chosen to come to Freedom School), but I nevertheless get the feeling that the education they get in [McComb] is better than they would get were they to be educated in Harlem, N.Y.

Life in the freedom house was tense. The civil rights workers' anxiety grew worse with each bomb blast, which usually could be heard all over town. "The pain increases with each bombing," SNCC field secretary Mendy Samstein wrote in the *Student Voice* on 23 September 1964. At the bombing scenes, he said, police arrested only the victims, intimidated black citizens, and removed evidence before the FBI arrived. He said the civil rights workers felt helpless because they believed the police were cooperating with the bombers, who oddly remained at large even though McComb was a small town "where everyone knows everyone's business."

On 14 July 1964, the *Enterprise-Journal* reported that Mayor Gordon Burt had issued a statement pledging law and order in McComb and urging the public to cooperate with police and ignore the civil rights workers. "The unwanted and unwelcome presence of some members of COFO has created a distasteful situation in our city," the mayor declared. "Their presence here—and the conditions under which they reside—violates the good taste of both the white and the Negro community." McComb's summer of violence continued. In late July, two more churches were destroyed and bombs were thrown at the home of Charles Bryant, brother of Curtis Bryant. The Zion Hill Free Baptist Church, seven miles from McComb, burned July 17. Someone attempted to bomb the Rose Bower Missionary Baptist Church on July 23, but the church was only slightly damaged.

In these bombings, the *Enterprise-Journal* took police at their word that officers were struggling to find the bombers. For example, the Mt. Vernon Missionary Baptist Church burned July 21, and the *Enterprise-Journal* reported 22 July 1964 that the possibility of arson was "under relentless investigation" by Sheriff Warren and others. But church members and SNCC workers offered a different perspective in affidavits filed just after the bombings. "On the night of July 21, 1964," M. L. Brown attested, "no fire fighting equipment, from either city, county or state sources, ever showed up at Mount Vernon Church while it was burning. It burned to the ground." In a subsequent affidavit, Brown cast doubt on the tenacity with which police were investigating the crime: "The next morning, Wednesday, the sheriff asked me questions about whether we had any enemies or whether there was any quarrel in the congregation which might account for the burning. It seemed that the was trying to put the blame on some of our people for the burning." Similarly, after the Mount Canaan Baptist Church in Walthall County burned 5 August 1964, church members reported that deputies gathered evidence at the scene but did not interview church members. On other occasions church members complained that they had provided the police with ample evidence as to the identity of the bombers, but no arrests resulted. (Affidavits found in

Candy Brown papers, Wisconsin Historical Society.) Relying upon the police version of events, the *Enterprise-Journal* also had little coverage of the harassment of the civil rights workers by police or by McComb whites. COFO narratives of the events in McComb in summer and fall 1964 show that harassment was consistent.

On 22 July 1964, the *Enterprise-Journal* published an article about Albert W. Heffner. A longtime insurance agent in McComb and friend of Emmerich, Heffner had tried to diffuse the tension in McComb by inviting two civil rights workers to his home. Neighbors reported it to police, and harassing telephone calls and threats began. The *Enterprise-Journal* reported a statement from Heffner about the meeting. He said that the two white civil rights workers were in his home for a "conference," not entertainment. "The purpose of the conference was to let the civil rights workers hear the Mississippi point of view," Heffner said. "Nothing was done in my home or elsewhere which was not fully disclosed to law enforcement authorities. I have worked closely with the authorities for the best interests of our town and state." In the weeks that followed the Heffners were beset by obscene phone calls. Three of their family pets were killed. The harassment of the Heffners became so intense that Heffner, his wife, and two teen-age daughters—one just finishing a reign as Miss Mississippi—moved from McComb at the end of the summer. No one would speak out on the Heffners' behalf, including Emmerich. The *Enterprise-Journal* and other newspapers reported 8 September 1964 that Heffner had been afraid to speak publicly about McComb until he had moved his family out of town.

On August 15, a bomb exploded at the Burgland Super Market at Warren and Denwiddie Streets. The bomb blew a hole in the front of the building and attracted a crowd of blacks from the surrounding neighborhood, two of whom were arrested. The McComb police and Pike County sheriff's office raided the COFO house the night after the bombing, the *Enterprise-Journal* reported 17 August 1964, in a search for illegal liquor. None was found.

COFO took about fifty blacks to register to vote at the Pike County courthouse in Magnolia on August 18 and 19. They were observed by police, FBI agents, and representatives of the National Council of Churches. Sheriff Warren said that while registrants were welcome, he would allow no demonstrations, folk singing, and "no Nigerian tribal dancing anywhere around the courthouse." The *Enterprise-Journal* noted on August 19 that national TV network cameramen were on hand "to await and photograph 'blood and violence' " but saw no confrontations. COFO representatives were pleased at the turnout and announced in the *Enterprise-Journal* of 20 August 1964 that 300 civil rights workers would remain in Mississippi, including McComb, through the fall and winter.

Late August marked a turning point in the *Enterprise-Journal*'s coverage of the bombings. Previously, the newspaper had described the bombings straightforwardly, treating them as a genuine threat to the community. But on Friday, August 21, 1964, the *Enterprise-Journal* reported at length on a supposed bomb hoax. Lee Garrett, a young COFO worker, conceded that he had told police that a bomb had been placed under the home of a civil rights worker, and that the story had turned out to be false. Garrett explained that he had taken the report from a fellow civil rights worker and had believed it to be genuine. SNCC compilations of the significant events in McComb during 1964 make no mention of Garrett's report and so offer no further explanation of the event.

Whether the incident was a genuine hoax or just a miscommunication among SNCC workers, the *Enterprise-Journal*'s news coverage became increasingly skeptical in coming weeks, often repeating police officers' speculation that the bombings were not bombings at all, but were plants by the civil rights workers, probably to get attention. As Charles Gordon, the *Enterprise-Journal* reporter, wrote in reporting the initial bomb hoax on 21 August 1964, "The disclosure quickly touched off a renewed close look at all church fires and 'bombings' in the area in recent weeks." The *Enterprise-Journal* was to continue to use quotation marks to describe the "bombings" for weeks; its new bias in favor of the police version of events made its previous coverage seem subtle and even-handed by comparison.

A week later, when a bomb exploded on the front lawn of Willie J. Dillon, the *Enterprise-Journal* was openly skeptical. The headline of 28 August 1964 read, "8th 'Bombing' Contains Several Unusual Aspects." The story noted Dillon's two children had been attending a COFO-operated school and that an automobile apparently belonging to civil rights worker Stokely Carmichael was at the house. Dillon was arrested on charges of operating a garage without a license and illegally connecting his garage to an electrical line.

The bombings escalated. On September 8, four bombings were reported—a pool room in Bogue Chitto, a black church in Lincoln County, and two black residences. On September 9, the *Enterprise-Journal* reported that "Pike Has 12th 'Bombing' "; a stick of dynamite had exploded in the yard of a black preacher, who suffered a broken leg. The bombing of the Chisholm Mission A.M.E. church in Lincoln County was also reported; the church was slightly damaged.

Two more bombings followed almost two weeks later. The Society Hill Missionary Baptist Church was bombed early the morning of Sunday, September 20. The same night, the home of Alyene Quin, a black tavern owner and activist, was also bombed. A babysitter and Quin's two children escaped unharmed, and a mob of angry blacks surrounded police on the scene, forcing authorities to call out the state Highway Patrol. COFO later reported that two COFO workers quieted the crowd, which was armed and throwing rocks at police cars, resulting in arrests. Sheriff Warren told the *Enterprise-Journal* on 21 September 1964 that he believed that the bombings were "plants," and officers said they were investigating reports that civil rights workers had predicted that the church would be bombed.

The week that followed was tense in McComb. Under the headline, "Variety of Officers Study City 'Bombings,' " the *Enterprise-Journal* noted 22 September 1964 that a mass meeting of blacks was held at Society Hill Baptist Church. COFO workers were taken into custody for questioning, and the *Enterprise-Journal* noted the unkempt appearance and long hair of some of those arrested. Mayor Burt, Police Chief George Guy, and Sheriff Warren were all interviewed by NBC News, and each predicted that racial tension would subside in McComb with adequate police work. Emmerich said in his column that lie detector tests, if taken voluntarily, could clear the name of someone accused of a crime, an apparent reference to the refusal of two blacks to take lie detector tests when questioned about the bombing at the Quin home.

Warrants were issued on September 23 for twenty-four blacks charged, under Mississippi's new "criminal syndicalism" law, with conspiracy to incite violence or unlawful acts. For one of the first times all summer and fall, the newspaper published SNCC accusations against police, who denied reports—presumably carried in other media—that a McComb black had lost his goatee to a "pocketknife shave" while in jail and that roadblocks had been used in black areas of McComb. The same day, the newspaper published COFO criticisms of its news coverage, to the effect that reporting of the Quin bombing and the aftermath was "full of errors and outright falsehoods" released by police. Will Campbell of Saskatoon, Saskatchewan, accused the *Enterprise-Journal* of failing to report that a COFO worker "was responsible to a large extent for keeping the crowd from getting out of hand" after the bombing. The *Enterprise-Journal* article said that the newspaper's practice of quoting law officers was "normal procedure when investigations of crimes are reported."

The next day, two more black homes were bombed, including a residence just vacated by Artis Garner, a black former McComb policeman who was testifying that day about McComb before the Civil Rights Advisory Commission meeting in Greenwood. Garner told the Commission he quit the police because his superiors had threatened to fire him because he "knew too much." Garner, wire services reported 24 September 1964, said the McComb mayor and police chief were good friends of an alleged Klan leader and said local police "are almost positive who is doing the bombing."

Meantime, Alyene Quin and two other bombing victims were in Washington, meeting with Burke Marshall, assistant attorney general for civil rights, and White House aides. Jesse Harris, director of the COFO summer project, had written Marshall that integration opponents were striking out violently at civil rights workers once public attention had shifted away from Mississippi at summer's end. "We plead with you to take action before it is too late," Harris had written, according to the *Student Voice* of 23 September 1964. In Washington, Quin told Marshall her house had been bombed as retribution for civil rights activities. She said civil rights workers ate at her restaurant, that one of her daughters taught in a COFO school, and that two others attended classes. She told reporters she was incredulous that Sheriff Warren would accuse her of bombing her own house. "Do you think I would work 11 years to keep a house," she said in the *New York Times* of 23 September 1964, "and then plant a bomb under it while two of my children were in it?"

The three women then met with President Johnson, who assured them he would call McComb to see about releasing twenty-six blacks who had been jailed recently. The *New York Times* of 25 September 1964 identified the three as "alleged victims of racial terrorism" and noted that President Johnson had suggested possible federal action to alleviate the strife in McComb. Representative William Fitts Ryan of Manhattan met with the three women, the *Times* reported, and said he planned to ask the Justice Department to convene a grand jury in McComb to investigate possible "collusion" between local police and white terrorists.

The pressure was now on McComb, and Emmerich decided to speak out. The editor was clearly pained by the prospect of federal intervention in southwest Mississippi. In two signed front-page editorials 25 September 1964, published under the headlines "Attention: All Colored People" and "Attention: White and Colored," Emmerich pleaded for public cooperation to solve the bombings. He passed on Sheriff Warren's plea for bombing victims to report violence directly to authorities, not COFO. Emmerich also related a request by Warren and Prosecuting Attorney Robert S. Reeves for public contributions of reward money. The sheriff, as Emmerich recalled in his autobiography, had visited Emmerich's office that morning to ask for help (p. 143).

Emmerich was part of an informal committee of four who met to raise the reward. Three of the four, including Emmerich, met a few days later to discuss progress. The four were so concerned about secrecy that they held their meeting in a parked car on a McComb residential street, outlandish circumstances for a meeting of city leaders, but an indication of the high levels of tension and paranoia in McComb. After the meeting, Emmerich recalled in his autobiography, one of the members got an anonymous telephone call attempting to dissuade him raising any money, leading Emmerich to believe that the telephones of some committee members were tapped (pp. 143–145).

Emmerich had exercised little leadership until it was requested of him, but now the editor finally spoke out, though hesitantly. "The world's attention is focused on McComb," Emmerich, skirting close to criticizing police and city officials, wrote in his column of 25 September 1964. "Everyone privately asks, 'Why doesn't somebody do something?' " If the bombings continued, martial law might result, and business "would dry up," Emmerich wrote. The editor urged Mayor Burt and Chief Guy to meet to take "a completely new look" at the crisis. "It must be decided if the law is being fully applied in the enforcement of the law. . . . The reason for the failures of the past must be weighed, analyzed, re-evaluated and re-appraised." Emmerich said objectivity was needed in analyzing the crisis, but he coyly added that he was not criticizing the law in McComb, only offering a "compliment to its potential."

September 28, Emmerich reported that the reward money had grown to $5,000. "The economy of our community, involving employment, is threatened," Emmerich declared. He said he had specific proof of this threat to employment but declined to publish it "because the threat would be increased by so doing." In the same column, he noted that the *Enterprise-Journal* was not publishing the regular column by Drew Pearson because the column concerned McComb and could not be confirmed. Emmerich said Pearson's column could "add nothing but further deterioration of morale within the community."

An advertisement in the same day's *Enterprise-Journal* demonstrated how the stakes in McComb had suddenly changed. The escalation of the violence threatened the city's very being—now affecting whites as well as blacks—and prompting whites to protest, though somewhat belatedly. "We are no longer dealing with a question of segregation," said the ad, which offered rewards for information leading to the arrest and conviction of the bombers. "We are faced with the possibility that the life of this community is at stake." The newspaper also published, on page seven, a statement by COFO asking for federal intervention in McComb. "Local Negro citizens live in fear of arrest and violence in retaliation for any association with civil rights activity," the statement said. COFO's request was part of a lengthy article that included a transcript of the organization's listing of the violent events in McComb over the summer. The *Enterprise-Journal*'s bold decision to publish the transcript ran counter to standard practice in most Mississippi newspapers, which seldom gave space to activists' versions of events.

The next day, Sheriff Warren and Prosecuting Attorney Reeves felt compelled to respond to COFO criticisms. The two denied harassment arrests and defended police actions in an *Enterprise-Journal* article. Moreover, the two said that local law enforcement officials could have caught the bombers if blacks had properly notified police immediately after the incidents. Only weeks earlier, Warren had denied that the bombings were genuine; now he complained that blacks were hindering proper law enforcement. The tide had turned in McComb, not in favor of the civil rights workers, certainly, but against violence. The threat of federal intervention had increased official McComb's commitment to solving the bombings.

Governor Johnson visited McComb and ordered a state investigation into the violence, with a state information center to be established in Pike County to evaluate evidence. He said he had information that indicated that COFO was behind some of the bombings, although "some bombings were by white people," wire services reported 30 September 1964. He accused COFO of coercing blacks to participate in civil rights activities by threatening a withdrawal of welfare benefits.

Finally, on Wednesday, September 30, the first arrests were made in the bombings. Three whites—the first of almost a dozen men to be charged in the bombings—were arrested and charged with the bombing of the Quin home. The arrests followed a week in which the governor of Mississippi and the president of the United States had expressed an interest in a stepped-up investigation. But much more importantly, the arrests came on the heels of increased local sentiment to put a stop to the violence, evidenced by the success of Emmerich's committee in raising reward money and residents' critical questioning of police and city officials at a town hall meeting.

Emmerich wrote on 5 October 1964 that Governor Johnson had stepped up law enforcement in McComb to head off martial law, which if enacted would cripple McComb's efforts to attract new industry. "Should martial law be established in McComb—we repeat—business would dry up," Emmerich wrote. "All of us can imagine the effect it would have on an industry which at present is committed to be located here. . . . [I]t is easy to comprehend what the attitude of the industrialists would be should martial law be declared here." Emmerich, not citing his source for the information, reported that three units of integrated troops had been placed on alert to move into McComb to create "all-out massive integration of eating places, drug stores, etc., within McComb." In fact, the NAACP had asked Governor Johnson a week previously to declare martial law in McComb.

Emmerich's son, John Emmerich, a writer for the *Baltimore Sun*, contributed an editorial column to the *Enterprise-Journal* on 1 October 1964 pointing out that no matter who was to blame for the bombings, both Mississippi and McComb were suffering from the publicity. McComb's summer of bombings was earning news coverage in wire services and newspapers all over the country, Emmerich maintained. Anyone interested in McComb, "in more industry, in more and better jobs," had better work to restore order, he argued. "How?" Emmerich asked. "By dedicating themselves to the re-establishment and continued preservation of domestic tranquility. . . . The publicity is hurting. Bad."

While the bombings had ended in McComb, controversy swirled. Dozens of blacks remained in jail after their arrests in the rioting that followed the Quin bombing. With the bombers in jail, the senior Emmerich now wrote his strongest editorials urging responsibility in McComb. If the editor waited until after violence subsided to speak out boldly, he at least provided belated leadership for a beleaguered community at a critical time in its recovery from crisis. Emmerich issued an urgent appeal 14 October 1964 for an "intensive spiritual drive to establish responsible thinking and action" in McComb.

> Because of human frailty in a time of crisis the McComb area can be characterized by a vast void, a void where responsible action should prevail.
>
> Negro churches have been burned. Negro homes have been bombed—and the homes of some white people as well. A Negro store has been dynamited. And with a sense of irresponsibility we have blamed the Negroes for the burnings, the bombings, and the dynamiting.
>
> This is the ugly record of our community; the sordid story of McComb.

McComb's problems, Emmerich wrote, are problems of McComb people. "And McComb people must solve them."

In subsequent editorials on 15 and 16 October 1964, Emmerich reflected on the high cost of hate, the "unreality" of opposing black voting rights, and the need to support the U.S. Constitution. Typical of Emmerich's editorials is one concerning the recently enacted civil rights law. Emmerich's piece lays out the choices in and consequences of obeying or ignoring the measure, but stops short of urging a specific action beyond being responsible. "Shall we ignore the laws enacted by Congress?" Emmerich asked 21 October 1964. "Every responsible man, woman and child must answer this question for himself or herself. . . . Shall we uphold government by law or government by men? . . . Where men today are free it is because this question was answered as free men must." In another editorial two days later, Emmerich urged McComb to adopt "a responsible, positive program." He said McComb could profit by emulating Tupelo, which had bypassed racial tensions by emphasizing economic development. "The positive economic goal for the McComb area," Emmerich wrote, "must be full employment and gainful employment for all of our people, whites and Negroes."

On October 23, nine of the men charged in the bombings entered guilty or no contest pleas and were given suspended sentences. Circuit Judge W. H. Watkins said all of the men were from good families who had been unduly provoked. He told the men that they had been "guilty of sedition, only slightly less than treason." The judge told the men, the *Enterprise-Journal* reported 23 October 1964, that if racial violence reemerged in McComb, probation would be revoked for all nine whether or not they were participants.

The suspended sentences were condemned inside and outside of Mississippi, the *Enterprise-Journal* reported 27 October 1964. The Greenville *Delta Democrat-Times* called the sentences astounding and said they were too light to deter future incidents. WDAM-TV in Hattiesburg editorialized that "there is room for serious question" when such meager justice is given to those who had given the state such a black eye. The *New York Times* said in an editorial 26 October 1964 that the sentences were sadly representative of so-called Mississippi justice. Emmerich, however, defended Watkins' decision. In his autobiography, he said the sentences amounted to an indictment of the entire community and were effective. "It was generally believed that the dynamiters had had the support of some leading citizens in the community," Emmerich said. "Despite the criticism, which came largely from other states, the dynamiting, the violence, and the bombing of homes and churches came to a sudden halt" (pp. 146–147).

J. Oliver Emmerich and the McComb Enterprise-Journal

Longtime Mississippi journalist Wilson F. Minor, writing in the New Orleans *Times-Picayune* of 1 November 1964, said that the sentences were significant because they were the first Mississippi cases in recent years to make felony charges stick in a racial crime. The outcry against the sentences, Minor wrote, overlooked the fact that an entire community was effectively placed on probation.

But if McComb seemed calm, the segregationists had the parting shot. The front window of the *Enterprise-Journal* was shot out in early November. A wire service reporter noted in the Columbia, South Carolina, *State* of 15 November 1964 that the incident had followed Emmerich's moderate editorials against the reign of violence. "The shot, fired at night, was certainly both evidence and a warning that the voice of moderation was not safe yet."

Emmerich's committee that had raised the reward money grew to eight, then ten, then twenty people. Finally a mass meeting was held in McComb in early November that led to the drafting of the statement of principles, which was signed by 650 residents and published in the *Enterprise-Journal* of 17 November 1964. The principles upheld law and order and favored greater communication between the races, and it opposed extremism, harassment arrests, and economic threats.

> The great majority of our citizens believe in law and order and are against violence of any kind. In spite of this, acts of terrorism have been committed numerous times against citizens both Negro and white.
>
> We believe the time has come for responsible people to speak out for what is right and against what is wrong. For too long we have let the extremists on both sides bring our community close to chaos.
>
> There is only one responsible stance we can take: and that is for equal treatment under the law for all citizens regardless of race, creed, position or wealth; for making our protests within the framework of the law; and for obeying the laws of the land regardless of our personal feelings. Certain of these laws may be contrary to our traditions, customs, or beliefs, but as God-

fearing men and women, and as citizens of these United States, we see no other honorable course to follow.

After the principles were published, Emmerich recalled in *Two Faces of Janus*, "Immediately the atmosphere, long charged as with electricity, cleared. The citizenry had finally evinced responsible concern" (p. 149). The *Enterprise-Journal* reprinted the statement of principles in an editorial 18 November 1964 as a show of the newspaper's support. "We regard it," the editorial said, "as a responsible position purposed to present a positive program which is in contrast with the repeated failures to find a solution through negation." SNCC workers, the *Student Voice* reported 25 November 1964, believed the statement of principles had been rushed into print to beat by one day the NAACP's planned desegregation of McComb businesses, a test of the new 1964 Civil Rights Act.

The statement of principles was hailed widely. In the New Orleans *Times-Picayune* of 22 November 1964, Minor called it "a national documentary of the triumph of the American sense of justice and citizenship." Pearson's column said the statement was "largely inspired by the courageous crusading of one lone newspaper editor," Emmerich. The *Newsweek* edition of 30 November 1964 called Emmerich the "untitled leader" of the businessmen who raised reward money for the arrest of the terrorists. The *New York Times* of 19 and 20 November 1964 hailed the statement of principles as encouraging news and noted that the business leaders who drafted them were "spurred by editorials in the local newspaper." The *Enterprise-Journal* recounted a long list of positive media reports about McComb and commented on 19 November 1964, "We believe this is good. The value of this kind of publicity cannot be measured in dollars."

The NAACP's planned desegregation of McComb's restaurants, motels, and a theater on 18 November 1964 occurred without incident. Twenty blacks—ten men and ten women—desegregated McComb's business district to test the new civil rights law while the news media and police officers looked on. The *New York Times* noted in a front-page article 19 November 1964 that McComb had desegregated peacefully, which McComb City Police Committee chairman John White said resulted from community pressure. "Any time the power structure of a community takes a stand against violence, it certainly curtails the possibility of trouble," said

White. That fact, the *Times* editorialized on 20 November 1964, should be a moral for every other Southern city facing racial strife.

McComb had taken a tentative first step toward racial harmony, though that goal lay some years in the future. At the very least, the worst of the violent opposition was over.

What, then, was the role of Emmerich and the *Enterprise-Journal*? Emmerich reflected the changing racial mores of his times, and he offered some leadership to his community at critical junctures. But his writing was far afield from the brash, integrationist editorials of Ira B. Harkey, Jr. of the Pascagoula *Chronicle*.

After McComb's crisis had ended, Emmerich liked to recall that the town's racial turmoil was like a feverish boil. Tampering with a boil too early only aggravates it and causes it to fester. The boil should be allowed to run its course and then be lanced at the proper time. Emmerich believed that had he tackled the racial issues directly and early in the crisis, he would have been ostracized and rendered ineffective, Dunagin recalled. Only by waiting to urge responsible action until late in the crisis, when McComb citizens were ready for such leadership, could Emmerich editorialize effectively. Because Emmerich reflected community change, he was able to lead it. In Emmerich's words penned for an unpublished manuscript, the boil of McComb's racial troubles "had to come to a head before it could be successfully lanced."

Unlike Harkey or Hazel Brannon Smith of the Lexington *Advertiser*, Emmerich did not win the Pulitzer Prize for his editorials. But neither did he lose his newspaper, as Smith ultimately did, or bitterly leave his hometown after being ostracized, as was Harkey after his editorials in defense of James Meredith's admission into the University of Mississippi. (Harkey was bitter about the Mississippi press, including Emmerich, whom he accused both of caving into the Citizens' Councils after the 1962 circulation boycott and of preventing his son John from writing crusading articles about race.) But Emmerich won national acclaim within the journalism community after the crisis. He won the 1964 editorial and public service awards presented by Sigma Delta Chi, The Society of Professional Journalists.

Dunagin maintained that the *Enterprise-Journal*'s contribution to the racial crisis in McComb was to offer to the public a complete report of the violence and reaction to it. There's little doubt, Dunagin recalled, that he and the *Enterprise-Journal*'s other reporter, Charles Gordon, reflected the dominant Mississippi mores in their reporting and too often relied far too heavily on police accounts of events. But, the McComb newspaper was at least willing to cover racial turmoil when many Mississippi newspapers were ignoring it. The *Enterprise-Journal* did indeed cover far more news related to local civil rights activity than did the vast majority of other Mississippi newspapers. As a result, the newspaper received threats from hoodlums and pleas from mainstream businessmen not to play up civil rights-related news. COFO workers, mindful of the vast extent of other events that were not being covered, encouraged the newspaper's coverage and, Dunagin recalled, even provided tips to *Enterprise-Journal* staffers.

Emmerich said that his life philosophy was to have "the hide of a rhino and the memory of an ostrich," that is, a thick skin against criticism and a capacity to forgive. He also believed in changing his opinion when conditions warranted. A reader once pointed out to him that a recent editorial contradicted the editorial opinion of just a few months back. "This must be the case sometimes," Emmerich replied in the *Enterprise-Journal* of 28 September 1964, "if the editorial page responsibly is keeping up with the changing times." Emmerich changed as Mississippi changed—slowly—but at least he reflected the first steps of progress in a state that previously had brooked no challenge to the racial status quo.

References

Branch, Taylor. *Parting the Waters*. (New York: Simon and Schuster, 1988).

Davies, David R. "J. Oliver Emmerich and the McComb *Enterprise-Journal*." *Journal of Mississippi History* 57 (February 1995): 1–23. This chapter is adapted from that article.

Dunagin, Charles. Interview. 7 April 1994.

Emmerich, J. Oliver. *Two Faces of Janus*. (Jackson, Miss.: University and College Press of Mississippi, 1973).

———. J. Oliver Emmerich Papers. Mitchell Memorial Library, Mississippi State University.

Sellers, Cleveland. *The River of No Return*. (1973, reprint ed., Jackson: University Press of Mississippi, 1990).

Silver, James W. *Mississippi: The Closed Society*. (New York: Harcourt, Brace & World, 1963).

Williams, Roger W. "Newspapers of the South." *Columbia Journalism Review*, Summer 1967.

George A. McLean and the *Tupelo Journal*

Laura Nan Fairley

> *God forbid that I should be remembered primarily as a newspaperman, or as a man of wealth and power. . . . If I can't be remembered primarily as one who sought to serve the best interests of all people of the community, then I hope that all memory of me will be blotted out.*
>
> —George A. McLean, writing in an untitled, undated manuscript

> *Are we treating our colored Mississippians as we would want to be treated? You and I both know the answer to that question.*
>
> —McLean, in a 1965 speech

* * *

For George Alonzo McLean, publisher of the *Tupelo Journal*, one thing mattered first and foremost—his community. The modest McLean was a hard-driving civic booster who worked methodically to bring agricultural and industrial diversification to Northeast Mississippi from the 1930s to the 1980s. As Tupelo prospered, largely through his leadership in community and economic development, he earned respect from leaders in Tupelo, Jackson, Washington D.C., and beyond.

In the cause of improving Tupelo, McLean had an impact in areas ranging from education to race relations. His leadership on community issues—including race—is credited with keeping Tupelo peaceful even as race-related violence swept Mississippi to the west and south in the 1960s. Though some derided him as too "liberal" for Mississippi, his writing on racial issues more often reflected the middle-of-the-road, behind-the-scenes approach to civic issues that characterized all of his work in Tupelo. Through the editorial pages of the *Journal*, McLean and editor Harry Rutherford presented carefully crafted arguments for progress in a state determined to cling to the past. Both believed that a low-key push for progress was the most effective route to change. Their vision of human development pushed the *Tupelo Journal* far beyond the norm for Mississippi newspapers of the era. Further, McLean put his preaching into practice. When he said he believed in equal opportunity for all, for example, he took practical steps to create opportunities for all. When he said Mississippians should be left to solve their own problems, he meant it; he was not employing the diversionary tactic so often used by other editors. He truly believed that he and other Mississippians could solve problems ranging from race relations to education. McLean and Rutherford's approach—similar to Hodding Carter, Jr.'s work in Greenville and J. Oliver Emmerich's in McComb—ultimately proved effective in the town they loved.

Though challenging Mississippi's racial mores was not McLean's primary motivation, his work had a profound effect on the lives of both black and white Mississippians in Tupelo and in Northeast Mississippi. McLean's crusades to improve the region's schools and economy helped to create a community that escaped the scars of racial conflict that marred so many other Mississippi towns in these years. His behind-the-scenes activity and low-key editorial style kept him largely out of the state and national spotlight, protecting him from Mississippi's rabid segregationists but denying him the national accolades he no doubt deserved as a progressive publisher in difficult times.

Though he did not accept school desegregation until it seemed inevitable, otherwise McLean was steady in his defense of equal rights for all Mississippians, blacks included. For these views, the editor's contemporaries tagged him a "moderate," a vague catchall term applied to anyone who eschewed the outright racism of Mississippi's closed society. Newspaper columnist Bill Minor, quoted in McLean's obituary published in the *Memphis Commercial Appeal* on 2 March 1983, praised McLean "for remaining a staunch supporter of federal social programs after many Mississippians became alienated from the federal government in the 1940s and 1950s." Minor also said McLean and Hodding Carter represented the few "moderate newspaper voices being heard in the state" during the civil rights struggles of the 1950s and 1960s. Minor, who covered much of this era, added, "He (McLean) had the courage to stand up for a philosophy that was against a great deal of the prevailing thought in Mississippi." James W. Silver, author of *Mississippi: The Closed Society*, singled out McLean's newspaper and those in Greenville, McComb, and Pascagoula as representative of "varying degrees of moderation" that could be found in the Mississippi press, offering sharp contrast with the "extremist" Jackson *Clarion-Ledger*. The *Journal* was a "beacon of progressive thinking, moderation and tolerance in Northeast Mississippi for many years," the Jackson *Capital Reporter* concluded on 15 January 1981. "There were some politicians (and some Mississippi editors) we recall back in those days who regarded McLean as a radical or subversive who was a danger to some of the state's revered customs."

Indeed, McLean's editorial overtures for equal opportunity and racial tolerance—understated though they were—often met with suspicion in 1960s Mississippi, though McLean never lost his effectiveness because of it. "There was a time some time ago," McLean recalled in an article in *Appalachian Views* in October 1981, "when I was considered a radical in my native state. Many people were correctly accusing me of being more interested in poor people, including black people, than in the upper classes." Despite such suspicions, McLean managed to maintain his place in the mainstream of his community, recalled Tupelo civic leader Jack Reed, Sr. McLean proved to be a more effective leader than other Mississippi editors, such as Carter or Ira B. Harkey, Jr., because he "moved within the system," Reed suggested in a 1999 interview. "He opposed all racists and was very liberal by Mississippi standards, yet he worked within the framework." Still, Reed said, "He was always controversial because he was either ahead of his time or too independent in his thinking or too liberal."

Laura Nan Fairley

* * *

McLean was born in Winona, Mississippi, in 1904. He was the youngest of six children, son of a lawyer and planter who had worked as a judge and state senator and owner of property scattered across several counties in Mississippi and Louisiana. The younger McLean earned a master's degree in religion from Boston University in 1928 after earning an undergraduate degree from the University of Mississippi. He also did graduate work in subjects ranging from sociology to psychology at the University of Chicago and at Stanford University. His out-of-state education had a great impact on young McLean. "He and the elder Hodding Carter were broadly educated," recalled Joe Rutherford, editorial page editor of the *Journal*, in a July 1999 interview. "When he went away from Mississippi for his education, he became liberated from views of the Old South early in life, long before he came to Tupelo."

After completing his education, McLean, a devout Presbyterian, at first thought his best method of ministry would be through Christian education. He accepted a teaching job at Adrian College in Michigan. Soon he moved to a faculty position at Southwestern at Memphis, known today as Rhodes College. The young professor was ousted from his faculty position, according to a 3 May 1999 article in the *Northeast Mississippi Daily Journal*, because "he had been organizing black tenant farmers in the Arkansas Delta when plantation owners appealed to longtime Memphis political boss E. H. Crump to curtail McLean's activities. McLean was suddenly informed that Southwestern had run out of money to continue funding his faculty position." These difficulties led McLean to a journalism career.

After a brief stint at a Grenada newspaper, McLean decided he wanted to buy his own journal, attracted by the notion that newspaper publishing would provide him with an effective tool for Christian service and ministry. Deidra Faye Jackson, in her 1995 University of Mississippi master's thesis on the publisher, noted that McLean's widow, Anna Keirsey McLean, said her husband believed running a newspaper would give him an opportunity to do more "than just preach at people." McLean himself, in a 1974 oral history interview with Kenneth McCarty, Jr., acknowledged his lack of formal training in journalism. "I had never had any experience or training in newspapering and in my wildest dreams had never planned to get into the newspaper profession, but I thought I would be able to express myself and do things through that medium that I had found impossible to do in the teaching profession or in religion or the church." Indeed, McLean would prove as willing to use his deep faith in defense of reason as others were willing to use religion as a justification for racism.

McLean took the reins of his struggling newspaper on June 1, 1934, undertaking a half-century of his own particular brand of ministry. He often said that he had bought "a bankrupt newspaper from a bankrupt bank"; the fledgling *Journal* had fewer than 500 paid subscribers in a town of 6,000 citizens. McLean set out to build a strong newspaper. From the first day, he decided to keep the newspaper's slogan, "Be just, fear not." He added his own touch that remains today: "A locally-owned newspaper dedicated to the service of God and mankind." McLean held the publisher's seat from the age of 29 until his death in 1983. By that time, the man with no previous journalism or business experience had transformed the paper into the 33,000-circulation *Northeast Mississippi Daily Journal,* one of the largest newspapers in the country published in a town the size of Tupelo. From his sparsely furnished office, McLean watched the *Journal's* circulation and his own personal fortune rise. Though he eventually earned millions, McLean always kept his modest style.

From his earliest days at the newspaper, McLean put his philosophy of giving back to the community into action. While he orchestrated the *Journal's* circulation growth, McLean also played a role in attracting manufacturing jobs. His efforts in areas ranging from industrial recruiting to overall community boosterism are still recognized as a major factor in contributing to the rise in manufacturing jobs in Tupelo, where the 1,000 industrial jobs in 1934 jumped to more than 13,000 four decades later. Lee County became the third largest manufacturing county in Mississippi by the 1980s. "I wanted to be a part of the effort to lift our people out of poverty and enable them to achieve a better way of life," McLean recalled of the Depression years in the *Appalachian Views* article. If effect, the *Tupelo Journal* was McLean's pulpit as he pushed for economic progress, agricultural diversification, and improvement of the lives of all local citizens.

The consequences of the red-haired McLean's dogged determination often put the publisher in the middle of controversy, particularly during his early years at the helm of the *Journal*. In fact, some trace McLean's later caution to 1937, when he sided with striking cotton mill workers not long after he took over the newspaper. Hodding Carter, Jr., recalled McLean's early years in a profile of Tupelo in the 17 February 1951 *Saturday Evening Post*. "Shortly after he bought the bankrupt *Journal*—then a weekly—McLean was in hot water. He learned that garment workers in some Mississippi towns were making as little as $3 a week, and began championing the cause of labor, organized and unorganized. The ensuring opposition almost put him out of business." Tom Pittman, former general manager of the *Journal* who worked with McLean from 1979 until the publisher's death, said the strike was a "defining moment" for young McLean, as his position prompted boycotts and protests that "almost put him under." It was then, according to Pittman, that McLean learned that "you need to do the right thing but you can't lead without people following you." Pittman, in a July 1999 interview, described McLean as a "liberal pragmatist" who, following the strike, tended to tone down public stands in order to be effective. The modest McLean was far from outspoken, according to current *Journal* editor Lloyd Gray, because the publisher was interested in "shedding more light than heat."

By 1936 McLean had expanded the *Journal* from a weekly to a daily, changing the name to the *Daily Journal*. By the age of 34, McLean began to earn national recognition, with *Nation* magazine naming him to its 1936 Honor Roll along with Supreme Court Justice Louis D. Brandeis and others. The magazine described McLean as a courageous editor who was successfully running a "liberal" newspaper. After returning from World War II duty in the United States Navy, McLean oversaw the *Journal*'s extensive local news and sports coverage, which won back readers lost in the 1930s. In 1947, McLean was able to purchase the only local competition, the *Tupelo Daily News*. In the postwar years, McLean began devoting the majority of his time to community development activities, delegating most of the responsibility of running the *Journal* to Bill Stroud, business manager. On the news side, McLean relied upon Harry Rutherford, his right-hand man through much of the publisher's newspaper career. Longtime associate Harry Martin said McLean tended to surround himself with competent people, associates who "would advise him not to get too far ahead" on controversial issues.

Harry Rutherford ran the news side of the operation with McLean's total trust and cooperation while the publisher pursued industrial prospects and other opportunities for Tupelo. Martin accompanied McLean on countless trips across the nation as the publisher worked hard to attract industrial prospects to Lee County. In addition to industrial recruits, McLean also brought home innovative ideas on how to improve agriculture, housing, and anything else that might benefit the community. The *Journal* was his prime vehicle for promoting those concepts.

In the meantime, Gray said Rutherford wrote most of the editorials for the *Journal*. The McLean-Rutherford duo shared the same views and collaborated on them. As Gray put in a July 1999 interview, "Whatever happened or whatever made it on the editorial page did not happen without George McLean's consent." Rutherford had joined the newspaper staff on 1 June 1936. His leadership was credited for helping the *Journal* grow from a small newspaper into the third largest daily in the state. Like McLean, he worked double-time, with the publisher's encouragement, on areas of concern such as regional development and improved housing. A graduate of the University of Missouri journalism school, Rutherford was named editor after returning to the newspaper from wartime service in the Navy. Joe Rutherford, no relation to Harry, suggested Rutherford's kind and compassionate approach balanced the square-jawed McLean's hot temper. He added, "McLean relied completely on Rutherford's editorial opinion. They worked in tandem." Both men were modest; neither liked to see his name or picture in the paper.

McLean, in the oral history interview, explained his perception of his role in the newsroom. "I don't write stories," McLean said. "I don't take photographs, I don't run machines; my basic interest is to be of service to my fellow man—my fellow Mississippians." McLean said that both he and Rutherford believed that a newspaper should serve its readers. "Our function is not just to have the latest headline, but to do a genuine service to the people of the area," McLean said. "The newspaper, as I see it, must be a constructive force and not simply a medium for someone to express (his) opinions or to make the most sensational approaches to the news." McLean's editorial philosophy was guided by his interest in developing Tupelo and a distaste for any controversy that might impede that goal. Under McLean's leadership and after, the *Journal* attempted to put issues into context and avoid "controversy for the sake of controversy," Gray explained. He acknowledged that McLean's approach was often misinterpreted as "cheerleading," but Gray suggested it was not that at all, just "vigorously pro-Tupelo." Gray believed that McLean was not above managing the news in terms of how much coverage he gave certain issues.

McLean, in a vision statement that was reprinted in the *Journal* on 1 January 1998, outlined his philosophy that continues to guide the newspaper today. "The good newspaper," he wrote, "adopts as one of its major objectives the unobtrusive establishment of a definite tone in its community built around high ethical standards, a cooperative spirit, a broadly based tolerance among all groups, a yearning for personal and community growth, a belief in God, service to man and hope for a better tomorrow." McLean's guiding principles also state that a good newspaper "emphasizes the good more than the bad." McLean seemed to put these principles into action, particularly in his economic development activities, which were always aimed at improving the lot of local people, both black and white. His concern for race relations was rooted in this vision, clearly based on McLean's notion that economic development was the foundation required for social change. No project, whether large or small, that could benefit Tupelo and surrounding counties was overlooked in McLean's grand scheme.

McLean's contributions to Tupelo's development were legion. Harry Rutherford pointed out in a tribute speech honoring McLean's 65th birthday that the publisher began working to promote the development of poultry-related jobs in Lee County soon after buying the newspaper. Rutherford said that "largely because of his efforts the first factory-type poultry production got under way in 1936, this later to become a twenty million dollar industry." He added that McLean was a leading booster of artificial breeding programs to improve cattle herds and even "gave away thousands of dollars worth of crimson clover seeds to farmers in the county."

Improving the Tupelo area one slow step at a time was McLean's method, and he eventually enlisted most of the town's civic leaders in his push for progress. Hodding Carter was not the only journalist to take note of what has become known as "the Tupelo Story." That story, for which McLean is given much credit for scripting, is built on the idea that the prosperity of city bankers and business leaders is directly connected to the success of outlying rural areas, a notion that the publisher preached from his earliest days at the *Journal.* That idea was put into practice when McLean worked to establish the Rural Community Development Program, a creative effort credited with laying the groundwork for future success in race relations. By including African Americans in the innovative project, McLean was stepping beyond the racial boundaries that normally excluded blacks.

On 20 August 1952, the innovative Tupelo approach spearheaded by McLean received national attention in a *Wall Street Journal* article by Victor J. Hillery, "Better Farming: The Tale of Tupelo Tells How it Pays and How Townsfolks Can Boost It." The article, describing the Community Development programs as a successful means of "encouraging rural development for the good of all," gave McLean credit for leading the movement. McLean, using one of his most frequent comments, explained in the article: "We told the farmers there's no Santa Claus in Washington, in Jackson . . . or in Tupelo, and that it was up to them to develop their own communities." This comment, used so frequently by McLean, indicates he believed from the start that local action could best solve local problems.

Carter reported in the *Saturday Evening Post* article, "The bankers do not take primary credit for what is happening in the Tupelo area. They point instead to the square-jawed forty-five-year-old George McLean." He continued, "It is hard to escape the conclusion that he is now Tupelo's dynamo. Most certainly it was he who put over the Rural Community Development Program, the amazingly far-reaching integration of agriculture and civic objectives which in its three years of existence has been copied by at least twenty other towns and cities from Louisiana to West Virginia." McLean, explaining the RCD program to Carter, said, "The idea is simple enough. We organize the farmers by community and offer the community, not individuals, prizes for such things as improved farm practices, new crops, increased efficiency in dairying, chicken raising and such. We hold community get-togethers every summer. And we constantly harp on good farm management." By 1950, 1,621 farm families in ten white and four black communities, were participating in the RCD contests. Because the communities were segregated, the individual organizations were also. However, the fact that the black communities were deliberately included in the programs was certainly a move forward for the times.

Carter described the program in the early 1950s. "It makes sense to everybody; to Odell Johnson, president of the Brewer community, who says it's nice to live in a place where everybody is working and learning together; to George McLean, who points out that every new farm dollar turns over five times in Tupelo before it leaves town; to Alice Little, Negro home-demonstration agent, who is getting help and encouragement in her work among the boys and girls who are already better farmers than their parents and will become even more useful citizens."

McLean, the professor-turned-publisher, was well versed in economic theories ranging from Adam Smith to Karl Marx. However, he turned to the Bible for his own much-expounded theory, which he said was entirely based on Luke 6:38, where Christ said, "Give and it shall be given to you," according to Joe Dove in the *Mississippi Business Journal* of November 1980. McLean, explaining his development theories to Dove in his always pragmatic terms, said: "I very strongly believe that the only way to prosperity is to put the money in the pockets of the people or there will be no retail sales, no bank deposits, no growth and no advertising in the newspaper. I believed that when I bought the *Journal* and I believe that today."

While Carter, the *Wall Street Journal* and national community development officials gave McLean much of the credit for the RCD and other projects, he wanted little recognition. Another saying attributed to McLean was, "There's no telling what we can do if we don't care who gets the credit," according to Pittman. Countless anecdotes about his behind-the-scenes efforts prove the point that McLean would often get the ball rolling on projects to improve everything from education to agriculture and then step quietly into the shadows to watch his dreams unfold. This modest style was particularly effective in creating opportunities for both blacks and whites during a time when a more aggressive approach would have surely met stubborn resistance.

When he could not get what he wanted through the system, Pittman said, McLean would try other avenues. For example, when advisers suggested Tupelo needed more warehouse space to attract new industries and local funds were not forthcoming, McLean paid for the construction of several warehouses out of his own pocket, moving the *Journal* offices into one and using the others as magnets for industry.

McLean's role in the community did not stop at economic development. The former professor viewed education as the key to progress and was "well ahead of recognition of that on the state level," according to Gray. The McLean obituary published in *The Clarion-Ledger* on 2 March 1983 noted that he paved the way for bringing one of the first Head Start programs in the nation to Tupelo. McLean was one of the founders of LIFT, Inc., a local Community Action Agency that provided Head Start and other services to the poor in Northeast Mississippi. This move was considered bold in a time when accepting federal funds was akin to accepting money from the devil in the view of some white Mississippians. It also reflects his level of personal commitment to creating opportunity for all—even if such action went against the grain of the dominant white society.

Again, it was not McLean's overt objective to push racial equality. But his sincere interest in the downtrodden would eventually help bring the same results. Editor Harry Rutherford recalled in a 1965 speech that McLean "took under his wing the forty or so poorest of Lee County's poor down in the Palmetto area a few weeks ago, helped line (up) jobs for the unemployed parents, provided school or day care for children who otherwise might never have learned to open a book, and even arranged transportation to get them to classes." This anecdote illustrates McLean's approach—action instead of rhetoric—that separates him from other Mississippi editors.

McLean, who drove old cars and lived in a modest home for a man of his means, preferred to spend his money on his passions, education and community development. In 1977, for example, he committed $1.1 million to pay for reading aides in Lee County schools, a move hailed by *The New York Times* as an unprecedented investment in public elementary schools. The reading aide program eventually served as a model for a statewide program established by the Mississippi Legislature in 1982.

The 15 January 1981 issue of *The Capital Reporter*, after McLean won the Tennessee Valley Authority's Distinguished Citizen Award, noted: "There are two Mississippi institutions that McLean set out recently to change: Those institutions are called ignorance and poverty. Public education has no greater friend than George McLean, a fact that was made a living reality when Tupelo was able to institute a biracial school system voluntarily while almost every other school district found itself involved in exhausting legal battles." These comments again illustrate how McLean's focus on the bigger picture eventually created positive results in terms of race relations even though he was not overtly pushing for such.

Clearly, McLean's vision of economic opportunity directly influenced his work in areas from race relations to education. In the McCarty interview, he said: "We have our head-start and our programs that move in to help black and white. All poor people are not black; there are more poor white people in Mississippi than black. We have our share of white and black poor, but we need to help these children; because they are the future of our state and of our nation, and every one of them deserves an opportunity to become what they should become."

The fact that race relations, at least on the surface, rarely deteriorated throughout the most heated period of the civil rights movement in Tupelo is credited in part to McLean, Rutherford, and other like-minded civic leaders. Other factors, however, came into play as well. When Hodding Carter visited Tupelo in the early 1950s, he found a town proud of its many firsts, including being the first city to acquire TVA power, to build "the first paved roads south of the Ohio River," and to establish Mississippi's first public library bookmobile. The civic discourse McLean encouraged in his actions and editorial pages was clearly alive and well in the Tupelo that Carter visited. He wrote, "If anything, Tupelo is overorganized—there appears to be a club of some kind, civic or religious, for every ten Tupeloans, and the eatin-meetin's dominate the social life. Community piety is strenuously expressed." Noting that Tupelo had been devastated by a tornado in April of 1936, which killed 203 citizens, injured hundreds, and caused $3 million in damage, Carter wrote, "It is as if the Tupeloans looked over the wreckage left by nature and said to one another, 'Well, it gives us a chance to clean things up anyway'. The result isn't old South, but new America." Numerous community leaders, including blacks, refer to the deadly tornado as a turning point for Tupelo.

Another factor that left Tupelo and Northeast Mississippi relatively unscathed during the worst days of civil rights turmoil was a simple matter of demographics. Carter pointed out in his 1951 *Saturday Evening Post* article that "in the five hill counties which comprise Tupelo's trade territory live some 175,00 mostly rural people. Unlike most of Mississippi's overall 50–50 division of the races, four-fifths of the hill farmers are white."

Harry Martin, a friend of McLean's from 1947 on, agreed that the Tupelo's relatively low minority population, seldom more than 22 percent African-American, had something to do with the area's lack of strife during the civil rights era. "We were never really an old Southern town like you found in the Delta," he suggested. "A lot of our success was because of demographics. Tupelo is in Appalachia. We were much more rooted in that culture than you would find in southern and western parts of the state. Here we never really had a plantation environment."

Donald Cunnigen, in "The Civil Rights Movement and Southern White Liberal Role Conflict," published in the Winter 1992 issue of *Southern Studies*, noted that a number of factors created different reactions to racial issues in different Mississippi communities. Those included, "the level of civil rights activism within the community, the community's racial composition, the level of anti-African-American sentiment in the white community, the community's level of economic prosperity, the community's level of education, and the relative cultural sophistication of the whites in the community." He contends that cross burnings and bombings forced other outspoken white Mississippians in communities where tensions ran high to a more obvious, perhaps even more dangerous and divisive, level of commitment to improving race relations than could be found in relatively peaceful communities such as Tupelo.

It might also be argued that McLean's push for improvements in economic conditions and education created an environment that allowed him to stay behind the scenes. McLean's early leadership in the community, not just demographics, clearly played a role in preventing the type of tensions that would have backed him into a corner during the civil rights movement. As it was, the publisher was able to quietly work to improve race relations in Northeast Mississippi, building on the foundation that he created in his early years as a publisher.

According to Martin and other close associates interviewed in 1999, McLean earned the trust and confidence of Tupelo's black leaders from his earliest days as a civic leader. "Black leaders met with him regularly in small groups or as individuals," Martin explained. "He was a person they could vent their frustrations and problems with. If they felt they had been in a situation where they had been mistreated, he was the person they would go to. He would listen." McLean, in a speech before the annual meeting of the Community Development Foundation on 7 May 1970, emphasized the importance of consensus building. "The practice of local citizens sitting down together and solving local problems or local misunderstandings rather than letting outside agitators come in and divide our people is a practice that has been followed for many, many years. As a newcomer to Tupelo I well recall elected officials sitting down with representative white and black citizens and discussing mutual problems and mutual responsibilities many years ago."

Kenneth Mayfield, an NAACP civil rights attorney in the 1970s, told Diedra Jackson that he best remembered McLean for his efforts to keep lines of communication between whites and blacks open. He said that "during the 1960s, while most of the country was grappling with racial conflicts, Tupelo experienced few problems. Some people attribute that to the white leadership that was able to get with the black leadership to keep a lid on everything here." Leadership indeed must have worked together, as Northeast Mississippi attracted considerably less civil rights activism than did other areas of the state. Two chronicles of civil rights activism in Mississippi, John Dittmer's *Local People* (1994) and Charles M. Payne's *I've Got the Light of Freedom* (1995), document no civil rights activism in Tupelo or in Lee County. That is not to say that none occurred, but it's clear civil rights activists chose to concentrate their efforts in other, more troubled regions of the state.

Besides working quietly to build better race relations in Tupelo, McLean and Rutherford eventually used the editorial pages of the *Journal* to take more obvious stands during the civil rights era. These stands are best reflected in *Journal* editorials on subjects representing some of the most dramatic conflicts in Mississippi—school integration, including the Ole Miss/Meredith crisis, the violence of the long, hot summer of 1964, and the ongoing role of segregationist politicians of the era. All of these events surely put McLean to the test, forcing him to slowly become more vocal on civil rights issues.

Leroy Henderson, Jr., completed an editorial analysis of the *Journal* covering the years 1934 to 1968 for his master's thesis at the University of

Southern Mississippi. In a June 1968 interview, McLean and Rutherford told Henderson "they were against organizations such as unions and the Ku Klux Klan, for birth control and equal rights, and that they both expressed such opinions in editorials." Henderson said McLean indicated that "the only policy he and Rutherford had was that he did not write anything Rutherford disagreed with, and Rutherford did not write anything he disagreed with."

He added that, despite the lack of a written policy, both McLean and Rutherford tried to balance their views with an understanding of their readers. Henderson suggested the tone of the *Journal*'s editorial page was influenced by McLean's efforts to "do good" from behind the scenes. Unlike the direct approach practiced by Ira Harkey, Jr., in Pascagoula, McLean's low-key approach kept him out of a firestorm of controversy sure to be generated by more confrontational editorials. According to Lloyd Gray, editorial positions were influenced by McLean's efforts to sell the benefits of racial reforms by tying them to economic interests. He added that McLean "was smart enough to know you could not tell anyone what to do. He preached enlightened self-interest."

Henderson's random sample of editorials from 1934 to 1968 found scant reference to racial issues, noting that the majority of editorials focused on religion, agriculture, education, politics, and attraction of industry. Despite the numbers indicated in Henderson's survey, McLean and Rutherford could no longer put racial conflict on the back burner as the issue came to the forefront in the 1960s, with race-related editorials increasing significantly during the Ole Miss crisis and throughout the summer of 1964.

The conclusions about McLean's role during the civil rights movement can perhaps be best illustrated by looking at several editorials up to and following the Ole Miss/Meredith crisis. These editorials illustrate many of McLean's characteristic traits, including his role as a civic preacher. The *Journal* editorials during this period are sprinkled with religious references, a technique used by other editors such as the Carters in Greenville, to call for reason and calm.

Gray described McLean's approach to the Ole Miss crisis as "the most responsible in the state other than Greenville's Hodding Carter." Joe Rutherford, who worked with McLean from 1972 until the publisher's death, agreed. He said the Ole Miss crisis was "personal" for McLean, with the *Journal* calling for an end to "futile resistance." Rutherford added that while McLean did not advocate integration, his stand during the tense days of Meredith's enrollment put the newspaper on the record in a profound way. The *Journal* was one of the few state newspapers who questioned Governor Ross Barnett's position on interposition. On 27 September 1962, the *Journal* editorial challenged Barnett. "He knows that no person, agency or state has ever been able to defy the authority of the government of the United States." The publisher was not afraid to use the *Journal*'s editorial page to take a stand for reason when little existed in the hours and days leading up to bloodshed in Oxford.

But such editorials were few in number in the days before Meredith's enrollment. While front page coverage frequently focused on the mounting crisis in Oxford, the *Journal* editorials turned the focus elsewhere. For example, while the 19 September 1962 issue included extensive front-page coverage, including a banner headline "Kennedy Phones Ross, Says Marshall Will Escort Negro," with photos and several news articles, the editorial that day was "When in Light, Reds turn to our Methods" attacking communist positions far from home.

However, a week later, the 27 September editorial came back to a seething Mississippi. This editorial reflected McLean's view that federal laws must be obeyed, which ran contrary to the resistance being encouraged by some other state newspapers. The editorial, "Point is Made—Now Let's Stop and Think," makes it clear that McLean was still hoping reason could stop a disaster in Oxford that would subsequently harm his priority, progress for Tupelo and Mississippi. That day's editorial captured the tension of the moments before violence erupted in Oxford. "The situation now is one which at any moment could find Mississippi citizens firing on the flag of our country. Or, on the other hand, it could find our state university closed in the first of a wave of shut-downs which in time could close every college, every high school, and every grammar school in the state."

Commenting on a Mississippi legislator's statement that "we must win this fight regardless of the cost . . . in human lives," the editorial responded with a defense of the law. "America is a nation of laws and interpretations of laws, with some of which any of us may at times find ourselves in heated disagreement. But to publicly or privately suggest opposing with force the duly constituted authority of the United States government in order to uphold anyone's personal interpretation of the Constitution in opposition to that of the federal courts, to which our Constitution gives authority, is little, if any, short of treason." McLean's concern for image is evident in the editorial statement that such "treason" would "be an act of rebellion worth a billion dollars in propaganda value to the Communists—and an act of suicide costing Mississippi ten billion dollars in lost economic development over the next couple of decades." The editorial predicted: "Nothing except disaster can now be achieved by pushing the issue past the explosive point. . . . Elected officials of the state of Mississippi have defied the duly constituted authority of the United States government. The people of Mississippi cannot possibly win or even come out with honor in such a contest. And the young people of our state are being made pawns in the battle as thoughtless opposing forces push toward the point of no return." McLean's call for calm would be ignored.

McLean's dismay as his predictions came true was evident in the editorial published on 2 October 1962, "God, Be Merciful To Me A Sinner." Calling the events at the Ole Miss campus "tragic beyond description," the editorial stated, "We have sown the seeds of hate and violence and of inflexible opinion and we have reaped violence, death and disgrace. Our University, its students, the people of Mississippi and the people of America have lost." Turning again to Christian values, the editorial continued, "Some of us have failed by doing or saying things that we should not have done or said. All of us have failed by not doing or saying something that would have helped create a Christ-like climate of opinion rather than permitting growth of a spirit of hate and violence."

McLean's *Journal*, in the 2 October 1962 editorial, noted that neither the NAACP or the White Citizens' Council were ". . . going to stop trying to force their point of view." The editorial then proposes a solution. "It is, therefore, imperative that the majority of the people of Mississippi and of America face this crisis and not be pulled violently into the conflict on either side. We cannot win our point by violence. That way all of us lose. We must learn to live together, to work together, to love our neighbor as ourselves. Only in this way can we avoid bitterness, hatred and conflict."

In view of the proximity of the editorial to the emotional rage sweeping the state prior to and following Meredith's enrollment, McLean's admonition to "learn to live together, to work together, to love our neighbors as ourselves" should be seen as a strong stand. By carefully casting views in terms of Christian principles, McLean proved more effective than taking a more outspoken stand in favor of the desegregation of Ole Miss.

Two days later, on 4 October 1962, the *Journal* editorial again desperately sought a way to approach the aftermath of Ole Miss violence by looking toward the future rather than by adding fuel to the flames with editorial ire. That editorial, "From Devastation Let Great College Rise," drew a parallel to Tupelo's recovery from the great tornado of 1936. Citing problems at the university such as faculty turn-over and "an overemphasis on football and beauty contests" that had been compounded by the Meredith crisis, the editorial found opportunity in the devastation. "For from its shattering experience Ole Miss, as the city of Tupelo did following its disastrous tornado of twenty-six years ago, can rebuild on an even finer and more solid basis than that which was destroyed."

Closer to home, *Journal* editorials and McLean's continued behind-the-scenes efforts would eventually influence the smooth desegregation of public schools in Tupelo and Lee County. However, like Hodding Carter, Jr., and other editors who questioned some aspects of the closed society, McLean was not an enthusiastic proponent of integration in the 1940s and 1950s, believing instead that improving conditions at segregated black schools was the correct path for all. *Journal* editorials during this period were holding to the line that separate but equal school systems were the best alternative for blacks and whites. Here again, McLean's views reflected those of other editors, such as Hodding Carter, Jr. Like Carter, McLean opposed the 1954 Brown decision. However, he was the only Mississippi editor who predicted economic implications of the decision, with an 18 August 1954 editorial that implied correctly that federal funding for schools might be used as a weapon to encourage compliance with Brown.

Like so many other white Southerners, even those who backed away from segregation's excesses, he could not imagine integration coming to pass in his lifetime. However, as early as 1947, McLean argued for equal opportunity. In a speech at the University of Mississippi on 15 May 1947, McLean lambasted fellow Mississippians over the treatment of African-

Americans, particularly for the failure to provide educational opportunities. "We, the white people," McLean declared, "stand indicted for our failure to develop one half of the people of Mississippi, the Negroes. Instead of treating them as a great human resource that could be trained to help raise our state to a higher level, we have treated them as a 'problem' and have tried to hold them down. The county schools for Negroes were built by gifts and the devoted work of the Negroes themselves. Yes, my good friends, Negroes have paid taxes to build good schools for you and me but the white people have not paid taxes to give the rural Negroes even shacks for schoolhouses."

Once again fitting the mold of earlier Southerners, McLean's views expressed in a 30 September 1958 editorial reflect his belief that race-related school problems were best solved locally and that anything less carried dire economic consequences. "And if left to solve our problems with a minimum of outside interference," the editorial stated, "Dixie leaders still have a good chance of solving the school crisis without loss of the traditional good will and friendship that have existed between races and which are important to our continued development."

A later *Journal* editorial on 20 March 1962 again calls for McLean's oft-repeated "good will" and matches sentiments expressed by other Southern publishers who expected the march toward full civil rights to proceed at a slow pace. "For as in most other instances it is the people seeking a short cut to uplifting and upgrading the 'disadvantaged' that are causing most of the friction in today's relations between white and colored. And once the members of both sides of the controversy realize that we have a situation definitely needing improvement but which cannot be corrected overnight or by any single compulsory action, there is no reason to believe that we can't achieve gains that will be both helpful to all and permanent in nature because they will be built on mutual understanding and good will."

However, *Journal* editorials eventually began to reflect a shift in McLean's view as he became convinced that desegregation was inevitable and much more immediate. He was at the forefront of editors who recognized that the issue had shifted from segregation to saving public schools and economic stability. In fact, the threat by Mississippi politicians to close public schools rather than integrate was greeted with horror by the former professor. Furthermore, the economic consequences of defying federal law were certainly not lost on McLean or other business leaders. He and Rutherford used those possible consequences in arguments for compliance with the law.

Conceding that Mississippi's efforts to fight the civil rights bill, including the expenditure of more than $100,000, had failed and noting that four Mississippi school systems had agreed to abide by the law and integrate in the coming school year, the *Journal* editorial of 10 August 1964 implied that all attempts to fight integration were futile. "Now with failure staring us in the face," the editorial stated, "it is time we shifted emphasis and started trying to convince our own people that we can do a better job of building a quality education system for white and colored alike than is being done in other states." A little more than a year later, a 28 October 1965 editorial reflects McLean's changing views as he suggested: "[W]e need to concentrate on doing whatever is necessary to build good schools rather than spending too much time debating the method of integration. . . . With the federal funds now becoming available, we in Mississippi should be able to develop really good schools for both white and colored pupils in every county."

Earlier, on 26 August 1964, the *Journal* editorial, "Too Cruel and Costly for Consideration," blasted the powerful Citizens' Council's suggestion that "going through life without an education is better than attending integrated classes." McLean was aghast. "Hundreds of thousands of Mississippians have already in recent years shown what they think of the Citizens' Council plan for ignorance by leaving the state. It is not difficult to imagine how this flight from Mississippi would be speeded up if our people took seriously the Citizens' Council proposal and for just one generation actually chose lifelong ignorance for their children rather than yielding to court orders for school integration."

Though the catalyst was federal pressure, *Journal* editorials and McLean's continual behind-the-scenes efforts influenced the smooth desegregation of public schools in Tupelo and Lee County in 1966. Tupelo city schools became the second school system to integrate following Greenville's lead. Tupelo High School was integrated in the first two years by the "freedom of choice" plan under which black high school seniors who wished to attend the traditionally white Tupelo High School were allowed to do so. By the third year of integration, all of Tupelo's ninth- and 10th-grade students were attending the formerly black Carver school, while Tupelo High School was fully integrated with all 11th and 12th grade students attending. According to Gray, "The school systems in Tupelo first integrated in 1966 without incident. The newspaper helped prepare the community and, except maybe in pockets in rural outlying areas, there was little resistance and private education faltered."

Although never an outspoken advocate of integration, McLean did make the connection between equal opportunity and progress. "The great need for Mississippi," McLean explained to McCarty, "is for people who will consider every person in Mississippi as a potential asset and, regardless of race, creed, color, section or any other thing, seek to do everything possible to develop them and give them increasing opportunities for growth and development so they can make the contribution that God intended them to make. Then we can really begin to move." Gray suggested that McLean had "a sense of fairness and justice and a strong sense of duty to the law." That outlook apparently influenced his changing views on integration. Gray noted, "His sense was that, because of the law of the land, integration was inevitable."

Robert Hereford, a Carver High School teacher, was one of the first black teachers who switched over to a position at Tupelo High. In his view, recorded in the 125th anniversary edition of the *Journal* in 1996, there was a difference in how Tupelo made the transition as compared to other Southern towns. Hereford, who later became assistant principal at Tupelo High School, said, "There were some problems, but there was never a crisis. People had decided that they would work together on their problems, so if one came up, we worked on it until it was solved." Jackson, in her thesis on McLean, said Kenneth Mayfield credited McLean and other white civic leaders in Tupelo for the smooth integration process because of a long-standing model of "working things out" behind the scenes.

Beyond integration, common threads found in *Journal* editorials between 1954 and 1965 include references to religion and the ever-present call for good will. McLean also consistently expressed his belief in locally based problem solving, often using the tactic of blaming "outside agitators," both black and white, for most of the race-related troubles in Mississippi. For example, the 29 October 1958 editorial bemoaned the fact that religion and other institutions were suffering because of the growing racial controversy. The editorial was in response to comments by Ross Barnett, "a probable candidate for governor in the coming year," who had told a Baptist church group that "Communists are exploiting church personnel to front their fight for integration." The editorial answered the candidate. "Mr. Barnett's words may leave for some the impression that if any of our ministers favor integration, they do so at the bidding of Communists rather than on the basis of their interpretation of the teaching of Jesus." The editorial continued: "During the difficult years ahead we in the South must learn to recognize that not everyone will see things alike and that often the specialized background of an individual will be responsible for the difference in his view points. If some ministers interpret the teachings of Jesus as supporting integration and some interpret those same words as supporting segregation each group must be respected for the sincerity of its beliefs." Even more frequently, *Journal* editorials reflected McLean's belief that local problems could be solved best by local people. McLean often put the blame for Mississippi's racial conflicts on the shoulders of "agitators," whether members of the Ku Klux Klan, Martin Luther King Jr., or the White Citizens' Council. All were equally contemptible to McLean—perhaps because all, in one way or another, challenged his view of the world. One aspect of his disdain for "troublemakers" was obviously his fear that any negative disruptions could mar his farsighted plans for progress. *Journal* editorials spared neither side. While balancing attacks on both races, editorials reflect McLean's conviction that Tupeloans could best handle local problems.

For example, in a 2 October 1961 editorial, "Proposed New 'Army' Can Hurt Negro Cause," the newspaper blasted Dr. Martin Luther King, Jr. and Southern Christian Leadership Conference plans to send a "nonviolent army" into the South. According to the editorial, such action would be enough to "set most communities automatically against whatever program it is trying to put over." It concluded: "And this business of trying to change political structure, combined with invasions by outsiders who look upon themselves as some kind of holy army, indicates a resort to lawlessness which will make it harder and harder for a community's local Negro leadership to get anywhere with improvements genuinely needed."

As late as 1964, McLean still believed, like other editors, that civil rights workers who descended on the state that summer were doing more harm than good. The *Journal* editorial of 21 August 1964, for example, suggested the more militant civil rights workers were "an irritant between the white and colored community, apparently achieving very little while causing great damage to human relations in communities all over the state." Although McLean was vehemently opposed to violence on any front, he was not ready to abandon his negative view of civil rights workers.

Cunnigen offered a possible explanation in his *Southern Studies* article. "Although white liberals were confused about their role, some of Mississippi's young African-Americans had a strong sense of direction. Many Mississippi white liberals were unable to accept the new forcefulness of the younger generation of African-Americans because it changed their role in a drastic manner." Such confusion might be evident in efforts to compare such groups as the NAACP and the White Citizens' Council in *Journal* editorials.

In one of its strongest editorial attacks on the Ku Klux Klan, the *Journal* editorial on 20 October 1965 suggested that Southerners had been strong critics of the Klan as they were closest to its terrorism. "And as our area sees the Klan for what it actually is," the editorial stated, "the best treatment we can give it is to ignore its meetings and rallies and money-making promotions just as in the past we have ignored COFO and similar integration movements in this area."

Earlier that month, the *Journal* editorial on 11 October 1965 attacked both the KKK and COFO and other groups such as the Freedom Democratic Party in the same breath. "One of the least understood paradoxes of our times is the fact that white extremist groups like the Ku Klux Klan damage most the white community they pretend to help while Negro extremist groups hurt worst the Negroes whom they are pretending to save."

Despite his opposition to the bold moves of a new generation of vocal civil rights workers, McLean continued to call for justice in areas such as voting rights. For example, on 30 July 1962, the *Journal* carried a strong editorial—for Mississippi editors of the time—in support of fair voting rights: "Amidst all of the awakening of the backward peoples in various parts of the world there are citizens of Mississippi, native born citizens,

citizens educated in our public schools, who have also awakened. These are our educated colored citizens. They have gone to school. They have met the requirements of citizenship and they want to be treated like any other citizen. When they are denied this lawful and legitimate right what agency set up by the State of Mississippi or by the counties of Mississippi or by the municipalities of Mississippi can they turn to in order to get fair and equal treatment under the law? Being a native-born Mississippian and having lived here most of our life we know there is no such state agency or local agency to help them get fair treatment."

The editorial continues to promote a common theme in *Journal* editorials, the need for cooperation between the races. "We think the future welfare of our state demands that the best people among the white and colored people work together in harmony for the improvement of all the people of our state. We think our future welfare depends upon improving the morals, the economic status, the health and the responsible citizenship of our state."

Another technique that McLean's *Journal* employed frequently during the civil rights era was an attempt at bolstering the state's image by attacking the North. His comments in the McCarty interview illustrate this view. "I think it is extremely important for the state of Mississippi to realize that because of our close relationship that we have had through the years, because we were such a large proportion black . . . there is no reason in the world we cannot take the reservoir of good will and learn to work and help them so that we can become one of the great areas of this nation; because we do not begin to have the type of animosity and alienation in our state that we have in Harlem or in Detroit or in Chicago or elsewhere." Both Carter and Emmerich expressed similar views; despite their stands questioning some aspects of Mississippi society, they continued to resent outside interpretations of race relations in Mississippi. Attacks on the national news media were a common trait in state newspapers during and after the summer of 1964.

Several *Journal* editorials suggested that race relations were as good in the South as in the North. "Some individual or small group of Mississippians—white or colored—at times breaks out into violence against some other individual or small group—also either white or colored," observed an editorial of 22 July 1964. "But as far as we know there still is no mass hatred in either race against the other as there apparently is in Harlem. And surely it is the prayer of all Mississippians that we will always keep this advantage over New York regardless of how deliberately misunderstood we frequently are." Another example of Southern boosterism can be seen in an editorial published on 31 August 1964. "Evidence is mounting that whatever the shortcomings in relations between the two races in the South, we still get along better than whites and Negro groups of the North, both of which jump at the chance to blame their problems on southerners— white and colored alike."

On the other hand, *Journal* editorials did not shy away from taking Mississippi politicians to task, usually by simply stressing the need for common sense and progressive thinking. Though no proponent of the 1954 Brown decision, a *Journal* editorial on 20 May 1954 expressed disapproval of state politicians who latched onto attacking the Supreme Court for political gain. In a later editorial, on 21 February 1962, the move by state officials to reject participation in federally funded urban renewal projects was lamented. "At the same time that America was entering a new age in space . . . here on the ground some of Mississippi's most influential politicians were plotting a backward step which, relatively speaking, was just about as big a retreat as John Glenn's space flight was an advance." Pointing out that programs to improve housing were working in Tupelo, the editorial said the ban on accepting federal funding out of the fear that "urban renewal was synonymous with integration" would result in "a group of die-hard segregationist legislators" blocking modernization across Mississippi.

A 22 October 1958 editorial suggested that the focus on race-related issues was diverting politicians' attention from "all other matters needing public attention and debate." The editorial stated: "For as soon as the candidates begin competing with each other to see which can talk the loudest, longest and most vehemently on the race question, all other issues will be shoved into the background." Throughout his career as publisher and community booster, McLean loathed anything that took the spotlight from his priority, economic development. Race-baiting politicians were no exception. "For if each of the candidates has a sincere desire to serve the people of Mississippi, he will recognize the danger of letting the race issue run wild. Then, and only then, will we have an opportunity to hear from the candidates really sound proposals for promoting the development of Mississippi, which in spite of our best efforts, still ranks 49th in most economic matters and which will slip even further behind if we permit our energy and attention to be centered exclusively on racial issues."

Another political stand in which McLean went against the white majority view came in 1964, when he endorsed Lyndon Johnson over U.S. Senator Barry Goldwater in the presidential campaign. According to Joe Rutherford, McLean's endorsement of LBJ had less to do with liberal views of civil rights than "his belief that friends in Washington would support TVA and other federal programs that would benefit Northeast Mississippi." In a television appearance on WCBI-TV in Columbus on November 2, the eve of the 1964 presidential election, McLean appeared to encourage votes for Johnson. His comments reflected his pragmatism as he stressed how voting Democratic would improve the chances of getting more federal funding for local projects. He predicted state voters would go for the conservative Goldwater based on "the mistaken leadership that we have received from our state political leaders." However, he added, "It is our very strong contention that if a half dozen or more counties in Northeast Mississippi vote in favor of the Democratic nominees that this will do more to demonstrate to the nation that not all Mississippians are prejudiced and violently antagonistic to America than anything that can be done at this time."

Later, in comments to McCarty, McLean further explained his opinion of segregationist politicians in Mississippi. "Unfortunately, many of our political leaders have reflected their peer group or have gained office by being for the masses. Then, of course, always behind all of this was the deep seated fear of the black. I don't understand this, because every true Mississippian that I know anything about, who is worth a thing, always had a few black people that (he) thinks a great deal of, and trusts more than (he) would a lot of white people. Why in the world we can't treat people on their own merits, I just don't understand."

Harry Martin, head of the Community Development Foundation that McLean and other business leaders founded in 1948, said in a July 1999 interview that the publisher's view of Ross Barnett and others made him a magnet for criticism. "He was considered liberal for the South and had his share of critics for that. If you heard some candidate speaking, they would get on him for that because they were doing what they felt they had to do to reach a certain group of voters."

During the long, hot summer of 1964, marked by murders and church burnings in southern parts of the state, the frequency of editorials on race-related issues increased dramatically. McLean's resolve to always find the positive in response to any crisis finally weakened. He did manage to stick with his common themes that stressed the need for law and order, good will, and even local control. But the *Journal* could no longer ignore the rising tide of anger. An editorial on 20 July 1964 reflected on earlier predictions that the South's first groups organized to defy the U.S. Supreme Court would eventually create "increasingly violent offspring which would break away from parent groups as the latter failed to prove fast enough—and tough enough—to satisfy the hoodlum elements on the fringes." By the summer of 1964 that concern was justified. "And rebel offshoots of the KKK—in a sense the 'grandchildren' of the South's early militant groups organized to defy the High Court's rulings—now are spreading terror across southern Mississippi," the July 20 editorial noted. The editorial blamed "hoodlums" who had taken over the Klan for bombings, floggings, church burnings, and murders in southwest Mississippi.

At the same time, the editorial suggested that "radicals" in groups such as CORE had taken the reins from former leaders of the integrationist movement associated with the NAACP and the Urban League. To stop the growing violence, the editorial suggested "outspoken support for law and order by responsible citizens in every community, coupled with firm, courageous leadership by our state officials, can discourage and possibly reverse the trend toward murder, arson and bombings among militant Mississippi white groups before hoodlums bring disaster to our state."

An eloquent editorial printed on 7 August 1964, written in the aftermath of the murders of three civil rights workers in Philadelphia, called the slayings "a crime, a tragedy . . . a black eye to all Mississippians." The editorial continued, "When our state presents to the world a live drama of lowest bestiality comparable with the worst conceived by Faulkner, there is strengthening in the American mind a conviction that not only was Faulkner eminently accurate in his description of hill country 'rednecks' but these characters were typically and exclusively of Mississippi, not a mere part of the good and bad in all humanity." Suggesting that violence had perhaps done permanent damage to the state's image, the editorial quoted the comments of a Massachusetts editor, Paul Bittinger, who had written on 2 July 1964: "Anyone at all familiar with Mississippi could not be surprised by the Philadelphia incident. This is redneck country—lawless, cruel and backward, a last frontier in both the physical and moral sense." The *Journal* editorial decried the fact that this was the image widely held of the state, adding sadly that "now this is the picture of Mississippi being brought to life by the tragic Philadelphia story."

Earlier, the 28 July 1964 editorial responded defensively to a syndicated article describing a "terror-wracked Mississippi." Again, it mirrors McLean's fear of any news or comment that would harm the state's image. The Chicago article had described the area as follows: "The hill folk, with their tenant shacks, tend to be 'radical.' They scrape at hot furrowed fields and hard infertile soil." The *Journal* defended its region. "It is true that much of our farm land is poor. And certainly at this season of the year the furrows are hot. But if the rest of the country gets the idea from the Chicago article that everybody in Northeast Mississippi is out following a mule, they are being misled. For actually all Lee County is as highly industrialized in relation to population as is the city of Chicago." The editorialists tried to respond with a positive spin. "But if one wants to get picayunish, as does the Chicago writer in pointing out that hog jowls and black eyed peas are still table staples in our state, we could point out that the percentage of families with two cars is three times as large in Lee County as it is in Chicago."

A 16 July 1964 editorial begged state leaders to speak out against violence as the state entered one of "the most critical periods of our history." "As more and more churches are burned in Mississippi and the shadow of other violence hangs heavy over our state," the editorial declared, "we feel that Gov. Johnson is challenged to speak out forcefully not once but as frequently as necessary to establish the preservation of law and order as the official policy of our state and the responsibility of all good citizens."

A month later, a 20 August 1964 editorial implied that the anger once directed at "outside agitators" was being directed inwardly. "Now groups within the same race are becoming angry and bitter with each other. In some areas of our state, school boards are split; city councils are split; churches are split, whole communities are split." Again, the editorial spells out the consequences of continued race-related turmoil, suggesting that while industrial prospects continued to visit the relatively calm Lee County area, they were staying away from the rest of the state. "In other words, at a time of peak expansion of American industry, there are signs that industry is beginning to shy away from much of Mississippi."

Commenting on reports that seventeen churches had been burned in Mississippi that summer, in a 29–30 August 1964 editorial, "Was it Really a Negro Church That Burned," the *Journal* once again used religion to make an argument for reason. "They are referred to in the news as Negro churches. But we have a feeling that referring to a church as white or Negro falls short of giving the full picture. For a church is more than a building. It is more than people. It is a spirit. And that spirit is Christ's ... the church building, though nothing more than clothing for the religious organizations, is actually Christ's building, we would not care to be among those who may have set fire to churches within our state this summer. We hope the period of church burning in Mississippi is over." This editorial reflects the similarities between McLean and Carter's stand and style, as the Delta publisher's newspaper had on 2 August 1964 bemoaned the fact that "native-born thugs" were using "the house of God as their favorite target."

However, the *Journal* editorial of 21 August 1964 also took the opportunity to suggest Tupelo was different from the rest of the state. "For there is much difference between this corner of Northeast Mississippi and some other sections of Mississippi as there is between our area and, say, Iowa." A 27 July 1964 editorial again distanced Tupelo from the violence that marred other sections of the state. "The fact that Northeast Mississippi has come this far through the widely heralded 'long, hot summer' without major incident is, we believe, an achievement in human relations which is a credit to all our people, both Negro and white." Instead of following the pattern of bombings and church burnings in south Mississippi, the editorial said Tupelo was escaping the violence because of "sound common sense by both the white people and the colored people of Northeast Mississippi." The editorial stated that common sense had "set our area apart from the rest of the state and from numerous other sections of the South and East as a place where racial relations are proceeding almost normally." The *Journal* pleaded for continued peace. "If we understand that our maintenance of near-normal relations thus far is a real achievement of which all Northeast Mississippi can be proud, there is good reason to believe that we in this area will at summer's end have met our first big test."

By the end of the most turbulent years of the civil rights movement, McLean's dream of a nonviolent passage through the most difficult years of civil rights unrest appears to have come true in his corner of Northeast Mississippi. In 1968, Tupelo earned national recognition as one of 10 cities, the first ever in the South, selected by the National Municipal League and *Look* magazine to receive the All America City Award. According to the 16 April 1968 issue of *Look*, "Tupelo's highly innovative school system, its housing program, recreation facilities and active economic structure are all modern, all successful and all completely integrated, thanks to civic common sense and constant interracial discussions at all levels."

The 125th anniversary edition of the *Journal* reported that the judges for the national competition were impressed with the "lack of racial strife in the city and its efforts to achieve racial harmony." In that same edition, Palmer Foster, a district Boy Scout executive and the only black representative on the Tupelo panel who traveled to Milwaukee as part of the All America City competition interview process, commented: "Naturally, they asked about the racial situation here. I think that the '36 tornado served a purpose in that it made us all work together and I don't think people, black or white, have ever forgotten that."

The *Look* article noted: "In 1936, little Tupelo was practically wiped out and blown away by a tornado. Somehow, that must have had something to do with the way things are now. As local OEO director Jack McDaniel says: 'Almost any way you cut it, this place comes up being a part of something other than Mississippi.'"

McLean worked hard to bring such distinction to Tupelo and Lee County. In the process of turning a bankrupt newspaper into a profitable, well-respected institution, McLean also remained true to his initial goals and helped bring better opportunities in education and employment to both blacks and whites of Northeast Mississippi.

A 1965 speech by McLean further reveals how his religious background provided the foundation that influenced his attitude toward race relations and equal opportunity from the start. "We have long known that man should not be discriminated against because God made them a different color. The colored man is God's child just as much as we are God's children and we knew in our hearts that to treat a man as inferior and as a second class citizen simply because God in His wisdom chose to give that man a darker skin than ours is to call unclean that which God has made. We know that equal educational opportunities, equal voting rights, equal employment rights, equal treatment under the law are basic in our treatment of others."

Vaughn Grisham, director of the George McLean Institute at the University of Mississippi, suggested in an opinion piece published in the *Northeast Mississippi Daily Journal* on 1 March 1993 that McLean's legacy has lasted long after his death. "Thousands of people in Northeast Mississippi never knew him personally or perhaps even knew of him, but only a few have not been touched by his influence," Grisham wrote. "He was instrumental in bringing the furniture industry to North Mississippi, was a key person in bringing thousands of other jobs to the area, a pioneer for kindergarten, the catalyst for the current four-lane highway program for the state, promoter and supporter of education at all levels, the founder of CREATE, (a public charitable corporation started in 1972 by McLean) which has supported community projects throughout the area, and one of the nation's premier community leaders."

Mississippi editor Jim Abbott of *The Enterprise-Tocsin*, in an editorial of 3 March 1983 following the publisher's death, described McLean, Hodding Carter, Jr., and J. Oliver Emmerich as "titans of the trade," noting that all three "advocated progressive economic advances for their communities, while battling consistently for human rights." And, editor Charles Dunagin, in comparing McLean to Oliver Emmerich in a 6 March 1983 *McComb Enterprise-Journal* editorial, noted that both men entered newspaper publishing during the hard days of the Great Depression, enduring the lean years of World War II to eventually earn considerable personal wealth. He described both publishers as "individualists who felt a keen sense of public responsibility and were able both financially and intellectually to transform that responsibility into solid actions and achievements."

Former Mississippi governor William Winter's "Politicians and the Press," in the May 1987 issue of the *Journal of Mississippi History* made similar comparisons. "Beginning in the depression years of the 1930s . . . there began to be heard the different voices of some progressive young editors who had come into places like Tupelo, Greenville, McComb and Pascagoula. While the larger papers in Jackson continued to thunder a message of opposition to any changes in the so-called Southern way of life, the fledgling group of newcomers started to write from a different point of view." Winter noted that about the time Carter arrived in Greenville, "a college professor named George McLean turned up in Tupelo."

John T. Kneebone's study of earlier prominent journalists, *Southern Liberal Journalists and the Issue of Race, 1920–1944*, well describes the dilemmas faced by McLean and other Mississippi editors. "Perhaps most importantly, the segregationists recognized that white southern unity was essential to overturning the *Brown* decision and treated the moderates as traitors. Whatever northern liberals thought of moderation's inadequacy, the segregationists saw it, in the words of a writer for the Citizens' Council, as no more than 'gradual surrender to creeping integration as an alternative to the galloping variety.'"

And that's exactly where McLean was in the 1950s and 1960s. Despite all his hopes for progress and his deeply held religious convictions about equal opportunity, the publisher could ill afford to go too far in either direction. Surveying the scene, McLean decided to "work within the system."

In the process, his newspaper apparently got his message of equating racial progress with economic progress across to his readers in Northeast Mississippi. And, perhaps, as Kneebone suggested, "The moderates did play a crucial role. By their dissent from massive resistance, they not only kept alive a measure of debate in the South, but they also provided evidence to the rest of the nation that southern white unity was not total."

McLean no doubt suffered from the conflicts other Southern white progressives were forced to encounter during the civil rights movement. From all indications, his approach was rooted in his past as the son of a Mississippi plantation owner and transformed by his futuristic vision and thirst for progress. Although nationally recognized for his community development efforts, McLean's achievements as a journalist in the civil rights years received little attention. However, his approach did help Tupelo proceed peacefully toward becoming a more integrated community. While his low-key approach toward civil rights earned him no Pulitzer Prize and little national applause, his efforts did help place his beloved city on more than one list as a progressive place. That achievement would certainly have been the highest prize in McLean's eyes.

McLean found a way to be both preacher and teacher through his role as a publisher. In the process, he helped build a foundation for improving race relations by actively improving economic and educational opportunities. McLean himself best stated the philosophy that guided his work. "We are all on this spaceship earth together; and if we're going to spend our time fighting each other, we're never going to achieve the good life, and there's nothing left for our children and for those who come after us," McLean said in the McCarty interview. "But if we learn to work together and communicate, then we can move."

"Men are God's methods," McLean declared in a 7 May 1970 speech, repeating a phrase he often used. "The world looks for more money, bigger buildings, better plans, wiser professionals, stronger institutions. God looks for better men and women." With the "Tupelo Story" of progress and peace continuing long after McLean's death, the publisher seems to have been successful in shedding more light than heat as he established his own brand of ministry in a Mississippi newsroom.

At the age of 77, McLean could look back and see progress. "I know we've come a long way," he wrote in his *Appalachian Views* article. "I can remember when there were no black schools of any consequence, when the black children had only little schools in churches and shacks with few teachers and no libraries. Today we are moving ahead, and there is great hope for our future. And I'm pleased to have had a small part in helping bring some of these changes for the betterment of Mississippi."

References

Crawford, Eugene Gregory. "Charlie Dobbins: Southern Liberal Journalist." Master's thesis, Auburn University, 1994.

Cunnigen, Donald. "The Civil Rights Movement and Southern White Liberal Role Conflict." *Southern Studies*, Winter 1992.

Foster, Eddie; Greer, Mike; Pinson, Charles; Pittman, Tom; and Rogers, Chris. "Leadership Legacy of Lee County—George McLean." November 8, 1984. Tupelo Public Library.

Henderson, Leroy. "Editorial Analysis of the Tupelo Daily Journal: 1934–1968." Master's thesis, University of Southern Mississippi, 1970.

Jackson, Deidra Faye. "George A. McLean: Profile of a People's Newspaper Publisher." Master's thesis, University of Mississippi, 1995.

Kneebone, John T. *Southern Liberal Journalists and the Issue of Race, 1920–1944*. (Chapel Hill, NC: The University of North Carolina Press, 1987).

McCarty, Jr., Kenneth G. "Interview with Mr. George McLean, Publisher, Owner of Tupelo Journal," for the Mississippi Oral History Program of The University of Southern Mississippi, Vol. 39, 1974, (photocopy). The University of Southern Mississippi, Special Collections.

McLean, George A. "A Good Newspaper Makes Community the Ongoing Story." Reprinted in the Thursday, January 1, 1998, *Northeast Mississippi Daily Journal*.

———. Untitled Manuscript. Special Collections, University of Mississippi, J. D. Williams Library, Oxford.

———. "The Next 100 Years—First, a Brief Look Back—Then, a Long Look Forward, Finally a Deep Look Within." Speech before annual meeting of Community Development Foundation. May 7, 1970. Special Collections, University of Mississippi, J. D. Williams Library, Oxford.

———. "Why Community Development?" Special Collections, J. D. Williams Library, University of Mississippi, Oxford.

———. "Civil Rights Agitation in Mississippi." 1965. Special Collection, J. D. Williams Library, University of Mississippi, Oxford.

———. Untitled script of WCBI-TV endorsement of L. B. Johnson. Monday, November 2, 1964. Special Collections. J. D. Williams Library, University of Mississippi, Oxford.

———. "Your Responsibility for the Development of Your Community: Speech before ODK, University of Mississippi." May 15, 1947. Special Collections. J. D. Williams Library, University of Mississippi, Oxford.

Rutherford, Harry. Speech: "Tribute to George McLean on His 65th Birthday" given on July 30, 1969. Special Collections. J. D. Williams Library, University of Mississippi, Oxford.

Silver, James W. *Mississippi: The Closed Society*. (New York: Harcourt, Brace & World, Inc., 1964).

Winter, William. "Politicians and the Press." *Journal of Mississippi History*. May 1987.

Interviews

Gray, Lloyd, editor, *Northeast Mississippi Daily Journal*. Interviewed July 22 1999.

Martin, Harry, director, Community Development Foundation. Interviewed July 22 1999.

Pittman, Tom, former general manager, *Northeast Mississippi Daily Journal*. Interviewed August 5 1999.

Reed, Jack, Sr. Interviewed July 23 1999.

Rutherford, Joe, editorial page editor, *Northeast Mississippi Daily Journal*. Interviewed July 22, 1999.

Ira B. Harkey, Jr., and the *Pascagoula Chronicle*

David L. Bennett

> *I won, but I lost, too....*
>
> *I could not remain in Pascagoula, could not bear to exist in the vacuum of ostracism that remained in force even after victory, could not function in a silence of total isolation as if I were underwater or in galactic space. I was a pariah. I do not know whether this was because hate had become a permanent attachment to my person and accompanied me everywhere, repulsing all among whom I moved, or whether I had become an ambulatory and ubiquitous monument to the shame of my fellow townsmen, galling their late-blooming consciences....*
>
> *I was told later that as I walked from The Chronicle office for the last time a reporter I had recently hired from upstate wrung his hands and drooled, "Boy, I can't wait to start writing nigger again!"*
>
> Ira B. Harkey, Jr., The Smell of Burning Crosses *(1967)*

* * *

In a place and time when men preached hate and killed for no reason but skin color, Ira Brown Harkey, Jr., stood at history's crossroads and cursed the evil of racism. As he watched his state sink into a moral and ideological abyss, Harkey remained a voice of passion and courage during Mississippi's bloodiest civil-rights battles of the early 1960s. Harkey, publisher and editor of the Pascagoula *Chronicle*, bitterly condemned race hate and pleaded for compassion in the face of the racial hysteria fueled by James Meredith's admission into the University of Mississippi.

As this chapter will show, Harkey was the first white journalist in Mississippi in the 1950s to lay bare the immorality of white repression and expose the state's long history of cruelty and injustice to blacks. He strengthened other editors' resolve to attack racism, helping to dismantle a form of apartheid that had thrived since slavery. He appealed to readers' religious beliefs and argued that prejudice was a vile sin. By framing his arguments in bold relief—words such as "sin," "hate," and "wickedness" resonated through most of his writings about race—he cast bigotry as a sickness that would eventually destroy society. While Harkey himself has often repeated that he "didn't change a single mind" during his fourteen years in Pascagoula, he planted and cultivated deep seeds of doubt that ultimately led to the closed society's unraveling. He was the first to challenge the racial status quo, the most outspoken, the most hated, and the most inflammatory of Mississippi's civil rights journalists, and though his efforts did not yield immediate change, his legacy of courage and vision endures as a vivid example of journalistic integrity.

Mississippi journalism's most resolute white defender of equal rights, Harkey disparaged attempts by whites to keep blacks subservient. He shamed church leaders for their racial insensitivity. He blasted political leaders for forsaking the black race, unleashing his most virulent criticism on Gov. Ross Barnett. He indicted fellow journalists for abdicating their duty and for abetting discrimination, and he targeted labor leaders for their betrayal of black workers.

He argued that Mississippians were making idiots of themselves as the nation watched. In an editorial on 2 May 1963, he criticized state officials for their archaic naivete in "denying the Negro his rights as an American citizen." He wrote that Mississippi leaders were "incomprehensibly stupid," and that racism was "against every tenet of democracy and every teaching of Christianity and is incorrigibly un-American." He refused to tone down his rhetoric; his voice was among the most passionate of the civil-rights struggle. Harkey repeatedly derided Barnett, the leader of a movement that had assumed "a peculiar God-given right to withhold citizenship from half our people."

After attacking Barnett in a series of editorials in 1962–63 following bloody riots at Ole Miss over the admission of Meredith, Harkey endured countless death threats, boycotts, dwindling circulation, and social alienation. He became one of Mississippi's most hated men, the despised "nigger lover" who "ridicules our great Governor Barnett," "calls niggers 'Mr.' and 'Mrs.'," "writes news stories so you can't tell who's a nigger and who ain't," he wrote in *The Smell of Burning Crosses* (1967). No one came to his aid; no one defended him.

Harkey's ordeal illustrated the degree to which intimidation shaped Mississippi society. Mississippi in the 1950s was an American apartheid, a rigid system of racial segregation so entrenched that any challenge to perceived white supremacy brought swift criticism and condemnation from the state's white press. Economic, social, and educational barriers had constructed a vast gulf between the races, creating a racial status quo in which blacks were consigned to lives of poverty and servility. The prevailing orthodoxy of this closed society, as University of Mississippi historian James Silver has called it, held that whites and blacks were not equal and that neither race wanted nor was prepared for an integrated society. The state's white newspaper editors repeated a familiar refrain: Good colored folks know their place and are happy there. Few editors questioned the existing social order; most harshly denounced any suggestion of racial desegregation. The concept of equality of the races seemed to them inconceivable and unworkable.

Harkey emerged as the quintessential voice in the wilderness, chastising and reproaching white Mississippi for its shameful treatment of blacks. His editorial viewpoint represented the first challenge by a white journalist to the state's existing hegemony, the first dent in the closed society's armor of security. As early as 1950, long before any other white journalist in the state had denounced white oppression of blacks, Harkey bemoaned the evil of racism, disputed the notion of white supremacy, and argued for equal opportunity. He promised that his newspaper would uphold the rights of all people, regardless of race, that he would be blind to skin color when publishing his newspaper, and that blacks and whites would be treated the same in his pages. He kept his promises.

Fear of white reprisal controlled the Mississippi press before and during the civil-rights struggle. No journalist before Harkey would dare risk his career, perhaps his life, by questioning the cherished doctrine of white supremacy; to do so was unthinkable. Retaliation was swift and unrelenting, as Harkey discovered when he first supported equality, infuriating the entrenched white power structure, which struck back with fury. Fellow journalists lashed out at him; politicians, educators, and even the clergy ridiculed him; he was ostracized, mocked, and belittled at every turn. Nonetheless, he forged ahead, determined to gain unprecedented freedoms for blacks.

Harkey railed against racial injustice. He lamented the folly of white superiority, deplored what he called disgraceful manipulation of blacks. Drawing on the lessons of his youth—when he never heard the word "nigger" in his home—and biblical teachings that showed him that all people had great worth, he forged a lonely career in Mississippi journalism, championing the rights of the state's poor and disenfranchised. He never wavered in his commitment to blacks, even when he became a hated outcast, reviled by most whites. In an age when Mississippi journalists sought tenaciously to hold on to vestiges of the past, Harkey fought for a future in which he hoped blacks and whites would unite to form an egalitarian society free from racism.

Harkey's editorials and other writings during his career in Pascagoula are best understood as jeremiads, a form of literary discourse that evolved out of the pulpit. The jeremiad, America's oldest distinctive literary genre, warns of impending calamity if people refuse to turn from their sins, which, in Harkey's writings, meant the sin of racism. Vivid biblical imagery and Protestant thought pervade Harkey's prose. He often asked, What would Jesus do if He were here? The editorials are secular sermons, excoriating white society for deserting the black race. Harkey framed racism as a moral wrong, an egregious sin that would forever be a squalid blot on Mississippi's history.

He wrote that racism illustrated humanity's capacity for evil and darkness. He warned that one day white Mississippians would agonize over the guilt and shame wrought by race hate. Over and over, this strong evangelical impulse manifested itself in Harkey's words. Harkey asked: Did God love all people or just white people? His argument struck raw nerves in Pascagoula, situated squarely in the Bible Belt. Sure that God was on his side, Harkey was fearless, condemning white society for blatant hypocrisy.

Harkey has always maintained that his motivation for taking the stands he took was simple. "I simply believed what I was taught in Sunday School about God loving all men," he said. "There's nothing complex about it. I thought all men were equal. That's all. There's no deeper explanation."

The Pascagoula editor's voice resonated deeply throughout the civil-rights struggle in Mississippi. From *Brown v. Board of Education* (1954), which ignited racial upheaval in the South, until 1964, six Southern editors won the Pulitzer Prize: Buford Boone of the *Tuscaloosa* (Ala.) *News* in 1957; Harry Ashmore of the *Arkansas Gazette* in 1958; Ralph McGill of the *Atlanta Constitution* in 1959; Lenoir Chambers of the *Norfolk Virginian-Pilot* in 1960; Harkey in 1963; and Hazel Brannon Smith of the *Lexington* (Miss.) *Advertiser* in 1964. Of the six, Harkey was the only open and avid supporter of integration—a path from which he never veered from 1949 until 1963. He was Mississippi's most incendiary voice, an in-your-face editorialist who infuriated the white power structure by attacking the racial hypocrisy that he claimed existed in all areas of life—religion, education, economics, industry, politics, law, and the press.

Harkey's editorials centered on three basic themes: (1) denunciation of racism as a vile scourge that threatened to rip apart Mississippi society; (2) condemnation of those segments of the power structure—politicians, preachers, educators, and journalists—that he considered most complicit in perpetuating racism; and (3) predictions of financial devastation if the state was unable to achieve racial harmony.

Harkey was smart enough to understand that economics would eventually close the racial divide. Whites controlled industry, owned the land, provided jobs, and managed the distribution of wealth. Convinced that blacks could compete financially with whites if given the opportunity, Harkey lobbied hard for equality of opportunity, positing that the entire state, whites and blacks alike, would benefit if poor black workers could be lifted up to the level of white workers.

Warning that Mississippi's racial intransigence would inevitably lead to chaos, Harkey wrote that his state would devolve into little more than a Third World country if it did not prudently address the race problem. He foresaw the rioting, murders, and bombings that would become common during the heat of the civil-rights struggle. Perhaps better than anyone, he understood the vindictiveness of the white power structure when it was threatened, for he had been a target of hate, physical retaliation, and abuse during much of his time in Pascagoula. He was snubbed, cursed, and challenged to fight during his forays along the Gulf Coast. He was a social leper, mocked and abhorred by white society.

Harkey's ordeal revealed much about the Mississippi of his time. A journalist questioning the existing order faced ridicule, alienation, and death—at least twice Harkey's enemies fired shots into his office, and death threats became common. He faced bitter and severe consequences throughout his Pascagoula career. Harkey admitted that the mention of his name emitted a high stench for decades after he was gone.

Harkey's belief in racial equality sustained him through his ordeals and triumphs. His was a simple faith in the brotherhood of men, and despite his own frailties and failings—he became an alcoholic and was divorced during his Mississippi siege—he clung to the conviction that all people deserved equal treatment. He was not a late convert to the civil-rights movement; indeed, he had advocated racial parity despite skin color from the moment he bought the *Chronicle* in 1949 to the moment he sold it in 1963.

Harkey formed his opinions about race early in life. He was born in New Orleans on 15 January 1918 to Flora B. Lewis and Ira Brown Harkey. He remembered a lesson he learned when he was 5 years old, when he and his grandmother were riding the streetcar and he saw "ragged children playing in the muddy open gutter beside the dirt street," he recalled in a letter of 16 April 1993. He asked why the children were dressed so shabbily. "Because they're colored," his grandmother told him. Those words left an abiding impression, as he wrote in the same letter, which revealed the strong evangelical impulse that echoed through most of his writings.

> I have not forgot those words in the seventy years since. They appear to me often. From them I came to believe that "because they're colored" was an invalid excuse for believing that any

man's worth is less than any other's simply because of the accident of his appearance. . . .

I believed, and wanted to believe, that there was a brotherhood of men under God. Nobody, I thought, was to be excluded from this brotherhood because of his position in life or the color of his skin, any more than he should be relegated to the rear because of the size of his feet or the shape of his nose. . . .

Because of these beliefs, all my life I instinctively took the side of the underdog, the American Negro, the Indian, the sharecropper, the laboring man, the meek and unassertive, anyone oppressed by anyone.

Harkey's belief in equality grew strong during his youth in New Orleans. A gifted student, he skipped half of his grades in grammar school before enrolling at Newman High School, a fine prep school. He made the honor roll his first two years, but then discovered "girls, automobiles, football and track and did only enough to get by." He was "a stupid kid," he told his granddaughter, Charlotte Bosarge, in a letter on 10 April 1988.

An outstanding athlete, the 5-foot-6, 157-pound Harkey starred as a tailback in football and as a sprinter in track. He had blazing speed; he ran the 100-yard dash in 9.9 seconds. In track, he finished second in the state in the broad jump. He credited athletics for instilling in him the competitiveness that marked his journalistic career. He graduated in 1935 and enrolled in the New Mexico Military Institute in Roswell for his first year of college.

He returned to New Orleans in 1936 and entered Tulane University's College of Commerce, which he hated. After a year as an indifferent student, he traveled to Santa Ana, California, where he got a job culling oranges, filling and loading barrels, and performing other manual labors at a citrus plant. He returned to New Orleans briefly to marry Marie E. Gore, who returned to Santa Ana with him.

By 1939, he became serious about his education and returned to Tulane, majoring in journalism. He breezed through his courses, making A's in every subject except for a few B's he made in his journalism classes. He also found time to work forty-eight hours a week as a reporter at the *New Orleans Times-Picayune* during his college years. He graduated in 1941.

Harkey and his wife had two children. But he chose to serve in World War II, joining the Navy as an ensign in May 1942 and reporting to his indoctrination at the Naval Training School at Harvard University, where he ranked first in his platoon in academics. He served as an instructor at training schools in Ohio and Kansas before a transfer to Pearl Harbor in 1943. The Navy made him a mobile correspondent, and he traveled aboard the USS *Hancock*, an aircraft carrier that engaged in brutal fighting throughout the Pacific, encountering countless Japanese kamikaze aircraft during the recapture of the Philippines.

Harkey experienced an epiphanic awakening in the western Pacific in 1945 when a 250-pound bomb ripped open his aircraft carrier, killing fifty-two of his friends. Harkey recounted the carnage in *Crosses* (1967).

> There was blood everywhere, ankle deep it seemed. I had read or heard that one reaction to observing butchered dead is, "My lord I didn't know they had so much blood in them." I know that I looked in astonishment at the blood, the thick bright red beautiful blood that oozed like a tide over the flight deck, eddying around the parcels of humans that lay on it, ebbing and flowing with the rhythm of the sea.

Men of all colors were dead—black, white, yellow, brown, red—and as Harkey watched their bodies being dumped into the ocean, he clearly understood that skin tone did not determine a man's worth. His writing again revealed his religious moorings—equality of people, an afterlife free from segregation—themes he would repeat over and over throughout his career.

> And now as the sacks plopped one by one into the sea I wondered how their contents could have been distinguishable in life, how any of the men could have been deemed more worthy than another because of the color of his skin any more than because of any physical and accidental characteristic. . . . Was death more feared by one than the other? Did steel and fire

hurt one less than another? Is the gap left by one in a family back home more achingly apparent than that left by another? Because of what they looked like? Because of the color of their skin, for example?

As I watched the blur of canvas sacks slip over the side the conviction came to me that the Negro, who is good enough to be gutted by an unsegregated explosion, to be trussed in an unsegregated sack, to be dumped into an unsegregated ocean and dispatched to an unsegregated heaven or hell, is just exactly good enough to live an unsegregated life in the nation of his birth. And I thought further that the Southern Negro, in his century of unemancipated emancipation, has shown himself through his infinite patience and incredible loyalty to be the best American there is. And I felt grateful to him. And I still do.

After his military service, during which he became a lieutenant, Harkey returned to New Orleans in 1946 and resumed work at the *Times-Picayune* as a reporter and magazine writer. He spent three years looking for a newspaper to buy—he had always wanted his own paper that he could shape in his image—but had little luck until he heard that the *Pascagoula Chronicle-Star*, a frail weekly, was for sale.

In 1949, Harkey negotiated the purchase of the *Chronicle* from Hazel Herring of Moss Point and her brother, W. B. Herring, president of the Pascagoula-Moss Point Bank, for $106,000. He retained Tristram Shandy Easton King, the previous editor of the paper, and King's wife Irene, a reporter, and made King a partner, giving him the opportunity to buy half the paper's stock even though King had been able to raise just $3,000 of the sale price.

Harkey instituted immediate changes when he bought the *Chronicle*. His first and most controversial was dropping all race tags; he refused to identify a person as either a black or a white unless race was pertinent to the story, as in the description of a fugitive. He declined to use "Colored" before a person's name, and he began using the courtesy title "Mrs." for black women. He did not segregate birth lists, awards, fraternal activities, and obituaries. The *Chronicle* treated blacks and whites the same in its news coverage, infuriating Mississippi racists.

Harkey's boldness in 1949 was startling—as late as 1965 no paper in the state had followed his lead and dropped the "Negro" and "Colored" tags. Harkey thought it absurd that editors of other newspapers would employ drastic tactics to keep the races separated in their columns. Even in obituaries, blacks were treated as inferior.

"One of the least known injustices inflicted on the Southern Negro is the newspaper tag that he cannot escape even in death," Harkey wrote in *Crosses* (1967). "In print he is never a man. He is a Negro, negro or colored. His wife is not a woman. She is colored, Negro, negro, Negress or negress. Indeed, she is not even allowed to be his wife in most Southern newspapers, being denied the title of Mrs. no matter how legally married she may be. . . ."

Journalists, police, educators, and the clergy conspired to treat blacks shamefully, Harkey wrote. In *Crosses* (1967), he recalled an explosion he covered at a shipyard in Pascagoula in 1950. As he was running through the shipyard, he passed a deputy sheriff and asked him if anybody was hurt. "Two men were hurt and a nigger was killed," the deputy said.

Newspaper editors showed blacks little respect, and the editor who confused a white and a black paid swiftly for his carelessness. "Occasionally, a fortunate white person is tagged Negro in a news story," Harkey wrote in *Crosses*. "This is a libel in Mississippi, an open and shut case, and is worth from $800 to $1,000 to the plaintiff. Very rarely does a case go to court. Most newspapers settle without quibble. I am always amused at the horror-stricken tone of apologies directed to aggrieved whites mislabeled in this way."

Harkey shocked the Mississippi Press Association in June 1950 when he spoke on "How the *Pascagoula Chronicle-Star* and *Moss Point Advertiser* Handles the Negro in the News." He ignited a maelstrom of denunciation with his speech. "I nearly didn't get out alive," Harkey said in a speech to the MPA in June 1993. "One editor wrote that I caused a panic. Another that I nearly caused a stampede. . . . All the editors went home certain that I had at last proved that I was what they had known and claimed all along, that I was a communist. Maybe the head red in the state."

Audience members sat open-mouthed, incredulous, stunned by the blasphemy they heard in his 1950 speech. Harkey advocated not only fair treatment for the races in newspapers but also argued for equality in all areas of life. He spoke passionately and eloquently, urging his colleagues to join him in promoting racial harmony. He laced his speech with jeremiads, again drawing on religious themes and casting race hate as a despicable evil.

> Mississippi will not abandon its forty-eighth ranking among states until it starts treating the Negro as a man instead of a second class citizen.... How reasonable is it to hate millions of fellow Americans because their skin is black? No more logical than it is to hate all tall men, all men with blue eyes, all men with red hair, all men who wear green shirts. The Negro is not a lesser man because he is black, but a lesser man exactly for the same reasons that many a white is a lesser man—he doesn't have a chance.
>
> ... If the Mississippi Negro and his poor white neighbor, through equal education and opportunity, can be transformed into a healthy and productive citizen, every resident of Mississippi will be benefited. It can be done. And the first step is to treat him like a man.

The speech was simply an extension of the same theme Harkey had repeated since he bought the *Chronicle*. In an editorial on 23 December 1949, he wrote that his paper would "uphold unfailingly the rights of every man ... whether he be white, black, yellow, green or pastel shades in-between ... We believe that the only classes of people are male and female, good and bad."

Following Harkey's talk to the MPA, people from all over the nation flooded him with mail, most of it endorsing what he had said. Doubleday asked him to write a book about his beliefs and his experiences with race in the Deep South. His speech was widely circulated and reprinted by the Southern Conference on Human Welfare. It also made him instant enemies among the Mississippi press; Harkey traded critical volleys with several journalists, particularly with Tom Ethridge, a columnist and editorial writer for the Jackson *Clarion-Ledger* who vehemently opposed equality and served as a voice for Mississippi's most racist elements.

Harkey never tried to hide his disdain for journalists in his state. In *Crosses*, he recalled that most of them were incompetent.

> Only a bare handful of them are newspapermen. The rest are former paper salesmen, Linotype operators, truck drivers, shoe clerks or inheritors of the business, and they run their newspapers on the same principles they would sell paper, set type, drive trucks and fit shoes. The concept of freedom of the press is to them a license unencumbered with responsibilities. They are morally impotent and intellectually bankrupt.

But other than swapping criticism with fellow writers and incurring the wrath of segregationists, Harkey enjoyed a relatively peaceful first five years in Pascagoula. He showed that he could manage a newspaper, increasing the *Chronicle*'s circulation by 25 percent to more than 5,000 readers and making the paper a strong financial force by 1954. He expanded local news coverage, crafted lively features about life on the Gulf Coast, improved the writing and layout, and introduced a strong editorial page that became a widely read forum for discussion. He wrote bold, evocative columns and editorials, and welcomed dissenting views. Readers may have detested Harkey as a person. Nevertheless, they bought his paper, one of the state's best. He had transformed a failing weekly into a viable newspaper, and readers responded by embracing the paper in record numbers.

Harkey faced a crisis in 1954 when he predicted that the U.S. Supreme Court would find racial segregation in public schools unconstitutional in *Brown v. Board of Education*, the historic ruling that shattered the separate-but-equal law that sanctioned organized discrimination. White racists immediately sprang into action, claiming that school mixing would lead to mongrelization of the races and to the destruction of Mississippi's educational system.

In an editorial on 21 May 1954, Harkey told Mississippi leaders to prepare for integration, to accept it, and to formulate plans to make the transition as seamlessly and painlessly as necessary. Supreme Court justices were unanimous in their *Brown* opinion, voting 9–0 to end segregation, and Harkey urged readers to prepare for the inevitable.

> We were disappointed at the reaction of Mississippi's top politicians, which was to call for immediate planning toward subverting the ruling. If the principle of segregation is unconstitutional, it appears likely that any schemes rigged to perpetuate the principle would also be unconstitutional. What then would Mississippi do? Abandon education of its youth? Secede again from the United States?
>
> . . . Let us not be fooled by disparagement of the Supreme Court ruling as a "trick" or a "political ruling." . . . Democracy cannot exist when any blameless man receives from his state a lesser share of its bounty merely because of an involuntary and purely accidental physical characteristic.

The landmark ruling was "greeted by the Mississippi press with predictable stupidity," Harkey wrote in *Crosses* (1967). "Editors answered with defiance, many with all sorts of childishly proposed subterfuges. Some called for closing the public schools and letting Negro children go without any education at all. . . . They felt . . . that the matter could be kept in litigation 'for a hundred years.'"

After Harkey ran a series of editorials praising the Supreme Court ruling, the Ku Klux Klan burned a six-foot white cross in his front yard. He recalled the incident in his autobiography.

> One of my startled children first saw the blaze in front of our home and ran screaming to his mother. White-faced, round-eyed, she called me. I went out and hosed the evil thing. A message had been left, painted on a piece of brown corrugated cardboard. "We do not appreciate niggerlovers. We are watching you. KKK." A few weeks before, Tommy Harper, the local Klan head, had stopped by for a chat. His unblinking snake-eyes fixed on mine, he had told me, "If any niggers try to register at white schools next month, we're not gonna bother them.

> The one we'll get is the white man that's behind them and we know who he is."
>
> No one not rooted in the South can understand the full terror of a cross burning, this classic threat from the Klan. It is like the voice of doom, the sentence of death, the placing of the victim beyond the pale. Marking him for punishment by some of the most ruthless thugs in the history of mankind. I did not let my wife and children see how profoundly I was shaken.

The Klan maintains a violent and ugly tradition in Southern lore. Many people in the South know a Klansman, or have kinfolks or friends with ties to the Klan. From an early age, children of the South, black and white alike, are told stories of sinister men in white robes committing egregious crimes against blacks with unremitting brutality. Passed from generation to generation, the Klan's legend grows, spawning fear. Dread of the KKK is particularly strong in the South, simply because the Klan is an ever-present threat. To encounter these men is a harrowing experience, as Harkey details in the passage above.

After the Klan's fury subsided and the outrage over *Brown* abated, Mississippians contented themselves with the belief that their schools would never be integrated. Their political leaders, the press, business and industry, and education allied to assure citizens the threat would never become reality. Harkey promised that school integration was coming and suggested a plan to integrate schools over a 20-year period. Few readers believed that Mississippi schools would ever desegregate; they largely tuned out Harkey's prediction.

Harkey's open support of school integration in 1954 did not hurt his paper financially. The *Chronicle* became Mississippi's largest weekly, and Harkey became one of the state's most honored writers, winning yearly awards from the Mississippi Press Association.

Speaking before the Alabama Press Association in March 1954, Harkey attributed the *Chronicle*'s success to three factors: localization of news, fine features, and the use of editorials. In the March 1954 edition of the Alabama Publisher, Harkey said editors should understand "the absolute necessity of stating your opinions on public issues."

He told APA members that he was continually "amazed at the readership that editorials in a weekly newspaper can attract." He added: "People will come in from the woods, bare-footed, with wild eyes, people you wouldn't think could read at all, yet they not only understand your editorial but can point out several angles you overlooked."

Harkey told editors to avoid "my own spectacular failing, irony, sarcasm, and any form of subtlety, or instead of being merely interesting you'll be confusing." He failed to heed his own advice; when race became a white-hot issue in his pages, sarcasm and irony became his two main editorial weapons.

Despite rhetorical duels with fellow journalists, customary spats with politicians and educators, and the weight of being the state's most ardent integrationist, Harkey enjoyed a relatively serene period from the mid-1950s to the early 1960s. He and his wife had six children. His newspaper grew and prospered; Harkey made it a semi-weekly in 1957 and planned to take it daily, which he did in 1961. He was in the Rotary Club, participated in civic functions, and navigated freely, if awkwardly, through Pascagoula society, such as it was. He was snubbed and cursed occasionally for his racial beliefs, but he had grown used to verbal jousts over the years, and he had learned how to handle them with dignity.

He remained a controversial figure, of course, but no organized hate groups threatened him, no one swore to kill him, and his presence at public meetings did not engender rancor or hostility. He was not a social gadabout, but neither was he was a target.

His paper continued to grow; circulation neared 6,000 by 1957, making the *Chronicle* the state's only weekly with more than 5,000 subscribers and the Deep South's largest audited weekly. Buoyed by increased revenue and readers, Harkey made the paper a semi-weekly, publishing on Tuesdays and Fridays. Harkey told the *Mississippi Press* in October 1957 that his paper sorely needed to expand. He said the *Chronicle* had grown "beyond the mechanical limits for one edition a week." He had too much news and too little space, he added, and his paper needed to adjust to the growth in the Pascagoula-Moss Point area. Advertisers were pressuring him to give their businesses more exposure.

Despite the *Chronicle's* success, Harkey's relationship with Easton King, his co-publisher, deteriorated over the years. Harkey promoted King to publisher within six months after he bought the paper in 1949, although Harkey remained the true power at the *Chronicle*. The two coexisted efficiently but not always peacefully. King boasted that he owned the paper and took credit for its accomplishments.

"Stupidly I was amused at King's pretense that he ran the paper," Harkey wrote in a letter in October 1994. "I continued to give King raises, setting my own pay at his rate. But he never paid me a cent for the stock he was supposed to be buying, although he participated as half-owner. With his growing affluence he built a house, sent his daughter to college, but made no payment to me."

In 1953, tired of King's stalling, Harkey tore up their contract, removing King as a co-owner. Harkey gave King 15 percent of the company stock but stripped him of any legitimate power. Their relationship further deteriorated when the *Chronicle* printed civil-rights activist's P. D. East's book about his life. King took full credit for the project, published in the late 1950s, and East thanked King effusively for all his work and cooperation in bringing the publication to fruition. East never mentioned Harkey's name, never thanked Harkey for funding the printing. He and King were friends, and King led East to think he was donating the work. Thus, all the praise went to King, who was only a peripheral player at best. Harkey was furious. "It was one thing for King to strut about Pascagoula as THE Chronicle," Harkey wrote in the same letter. "It was another for this fiction to appear in a nationally circulated book. . . . My resentment boiled so that I could hardly think of anything else."

Harkey demoted King to associate editor and publisher. He told East to find another publisher. And finally, in 1961, when King made pay demands, Harkey fired him and filed suit seeking repayment of $5,600 in cash advances made to King over the years and of $3,200 in purchases made by Irene. Harkey won a suit in county court but did not obtain a judgment. "King sold his fifteen percent of Chronicle stock to a local couple," Harkey wrote in the October 1994 letter. "An alcoholic with a heart problem, he moved to New Orleans and died in 1965.

"I also am an alcoholic," Harkey continued with a rare admission, "as was my first wife and mother of my children who died in 1994. We separated in April 1959, I moved out, managed to stop drinking. I have not had a drop since 4:30 a.m. 30 May 1960, thirty-four parched miserable years."

Harkey's life changed irrevocably in the summer of 1962. As James Meredith made plans to enroll at Ole Miss, fueling a racial hysteria that swept the state, Harkey warned of the consequences that would follow if Mississippi defied federal law. Few listened to his advice, least of all Ross Barnett, who vowed never to give in to the mandates of President John F. Kennedy. Harkey excoriated Barnett, who "was going to let blood flow in order to prove how staunchly he opposed the extension of the rights of citizenship to half the people of Mississippi," Harkey wrote in his autobiography.

Harkey was confident Barnett would surrender to reason. To do otherwise would constitute an act of madness, Harkey thought. With the nation watching, Barnett could not afford to risk Mississippi's future.

The Meredith case had been winding through the courts since 1961 when Meredith, a 29-year-old Air Force veteran, sued to gain admission to Ole Miss. Harkey lamented the folly of Ole Miss even trying to fight integration, pointing out that many blacks had attended the school long before Meredith applied. Harkey argued that other blacks of varying degrees of blackness had long frequented Ole Miss, and that no white in Mississippi could prove that he was not indeed black.

". . . the state is full of obvious physical Negroes of varying shades of tan living as social whites whose parents or grandparents had 'passed,' " Harkey wrote. In fact, as early as 1945, Harry S. Murphy, Jr., a light-skinned black, had attended Ole Miss, Harkey noted.

Justice Hugo Black ordered the university to admit Meredith on 10 September 1962, following a 9–0 vote by the High Court. Three nights later, Barnett appeared on statewide television to give his response. Harkey was certain the governor would accept the inevitable and allow Ole Miss to admit Meredith peacefully. Barnett refused, summoning up the law of "interposition" and invoking it as a barrier between the federal government and the rights of his state—a desperate and ill-guided attempt to circumvent the ruling. Politicians around the state joined Barnett, promising to go to jail with him if they had to.

Harkey was shocked. On 14 September 1962—the day after Barnett's speech—he lashed out in an editorial, again using the jeremiad, his key literary tact, to promise ruin and devastation if Mississippi did not mend its ways.

> [Barnett] called upon officials to defy the United States and he vowed again that Ole Miss will not be integrated . . . Barnett will either back down or he will destroy our educational system. His words last night made it virtually impossible that he will back down. . . .
>
> But it is not "the Kennedy administration" that is making demands upon Mississippi. It is democracy itself, it is the whole of humanity. These surely will not back down either. Barnett has asked them to force us to comply. They will, and the process can ruin Mississippi.

Harkey continued to criticize Barnett in a series of incendiary editorials. He ripped other politicians for siding with the governor, calling their behavior shameless and cowardly. When twenty-six office holders in Hinds County signed a resolution supporting Barnett and promising to go to jail with him if needed, Harkey praised Allen Thompson, the mayor of Jackson, for refusing to sign. "Comforting to know there is one mature man among the kids holding public office in our state capital," Harkey wrote in an editorial on 27 July 1962. "On the face of it, the resolution expressed a noble sentiment. But the signers meant just the opposite of what they said. They will go to jail, they said, in support of what they interpret the Constitution to be. It happens that, in most cases, this is exactly the opposite of what the Constitution is."

In a column that was reprinted nationally, "Confusing times, dangerous times," published on 19 September 1962, Harkey claimed that Barnett had chosen suicide by challenging the federal government. The editor promised that the United States government would respond with necessary force.

> A pall of contradiction covers our state as if every one of us had developed schizophrenia. . . .
>
> Gov. Barnett knows full well how laws are enforced when the lawless are defiant. . . . How do you think the United States

will enforce the law now? By sending in the Peace Corps? Postmen? Soil conservationists? When laws are ignored, force is applied. Gov. Barnett knows that. . . .

In a madhouse's din, Mississippi waits. God help Mississippi.

Harkey noted blatant hypocrisy in Mississippi's political stance. The state's politicians and newspapers had long advocated a "fight to the finish," yet they were now asking the federal government not to send marshals into the state to enforce the law. They called upon citizens not to resort to violence while they advocated a battle to the end. Harkey asked: "How can we defy the law 'to the finish' without resorting to violence?"

Harkey praised Judge Sidney Mize of Gulfport, "the first person to decline Gov. Barnett's invitation to go to jail." Agreeing with an earlier ruling in the federal court of appeals, Mize ordered Ole Miss to admit Meredith immediately.

As Harkey's attacks on Barnett mounted, opponents organized to silence him. The Jackson County Citizens Emergency Unit sprang to life under the lead of the county sheriff, James Ira Grimsley, "a bloated harddrinking semiliterate ruffian," Harkey recalled in his autobiography. Meeting in the Jackson County Courthouse several times a week, the Unit conspired to retaliate against Harkey, to boycott businesses that employed or catered to blacks, and to protect the cherished doctrine of white supremacy.

Boasting of 600 members, the Unit attracted members from most segments of society, though its plans were largely articulated and implemented by the most extreme racists, a hard-core group of thugs who used violence to terrorize Pascagoula citizens into conformity. The group's leading objective was to silence Harkey and to run the *Chronicle* out of business if possible.

Harkey despised Grimsley, whose office sanctioned and coordinated the activities of the Unit. Though he denied it publicly, Grimsley was clearly the terrorist group's leader, arranging for meetings in the county courthouse and using his deputies to institute its edicts, Harkey wrote.

Grimsley and twenty of his followers returned from the riots at Ole Miss following Meredith's admission as heroes because of their bonecracking, skull-smashing expertise. They were extremely dangerous, Harkey wrote in his autobiography, but they were also extremely stupid. They spread terror throughout the county, and Harkey was one of their prime targets.

They organized a boycott of the *Chronicle*; they threatened subscribers and advertisers; they issued death threats to Harkey; they launched a campaign of hate and abuse that silenced anyone who might have sided with Harkey.

"In Pascagoula, there was no power to which I could turn for help," Harkey wrote in *Crosses*. ". . . City and county police authorities shrugged. Other newspapers in Mississippi and those in the city of Mobile in nearby Alabama, had already grabbed up the cudgel of bigotry . . . The *Chronicle* was, as was pointed out in the viciously racist Jackson *Daily News* of the state capital, 'the only newspaper to oppose the chartered (sic) course of Mississippi.' "

The riots at Ole Miss left Harkey almost speechless. His greatest fear had become reality. Any hope for a peaceful reconciliation of the racial problem in Mississippi had disappeared, and anarchy had ensued. Harkey recounted his pain in *Crosses*, again drawing on his religious beliefs, as his references to the goodness of men and hell illustrate, to issue a harsh jeremiad.

> I thought I would lose my mind. Despite the unassailable facts, my mind rejected what had happened at Ole Miss. I could not reconcile all I had been taught and believed about the ultimate goodness of men with what the newspapers and television reports showed that men—the leaders of my state—had done at Oxford. And what came after October 1 was as bad. There was no recoil of remorse. . . . Mississippians exulted in rebellion, hailed murder, raised Barnett to sainthood and assigned John Kennedy to perfidy with Tojo, Hitler and Castro.

Harkey fought back through his editorials, lashing out at those responsible for the mayhem at Oxford and pleading for racial understanding. He worried that state leaders would actually close Ole Miss rather than integrate; he thought it insane that their mistakes in judgment now seriously jeopardized higher education throughout the state.

Ira B. Harkey, Jr., and the Pascagoula Chronicle

The dismantling of the educational system, of course, would lead to a dismantling of industry, of culture, of the ability of Mississippians to make a living. Harkey doubted if anyone had analyzed the long-range effects: businesses would leave the state, the economic structure would collapse, citizens would exit in large numbers to find work in other states, and technological advancement would cease, leaving the state in basically the same condition as a Third World country.

He lamented the sorry spectacle Mississippi had made of itself, and voiced fear that its leaders were foolish enough to allow the racial madness to continue. In an editorial on 14 November 1962 titled "Perfectly capable of closing Ole Miss," he shared his dismay.

> Anywhere else in the United States, the suggestion that a state university be closed down for any reason at all would not rise to the level of public discussion. Such a suggestion could not originate outside a lunatic academy.
>
> But in our state—where the leaders for eight years led us to believe we would not be required to obey the same laws that others must obey, whose leaders called out the mobs to let blood in senseless opposition to the will of the nation . . . —in this state we had better discuss the possibility. Now. . . . If we now let them convince us that it is proper to close Ole Miss and destroy a century of cultural advancement, then maybe we do not deserve any better than to be led by owners of grammar-school intellects and of attitudes that most humans left behind somewhere in history.

Harkey contended that economics would ultimately lead to integration, and that Mississippians were wise enough to realize that. Dollars would speak more eloquently that misguided logic, he posited. Half the state's workforce could not be denied work, could not be discriminated against, without their absence eventually destroying the other half. It was his wisest observation: in the end, discrimination became a financial issue. Industry knew it could not survive without black workers; the economy would nose-dive without blacks as full participants. Throughout Mississippi blacks were important to the economy as underpaid, low-wage workers.

In an editorial on 20 November 1962, Harkey quoted Dr. Sam S. Talbert, head of the journalism department at Ole Miss: "Every job in every factory in Mississippi is in some way related to knowledge originating in a university," Talbert said. "The automobiles we drive, the fertilizer and poisons we use on our crops, this whole electronic era and the atomic era ahead are by-products of university training and research."

Talbert issued a grievous warning: "Let no one be misled. Only the sorriest kind of industry would move to a state where the children of workers and executives could not attend accredited institutions, nor to a state whose institutions ceased to educate first class executives, scientists, engineers, and enlightened community leaders."

Harkey chastised the state's leaders for remaining silent in the months and years leading up to the Ole Miss explosion. When a few voices denounced the riots, Harkey answered them. In an editorial on 9 October 1962, he wrote that their silence had led to bloodshed.

> It is heartening that responsible leaders throughout Mississippi are now raising their voices on behalf of law, order and decency in our state. It is pathetic, though, that they waited until it was too late, that they remained mute during the eight years that Mississippi built up its head of hate, that many of those now calling for decency actually abetted that build-up merely by saying nothing.
>
> There is no fun in this instance in saying I told you so. What we said would happen—and what has now happened—is too horrible and the shame is too great to bear taunts from any quarter. We pray, however, that the voices now calling for order will continue to do so forever and ever.
>
> For eight years, since the 1954 Supreme Court ruling that cast out the separate-but-equal doctrine, our state has heard nothing but violent talk from its leaders. Only one or two politicians, almost no religious leaders and less than a half-handful of newspapers tried to warn of the calamity that was being prepared.

A powerful white ally finally emerged for Harkey in Pascagoula: Claude Ramsey, state president of the AFL-CIO—the first person to publicly defend Harkey and the *Chronicle*. Black groups such as the NAACP had endorsed Harkey's views, but Ramsey represented the first significant crack in the armor of white supremacy. Speaking before union members at Ingalls Shipbuilding in November 1962, Ramsey called the *Chronicle* a friend and an organ that promoted the best interests of Ingalls, one of the largest employers on the Gulf Coast. Ramsey spoke in terms the workers could understand: A racial explosion in Pascagoula could cost the company its federal contracts, he said, and cost them their paychecks. He urged the workers to accept the paper as an ally, and to cease all efforts to destroy it.

Harkey was astonished by Ramsey's courage. "He risked his neck," Harkey said. "That particular branch of the KKK around Pascagoula and Moss Point had some of the most brutal and ruthless men I had ever met. I mean, those people would kill you. But that didn't seem to faze Ramsey. He saved my bacon. I still can't see how he got away with it."

Ramsey's talk came at a fortuitous time for Harkey. The *Chronicle*'s circulation was declining; advertisers were bailing out; Harkey failed to make any money in December, a paper's most profitable month. Harkey had fired heated salvos at the Unit for two months, and the "goons," as he called them, had struck back with boycotts, shots into his office, death threats, and promises of violence. Harkey stared them down.

In an editorial on 26 October 1962 that was circulated and reprinted nationwide, Harkey vowed never to give in to the racists. Titled "A drift from reality, for drunks and loons," the editorial targeted Sheriff Grimsley, whom Harkey said was the Unit's head goon.

Harkey told his readers that a terrorist group was seeking to destroy his newspaper, and he implicated Grimsley as its leader. He commented on a speech Grimsley had given to his followers, calling it "a drift from reality, a nightmare, a situation that in a work of fiction would be too fantastic to be believed other than by children, loons and drunks." He attacked Grimsley for blatant lies and promised to reveal "the flood of corruption that has engulfed our county during the past two years." He threatened to reveal the gambling and prostitution that he claimed had flourished with Grimsley as sheriff.

Harkey appealed to his readers to remain loyal to the *Chronicle*. In an editorial on 12 November 1962, he told his readers that "just as spite and hate will never build a going concern, spite and hate will not sink an enterprise that is honestly run and supplies a genuine need." He promised his paper would never sell its integrity and never compromise.

During Harkey's darkest moments, help came from the federal government. Ashton Phelps, publisher of the New Orleans *Time-Picayune*, aided Harkey at the urging of Harkey's father, a wealthy businessman who served on the board of directors of the *Picayune*. Born in Scott County, Miss., Ira, Sr. headed five Coca-Cola bottling plants, a vinegar plant, and a fruit flavoring plant that supplied flavors for soft drinks, candy, and other goodies.

Phelps called a high-ranking official in the U.S. Justice Department, and the official dispatched agents to Pascagoula to investigate civil-rights violations by those forces who were attempting to destroy the *Chronicle*.

"Their intervention helped considerably," Harkey said. "That was a tough time for us, but the FBI helped us out. The FBI told me that these guys in the Unit were scared to death of the FBI; they were practically crying, the yellow bastards."

The Unit entered a deep funk, almost sinking into oblivion. The *Chronicle* had always slipped spies into the meetings, and the spies reported that in late spring 1963, at the last meeting the newspaper infiltrated, only 22 members had attended, far from the reported high of 600 during fall 1962.

Radio station WNET in New York City also rallied support for Harkey. On a newscast on 23 January 1963, commentator Dee Finch said he planned to buy a subscription to the *Chronicle* and suggested listeners follow him. More than 500 callers to the station in a two-hour period pledged to subscribe to the paper. Advertising agencies called to say they planned to place their clients' ads in the *Chronicle*. After a ten-minute feature on Harkey later in the day, 250 listeners promised to subscribe to his paper. Taped interviews by Harkey and Sheriff Grimsley were played during the feature.

With the Unit neutralized, Harkey seized the momentum. He began to win back his advertisers, and circulation rebounded to 8,500, 15 percent higher than at any time in history. Winning the Pulitzer Prize in May 1963 enhanced his status. In addition to the new subscribers from the New York area, the *Chronicle* attracted white and black readers alike from the Gulf Coast, many of whom were lured by the contentious debate over integration featured in the paper's pages. Harkey's outspokenness and his solicitation of opposing views made the *Chronicle* a topical, highly readable paper. Letters to the editor routinely contained bitter denunciations of Harkey; indeed, his paper served as an open platform in which citizens were free to air their views on race.

Harkey's Pulitzer infuriated Mississippi editors, who harshly criticized the Pulitzer Awards Committee for giving "the nigger-loving traitor" its top award. Only a handful of journalists congratulated him: Charles Nutter of Picayune, Hazel Brannon Smith of Lexington, Hodding Carter Jr. of Greenville, H. H. Chrisler of Bay Springs, and Phil Mullen of Canton.

"You're the bravest man in Mississippi, and congratulations for your greatest of editorial recognitions," Mullen said in a letter on 9 May 1963. Mullen told Harkey to keep fighting despite the opposition, pointing out that friends could be fickle. Mullen added: "I was thinking about friends the other day: Did you know that Bill Faulkner never had any really intimate friends? Not in Oxford anyway. We have quailed for you with every one of your issues of recent months but certainly do appreciate receiving them."

Nutter, who became an Associated Press correspondent in Spain and later was the AP bureau chief in New Orleans, told Harkey in a letter on 9 May 1963 that he hoped Harkey's Pulitzer would "stiffen the backbone of other editors, although I am not sure it will." Nutter was confident that most other state journalists would attack Harkey with a primal vengeance, and he was correct.

Hate and vitriol filled Mississippi newspapers after Harkey's triumph. Writers ridiculed the Pulitzer Committee, belittled the prize, questioned Harkey's motives, and wrote openly about a communist conspiracy to destroy Mississippi from the inside by planting traitors such as Harkey. In *Crosses* (1967), Harkey reprinted an article by John G. Gibson of Magnolia:

> Any Mississippi editor who craves and seeks the national spotlight can easily have it focused upon him (and become literate) simply by writing what conforms to the socialistic and commu-

nistic trends of the hour. He must be willing to close his eyes to history, join the ranks of the pacifists under the guise of law and order and decency, ignore principle and fundamentals, get in the hog wallow of slime and maggots, and say to hell with my race, my country and my God. Then he will become a great and literate editor. Hogwash!

Tom Ethridge of the Jackson *Clarion Ledger* mocked Harkey's Pulitzer in a column on 21 May 1963. "Since Mississippi is a key area," he wrote, "any journalistic quisling here can put himself in line for the Pulitzer editorial award by singing the surrender song so dear to the mix-minded board of Pulitzer judges."

Ethridge wrote that "it also helps to be a Southern integrationist in the right place at the right time." He called New York's Columbia University, home of the Pulitzer, a "fountainhead of race-mixing ideologies and one-world radicalism."

Harkey told Publishers' Auxiliary on 11 May 1963 that he knew the Jackson dailies (the *Clarion Ledger* and the *Daily News*) suspected he would win the prize because both had "been writing hate editorials during the past few weeks belittling the Pulitzer Prizes and saying only left-wing editors could win."

William Faulkner captured the Pulitzer for fiction writing on the same day Harkey won his. Harkey believed Faulkner was the greatest man Mississippi had ever produced. "They called Faulkner a traitor, but no man has ever loved Mississippi more," Harkey told Publishers' Auxiliary. "Some call me a traitor, too, but how could I be a traitor because I was never a part of that cause."

Harkey fired back at his critics in the Mississippi press. In an editorial on 17 May 1963, he wrote: "A Pulitzer Prize is the greatest honor that can come to a newspaperman. So great an honor that if he lives 100 years after receiving one, he will be identified every single day of his life as the 'Pulitzer Prize-winning editor.'"

He added: "In all inhumility we say that the pygmies attempting to belittle the Pulitzer Prize are as ludicrous as jackals faulting a lion. The truth is that 100 percent of newspaper editors, including all of them in

Mississippi, would give several years' profits and several years of their lives to win a Pulitzer."

Two days after winning the award, Harkey appeared at a meeting of the Pascagoula Rotary Club. Members ignored him. "One brave person, City Judge Red Watts, told me in a loud voice that the Pulitzer was not only an honor for me but an honor for the community," Harkey wrote. "Heads turned away, not one voice seconded Red's thought. Until then, all through the fourteen years of campaigning for civil rights, I had had no inkling that Red agreed with me on anything. I nearly kissed him."

Harkey answered fellow journalists in an editorial on 4 June 1963, scorching his critics with biting sarcasm, again invoking religious themes.

> ... Envious hacks have charged that the writing that won this year's Pulitzer Prize was "against Mississippi," "knock Mississippi," when in truth the editorials did exactly 180 degrees the opposite. The editorials were against race hate, against the unchristian doctrine of white supremacy, against the demagoguery of political leaders that nailed Mississippi's name at the top of the western hemisphere's infamy list. The writing was "against" those who have come very close to destroying Mississippi. . . . The lowest elements in our society are ruling our state. But there will come a day when the hateist press will be ignored, the hateist politician will spew his venom to empty spaces and Mississippi's fair name will be extricated from the disgrace into which the hateists have thrust it.

Harkey always felt that he never received just credit for winning his award. As late as 1989, he was still fighting a battle to get Mississippians to acknowledge his prize. In a letter on 31 October 1989 to the director of the Center for the Study of Southern Culture at the University of Mississippi, he revealed his frustration after he read an article that omitted him.

> A brief visit to a library would have revealed to the author of referenced article a notable fact in country newspapers: two Mississippi editors won Pulitzer Prizes for editorial writing in successive years.

David L. Bennett

> This author mentions Hazel Smith, who won in 1964, but not Ira Harkey, who won in 1963 for editorials before, during and after the Ole Miss-Meredith turmoil of 1962. . . .
> The Southern Regional Council said that his was "the most compelling voice" heard in Mississippi during the struggle, "alternately cajoling and shaming white Mississippi." The *Columbia* (University) *Journalism Review* said that Harkey was "perhaps the stoutest representative" of the few Mississippi editors who opposed Gov. Ross Barnett's "never" stance, making others "seem slow or equivocating."
> Harkey tells of his fourteen-year civil rights work in his book *The Smell of Burning Crosses*, which went to three printings, is found in many libraries and is still used even in 1989 as a text in some journalism classes.
> The author of the referenced ESC paragraph mentions Hodding Carter besides Hazel Smith. He evidently does not know that Hodding won his Pulitzer nearly twenty years before the civil rights movement, and not for editorials on Negro rights but about treatment of Japanese-Americans.

A month after Harkey won his prize, the Mississippi Press Association held its annual convention in June 1963. Not once during the three days did anyone mention Harkey's Pulitzer.

Harkey took particular delight in parading the Pulitzer before his fellow Mississippi journalists, most of whom had deserted him during the racial madness of Oxford. Harkey ripped his former colleagues in *Crosses* (1967).

> The sins of the press spreadeagled the whole sorry scene of racism in Mississippi. The press not only allowed the failures of the schools and the churches to go unnoted and the better element of the white public to remain ignorant of the failures, but actively promoted these failures. Any deviation from the established doctrine of white supremacy on the part of either brought swift condemnation from watchful editors. The press not only allowed the politicians and lawyers and their business

and industry allies to use hatred as an escalator to power, but in most cases became their active partner. And in order to reach the same goal: power and its financial spoils. . . .

Thus it is that a proud profession—journalism—which in the past has listed among its practitioners some of the most courageous, learned, selfless and cultured Southern gentlemen, degenerated into an agency for the propagation of the ideals of the lowest elements in our society.

Harkey did not squander all his criticism on the press; he also indicted the clergy for shameless hypocrisy. In one of his most famous editorials, published in the *Chronicle* on 21 November 1962, he articulated his thoughts about Christianity, harshly criticizing religion as it was practiced in Mississippi. Harkey quoted a letter from Ross Barnett's cousin, a missionary to Nigeria, to condemn religious bigotry, and evangelical themes saturated his writing.

"You send us out here to preach that Christ died for all men," wrote Atonina Canzoneri to a Mississippi Baptist newspaper, "then you make a travesty of our message by refusing to associate with some of them because of the color of their skin."

This is the basic cause of the Mississippi schizophrenia, the incredible disease that allows us to claim that we are at one and the same time Christians and white supremists, when there are no two attitudes more incompatible than these.

Harkey called Christianity in Mississippi "a white man's fraternity . . . There is only one God, but he is God only for certain people, people who look and think like we do."

Harkey wrote that a person who attempted to practice the Christian virtues of tolerance and compassion in Mississippi was "cursed as a liberal, a leftist, a communist, a nigger-lover." He wondered whose side Christ would choose: "If He were to visit us here, now, by whose side would He stand, beside the brick-throwing, foulmouthed, destroying, profaning, slavering members of the mob and their 'rich folk' eggers-on, or beside the trembling victim of their hate?" He closed by writing that "there cannot be one brand of Christianity for Mississippi and another for Nigeria and the rest of the world."

As a result of his editorials, Harkey and his newspaper were deluged by hate in all its many forms. From November 1962 until May 1963, Harkey fought a bitter battle to keep his newspaper solvent. Even as he reversed his newspaper's financial setbacks, he became a pariah, tolerated by most of Pascagoula's citizens but harshly abused by others. Shots were twice fired into his newspaper office. Callers threatened to kill him. People snubbed him on the streets, cursed him, mocked him, and challenged him. Harkey carried a Smith & Wesson .38 pistol in his belt at all times. Even after the Unit lost most of its influence, dropping from 600 members to a few hard-core believers who were essentially harmless, Harkey still could not relax—too many enemies lurked. Though the Unit was largely impotent by May 1963, many people along the Gulf Coast still embraced its view that integration was a vile institution that must never become a reality. The slightest spark could have ignited such a racial tinderbox, inflaming passions yet again. And indeed, on the very day Harkey left Pascagoula for good, in July 1963, extremist sentiment manifested itself anew when the new owner of the *Chronicle* disavowed Harkey's beliefs and turned the paper into a hate sheet filled with inflammatory racist rhetoric.

"The organized opposition against me is out of business but that doesn't make me a whole lot more comfortable," Harkey told *Newsweek* in June 1963. "I have no friends here. Nobody can afford to associate with me openly. . . . I'm no fanatic, no John Brown. In my business, I have to say what I think and write about what's important. Right now, in Mississippi, the important story is the wretched condition we're in."

"People down here don't hate him," a fellow journalist, who remained nameless, told *Newsweek* in June 1963. "They treat him a lot like they'd treat their dog. Once in a while someone will pat him on the head but most of the time they want to kick him in the backside. You've got to admire Ira for what he's stood up to, but he seems to have a chip on his shoulder all the time. If he doesn't watch it he might become a professional martyr."

Harkey continued his assaults on racists until July 1963, when he sold the *Chronicle* to Ralph Nicholson of Tallahassee, Fla., ending his 14-year career in Pascagoula. Harkey had been trying to sell the *Chronicle* for four years, since separating from his first wife in 1959. When Harkey nursed the paper back from the boycotts and made it more profitable than ever in 1963, Nicholson stepped forward to buy the paper—and finally made the financial offer Harkey had been waiting for.

Harkey had bought the weekly paper for $106,000 in 1949. He had converted it into a semi-weekly in 1957 and made it a daily in 1961. Nicholson offered him more than $1 million in 1963—eleven times what Harkey had paid for the *Chronicle*. In a letter in 1992 to Bill Minor, a veteran political columnist in Jackson, Harkey explained his decision to sell the paper—the first time he had shared these thoughts with anyone. He admitted that he had been asking an astronomical figure for the *Chronicle*.

Harkey detailed the sale to Minor: "When the Kanter agency showed with my price of more than $1 million, I took it and went to Reno for a divorce. (I'd been told by lawyers that a contested divorce in Mississippi would not be granted.)

"I didn't leave with my tail between my legs. The record, and my personality and character prove otherwise. I got eleven and a half times more for the *Chronicle* than I had paid for it. It obviously was not a business in ruin and I was not an owner being chased out. This is the first time I've spelled this out for anybody. . . . I'd had 14 years in the lead, was the first, had done all I could, and personal reasons made me take the buy offer I'd been seeking for four years."

Nicholson promised Harkey that he would make no editorial changes, that he would not ally with racists. He immediately broke the promise, siding with the segregationists.

"He convinced me he was a liberal," Harkey told the Newport (R.I.) *Daily News* on 11 April 1964. "He was a strong Quaker from Pennsylvania and I had no reason not to believe him. I was wrong, though, for as soon as he took it over, all liberal views concerning rights for Negroes promptly disappeared from the paper."

After the sale, Harkey divorced Marie E. Gore in 1963. They had six children. He married Marion Marks, the mother of four children, in December 1963. He moved to Reno, Nev., in 1964 and began writing *Crosses*, his best-selling account of the racial hysteria he endured in Pascagoula.

He joined the Ohio State University journalism faculty in 1965, teaching a course in editorial writing and reporting and advising the campus newspaper, the *Lantern*. He earned his master's in journalism at Ohio State in 1967 and his doctorate, in political science, in 1973 at the same school.

Harkey focused on academia. He became Carnegie visiting professor at the University of Alaska in 1968–69, Dean Stone lecturer at the University of Montana in 1970, and Eric Allen lecturer at the University of Oregon in 1972. He was a widely sought speaker, traveling the country to dispense wisdom about the lessons he had learned about race; universities recruited him with lucrative offers to speak.

Despite his success, he could not escape the feeling that he had disappointed his beloved father. He felt a deep need to please his father, as he revealed in a letter on 14 September 1972.

> Dear Daddy:
> I still can't get out of my mind my hurt when you told me you were worried about me settling down, that I was flitting around too much. . . .
> It is noteworthy that at age 54 I still want and need your approval and am not happy when I receive disapproval. This is because I love you; otherwise I would not care. Be assured that your son is not flitting around aimlessly. He is busy, at worthwhile endeavors; he has put eleven people through college and beyond; he is famous within his profession; he harms no one; he is sought out by intelligent people. Who do you know has a son who does better?

After leaving Mississippi to pursue academia, Harkey severed ties with most acquaintances in the state. He visited occasionally, but his presence did not inspire joy. He waited thirty years to be officially honored by his state, which he was in June 1993 when he was inducted into the Mississippi Press Association Hall of Fame—an award few could have envisioned during his hate-filled years in Pascagoula. He had been nominated by a young editor from the *Amory Advertiser* that he had never heard of—Waid Prather.

Wanda Jacobs, publisher of the *Mississippi Press* of Pascagoula, introduced Harkey at the MPA convention. Jacobs, the first black woman publisher of a general newspaper in Mississippi, occupies Harkey's old job at the Pascagoula paper, although the *MP* is not the *Chronicle*'s successor, as Harkey reminds. After Harkey sold his paper to Nicholson in 1963, Nicholson abolished Harkey's anti-segregation editorial stand and turned the *Chronicle* into just another hate sheet. Five years later the *MP* bought the paper from Nicholson, ending its 120-year history.

"My induction is indicative of the changes that have been made in Mississippi," Harkey said in the *Mississippi Press* on 20 June 1993. "Wanda Jacobs is also indicative of these changes. The changes are nothing short of a miracle. There's a black man on the Mississippi Supreme Court and Mississippi has more blacks in public offices than any other state."

Harkey had chuckled at his acceptance in Mississippi during a speech he made at the University of Southern Mississippi on 28 October 1992, just six months before he entered the Hall of Fame. He had returned to Pascagoula several times and had been surprised by his reception.

"This is the funniest darn thing," he said. "I am a hero there. About eight years ago the Rotary Club invited me to come speak. The place was full. It went on for three hours. The local paper had five pictures of me throughout the paper and a yard-long story. The next year the Kiwanis Club invited me. Last year, my youngest son was elected DA of Jackson, George and Green Counties. . . . It's not the same old place."

Now retired and living near Kerrville, Texas, with his third wife, Virgia, Harkey is pleased and surprised by the racial harmony he has seen in Mississippi on his visits. He said he always knew that integration would succeed, that hate would give way to understanding. He again cast racism as a sin, equating it with hate, as he had done throughout his career. "It's a lot of trouble to hate," Harkey said. "Hate takes work, and it will end up destroying you. There was this marvelous sense of relief for the white man in Mississippi when all the racism and bitterness came to an end. I think white men had a deep sense of shame; they'd been carrying around all this guilt and hate for so long, and finally they were free of it."

Harkey said that he could never understand the hate he witnessed toward black people in his years in Mississippi. "My parents never used that word 'nigger' when I was growing up," he said. "I was always taught that you treat all men the same, that the color of a man's skin did not in any way determine his worth."

Harkey added: "How do you hate somebody just because their shade of skin is just a little bit different than the shade of your skin? I believe there is a brotherhood of men, and I believe we're supposed to love each other. That's what I was trying to tell people in Mississippi."

History has proved him correct. He understood Mississippi's racial dilemma far more clearly than anyone believed at the time.

In 1998, on his eightieth birthday, Harkey sold the private airplane he had used often for thirty years to travel around the country to universities, where he was in demand as a speaker, and to his business holdings.

"I used to be famous," he said with a quiet laugh. "But now there's not a big demand for me. I decided to ground myself and get rid of the plane because I was making so many mistakes in the air, most of them out of complacency because I'd flown so often. But a mistake in the air is not funny; it might kill you."

Always a strict planner, Harkey delineated a blueprint for his funeral in a letter dated 14 January 1992. He wants this funeral:

> Absolutely a must: a polished wooden coffin, not one of those monster copper or whatever metal ones. Undertakers the Lakewood Metairie people, saving everybody, including me, transport time. On my slab in the tomb have engraved Ira Brown Harkey Jr. PhD January 15, 1918—date of death.
>
> No viewing of the dear departed. At the tomb, I want a black (a true black, not a tan or a yellow) bass-baritone—say from Dillard, Xavier or Loyola music schools—to sing softly "Swing Low Sweet Chariot."
>
> Next have a Presbyterian minister say a few words—very few—I will lift up mine eyes . . . from whence maybe, and the 23rd.
>
> Then allow anyone who wants to to say a few words. Do not invite anyone to do this. Just ask if anyone wishes to sound off.
>
> Close with a sweet-voiced, white soprano softly singing "Dear Little Boy of Mine," the 1918 song Momma used to sing me to sleep with along with "Kentucky Babe."
>
> That will be -30-. Stop the press. Close the shop, walk away.

References

Broadus, Don. "Former Pass Publisher Joins the Hall of Fame." *Mississippi Press*, 20 June 1993, p. 1A.

"Chronicle-Star at Pascagoula Semi-weekly." *The Mississippi Press* (October 1957), p. 4.

Dorr, Bill. "Bitterness: A Little; Happiness: A Lot." *Publishers' Auxiliary*, 11 May 1963, p. 1.

———. "Another Mississippi Editor Survives the Pressure-group." *Publishers' Auxiliary*, 19 June 1963, p. 1.

Harkey, Ira B., Jr. Personal Papers. Madison, Wis.: University of Wisconsin Library.

———. *The Smell of Burning Crosses*. (Jacksonville, Ill.: Harris-Wolfe & Company, 1967).

"In a Madhouse's Din." *Newsweek*, 16 June 1963, p. 48.

"Mississippi Editor Talks to APA Group." *The Alabama Publisher* (March 1954), p. 1.

Morris, Ron. "Pulitzer Prize-winner Drafts Freedom Fight Book in Reno." *Nevada State Journal*, 23 May 1964, p. 9.

"New York City Radio Station Rallies Aid for Miss. Editor." *Editor & Publisher*, 2 February 1963, p. 11.

Niffert, Jane. "15-Year Crusade Like Living in Vacuum, Says Pulitzer Winner." *Newport Daily News*, 11 April 1964, p. 1.

Wilson F. (Bill) Minor and the New Orleans *Times-Picayune*

Lawrence N. Strout

Decades after the passage of the Civil Rights Act (1964) and the Voting Rights Act (1965), Wilson F. (Bill) Minor recounted in a 15 September 1999 interview how the two pieces of federal legislation, after years of struggle, unrest and violence in Mississippi, changed the state forever.[1] For the ten years leading up to those pieces of legislation, Minor witnessed, reported and commented about the turmoil associated with African-Americans fighting for the same rights as whites. Minor was no radical. He saw himself as a reporter, not a crusading columnist pushing for civil rights and desegregation. However, Minor used his weekly "Eyes on Mississippi" columns (and some news dispatches) in the *Times-Picayune* to subtly, and in the 1960s more overtly, discredit segregationist positions and promote integration.[2]

From the U.S. Supreme Court decision in *Brown v. the Board of Education* in 1954 until the passage of the Voting Rights Act in 1965, Minor's distaste for segregationists and their leaders in Mississippi government became progressively more apparent. A supporter of black civil rights and school integration, his writings in the New Orleans *Times-Picayune* from the Mississippi paper's bureau in Jackson steadily reflected a more "liberal" stance as the 1960s commenced. Most important, though, Minor wrote news accounts of what actually happened during the civil rights movement rather than espousing the (white) government position, which advocated keeping blacks as second class citizens. This is no small contribution and, given the racial climate in Mississippi, took great courage at times. Additionally, Minor was not an editor of a Mississippi newspaper. He was a front-line reporter and columnist for the most widely circulated daily in southern Louisiana, which made him an important voice informing the people of the greater New Orleans area and South Mississippi of what was happening throughout Mississippi.

Wilson F. Minor was born in Hammond, Louisiana, and grew up in nearby Bogalusa. He graduated from Tulane University and in 1942 was hired by the New Orleans *Times-Picayune*. After a stint serving his country in World War II, Minor was rehired in 1947 by the *Times-Picayune* and assigned to Jackson as its Mississippi correspondent. In Jackson from 1947 through the 1990s,[3] Minor watched and reported the transformation of Mississippi from the Old South to the New—a transformation that many would argue is still a work-in-progress. Minor's work won respect at both the regional and national level. Minor wrote for national publications such as the *New York Times*, the *Washington Post*, *Newsweek*, and *Newsday*. In the *Greenwood Commonwealth* of 4 October 1987, Mississippi editor John Emmerich paid tribute to Minor's accomplishments on Mississippi State University's acceptance of the longtime journalist's papers. Emmerich noted that in the early and mid-1960s, Minor "covered every tough civil rights story at a time when many reporters were considered the enemy" of segregationist white Mississippians. Minor has received nearly every major journalism award short of the Pulitzer Prize. And many of his awards have been, at least in part, related to the fair and accurate reporting and commentary about the civil rights movement in Mississippi.

Looking back on his long career in a 1999 interview, Minor marveled at Mississippi's transformation since the U.S. Supreme Court handed down its *Brown* decision on 17 May 1954. The "conventional wisdom" of the state's white leadership, Minor recalled, was that desegregation in Mississippi would not occur "in our lifetime." An 18 May 1954 *Times-Picayune* editorial reflected the common wisdom of the day, arguing that "the decision will do no service either to education or racial accommodation." It contended that the court's 1896 *Plessy v. Ferguson* ruling that "equal facilities" satisfied the intent of the Fourteenth Amendment, and that "approximately equal" schools for blacks existed. *Brown*'s declaration that "separate educational facilities are inherently unequal" was simply not true, the editorial concluded.

Minor reported in his "Eyes of Mississippi" column of 23 May 1954 that "Negro and white observers" believed that the U.S. Supreme Court decision would result in "no immediate changes in the historic pattern of separate school facilities in Mississippi." Minor wrote that anti-desegregation "government forces" would probably prevent enforcement of the court decision "for some years to come, if ever." Minor quoted State Superintendent of Education J. M. Tubb as saying that the state's equalization program offered the best solution to retaining segregation. And, Prof. J. D. Boyd of Utica, then president of the Negro Teachers Association of Mississippi, observed that if "quality" schools were provided for blacks in their own neighborhoods that the communities would "overwhelmingly" be in favor of remaining segregated.

At the end of Minor's May 23 piece, he offered convincing evidence that separate but equal was simply not the case in Mississippi. He documented 225,399 "Negro children" and 238,677 white children attending public schools in Mississippi in 1953. Yet, Mississippi spent about $8,816,670 for "instruction of the Negro children compared with $23,536,000 for instruction of the white children" (which was before a newly passed equalization program was to go into effect 1 July 1954). Minor did not criticize the discrepancy in funds for blacks versus whites, nor did he dwell on it or make a special effort to call readers' attention to it; he merely reported the facts and let them stand on their merit. Clearly, Minor was not satisfied with the journalistic principle of "objectivity," merely quoting people on both or all sides of a news story without digging independently for the truth.

In the months following *Brown*, Minor focused on Mississippi's strategy to maintain segregation, calling it a "grim political struggle." He wrote in a 20 June 1954 column that leaders of the segregationist movement, which included the most powerful men in the state, believed that the "best immediate hope" was for "voluntary segregation based on the cooperation of Negroes." Minor also reported state leaders' plans to create a "standby authority to do away with public schools" if the new equalization program was rejected, thus ensuring that state schools would not be integrated. However, as Minor pointed out, the abolition of public schools would have created a problem with the poll tax, which under the state Constitution went to fund public schools.

Nearly one month later, in a 19 July 1954 report, Minor described the legislative battle over a bill that would have awarded tuition grants to citizens who chose to send their children to private schools. Minor wrote that many legislators admitted that "anything they did now with the idea of circumventing school desegregation was little more than an exercise in futility." Minor reported that part of the debate about the private school tuition grants centered on excluding Catholic school students from the plan. This element of the debate was "less a conflict on the separation of church and state issue," Minor wrote, "than it was an underlying battle to keep any bill from passing." Minor, with a penchant for putting issues into perspective, wrote that since 90 percent of the private schools were parochial, few people would be able to take advantage of private tuition grants if Catholic schools were eliminated. Further, Minor wrote that "Mississippi has no tradition for private schools," and the bill would provide only $185 per year, which would "mean that any parent sending his child to private school would have to pay a sizable difference out of his pocket."

By the end of July 1954, Governor Hugh White called for a September 7 special session of the Legislature in order "to seek legislative authority to abolish public schools." This pronouncement came after a conference in which black leaders would not "guarantee voluntary school segregation." Minor, in a 31 July 1954 article, reported that both liberal and conservative black leaders proposed that blacks be given a free choice to attend schools nearest their homes, whatever the school's racial makeup; that the state start a program to eliminate the vast number of substandard schools provided for blacks; and that blacks be placed on policy-making boards affecting both races. White quoted *Jackson Advocate* editor Percy Greene, who called for equal public schools for blacks and whites and for Mississippi to "abolish segregation by force." Minor observed that whatever opposition to the abolition of public schools had existed earlier, it had been erased after the conference with black leaders because of their commitment to integration.

Wilson F. (Bill) Minor and the New Orleans Times-Picayune

After the frenzy surrounding *Brown* subsided, most elected officials and educators thought integration could be forestalled for decades, if not forever. Racial hostilities did not flare with such intensity again until 1962, when James Meredith made plans to enroll in the University of Mississippi. In 1962, still before school desegregation hit Mississippi to any degree, Minor continued to report the inequality of education in the state. A 7 January 1962 piece offered extensive detailed documentation taken from an unpublished education report that revealed that the "separate but equal" program was anything but equal. The share of "local" funds being provided clearly showed that $4 was being spent for each white child for every $1 spent for each black child. Minor listed the county-by-county discrepancy of money being allocated for whites versus blacks. He also wrote that of the 638 black schools, 330 failed to meet state accrediting standards as opposed to only five of the 642 white schools below accreditation standards. Other inadequacies in the black schools included substandard libraries, lack of school counselors, and inadequate curricula. Once again, Minor did not preach about the inequality of Mississippi schools. Instead, he obtained a copy of an unpublished Mississippi education report and disclosed indisputable numbers documenting that while "separate but equal" may have been sold to the public as workable, it clearly was not working for blacks.

The article did not draw any mail directly to Minor, but it did prompt Herbert Farrell, assistant superintendent of schools in Pascagoula, to send a letter dated 9 January 1962 to the State Superintendent of Education, J. M. Tubb. Farrell intended to set the record straight about the figures reported by Minor. He called the article a "case where the truth unaccompanied by an analysis and explanations" becomes "very unfair" to the educational system in Mississippi. Farrell wrote that Minor's report was a "prime example of the extortion of truth when placed in the hands of radicals, extremists and those who are determined to enforce punitive measures on some groups of people." Farrell complained that Tubb's response to Minor's article (which was published as a letter to the editor) was "inadequate in explaining to the public why such a variation could naturally exist." Farrell detailed the logical reasons for some of the discrepancies, including a contention that maintenance costs for the "Negro" schools were less than the white schools because the "Negro buildings are in much better condition than the white buildings." Finally, Farrell wrote to Tubb that if an "analysis of the report given to Mr. Minor" had been provided, it would have "greatly aided him in writing and presenting his article."

Nearly ten years after *Brown*, Minor conceded some progress had been made toward "separate but equal" in the Mississippi school system. Writing in his 17 May 1964 column, Minor declared that the effort to build a segregated system "evidently has paid off, both in buying time for the state in keeping the segregated system, and in the invironment [*sic*] of the welfare of its citizens, both white and Negro." Minor wrote that "politicians saw the threat of the federal courts hanging over their heads [and] . . . it has nevertheless pulled Mississippi up by the bootstraps in school facilities offered for both white and Negro children." Minor concluded that the "ten-year construction program may prove the state's best asset in obviating mass desegregation in years to come."

It was not until September 1964, more than ten years after *Brown*, that Minor could report on the beginning of desegregation in the Jackson Public Schools. Minor's introductory paragraph on a 14 September 1964 article about the opening of school declared that "Racial barriers in Mississippi's largest school district came down here Monday as thirty-nine Negro[es] first attended classes with white children in eight of the city's previously white schools." Minor, noting the peaceful grouping of blacks with whites, quoted a principal who said that a "white girl first grader offered a hair ribbon to a Negro girl in her class," and in another case, "A Negro boy asked a white lad if he could help him straighten his hair on the way to the lunchroom." On the other hand, Minor informed readers that at a school in one of the wealthier sections of Jackson, "a father and mother entered the building and asked to have their daughter withdrawn from the first grade when the lone Negro child in the school was placed in the same class."

Minor ended his article by reporting that some parents were already turning to private schools, including the three-year-old Jackson Academy, Southside Academy, and the soon-to-be-opened Bancroft School. Minor wrote, "The Jackson Citizens' Council, which has proposed to provide a system of private schools for parents who do not want to send their children to desegregated schools, has no facility ready for use . . . it has an option on a building in north Jackson."

It had taken more than ten years, but the inevitable was beginning in the city of Jackson. White children in 1964 were being joined, albeit in small numbers, by black children, and according to Minor's observations, the process was a long time in coming but did not spark any major incidents. Minor later recalled that there was a "sprinkling of integration in schools located in Leake County and in Jackson" during that year, but he noted that some Catholic schools had earlier become the first Mississippi schools to enroll blacks.

In the middle of the two-decade process of desegregation, one of the ugliest events of the civil rights movement in Mississippi occurred, and justice would not be served until the last decade of the Twentieth Century. On 5 February 1994, 73-year-old Byron De La Beckwith was found guilty of the 12 June 1963, assassination of civil rights leader Medgar Evers. Beckwith was sentenced to life in prison. Those not familiar with the case history observed a frail old man heading off to prison, not the white supremacist killer who had shot Evers in cold blood and then escaped justice twice in 1964, when all-white juries could not reach a verdict.

Minor covered the Evers case from the beginning. Initial articles focused strictly on the facts of the case. Minor revealed in a 13 June 1963 article that police had good leads, including information that a 51-year-old man from another county had been apprehended and questioned for several hours before being released. A person with a rifle standing 200 yards away shot and killed Evers. The bullet hit Evers in the right side of the back, passed through his right upper chest, and then projected through a front window and kitchen wall before falling on the Evers' kitchen table. Minor wrote that Evers "had been regarded by reporters as a usually reliable news source" who had preferred to hold local protests with "local Negro leadership, rather than bringing in well-known Negro leaders outside to direct the drive."

To no one's surprise, the Evers assassination spawned protests resulting in as many as ninety arrests in Jackson. Minor's 14 June 1963 account of the peaceful protest that prompted police violence hardly painted a pretty picture of Jackson officers, who "waded into one group of heckling onlookers with clubs." Minor labeled it an "ugly" episode.

> Some twenty city police and sheriffs' deputies surged into the tiny front yard and onto the front porch of a Negro home with clubs raised when a group of Negroes and several white integration workers had gathered after being told by police to move onto private property because they were booing and heckling officers who apprehended 82 young marchers in the street.

Minor further reported that a white professor from Tougaloo Southern Christian College, John Salter, was "hit by officers and pulled from the porch" and later had to be "led away bleeding from a wound on his head." Further, Minor wrote that a "15-year-old Negro girl who lived in the house was hit with a police club" and then the officers "surged inside the house when the girl went down." And finally, Minor noted that several black ministers had warned that "the conduct of the police may trigger serious racial violence on the part of Negroes."

Just two days later, Medgar Evers was laid to rest with mourners turning into what Minor described as a "bottle, brick throwing throng of Negroes. . . ." The violence, which resulted in at least twenty-seven arrests, began a 16 June 1963 story about Evers' funeral. "Some 250 helmeted police, highway patrolmen and deputies, with pistol and riot guns drawn, turned back the growing mob of angry Negroes a block from Capitol St.," Minor reported. The bulk of the article focused on the mourning of Evers by family, friends, and civil rights activists. Minor described Mrs. Evers as sitting "stoically, occasionally wiping a tear away" as Roy Wilkins, executive secretary of the NAACP, spoke about Evers' impact as a "symbol of our victory and of their defeat." Whether it was the police using unreasonable force against blacks and other civil rights advocates, or blacks creating violence without provocation, Minor's readers could count on an unbiased report, journalism very different from that of more partisan reporters and newspapers.

When Beckwith was arrested less than two weeks after Evers' death, Minor described the accused assassin as a "dapper 42 year old Greenwood white man with old Mississippi family ties." The 24 June 1963 story pictured Beckwith as "tanned and neatly dressed in a cocoa brown suit and a dark green tie, wearing white duck loafer style shoes" who "appeared cool and calm" as he was lead to and from the court building. Minor also wrote that friends described Beckwith as a "racial extremist and a member of the [White] Citizens' Council." Minor reported that a "longtime acquaintance" of Beckwith recalled him carrying a pistol to church "because of the possibility that Negroes may try to attend services." Minor also reported hard evidence that had been gathered, including a report that the murder weapon—a World War I Enfield rifle—bore fingerprints that matched Beckwith's. (In an interview, Minor said he does not believe that purely extremist racist beliefs caused Beckwith to murder Evers in cold blood. Minor believes that Beckwith was an "outcast" from society who was looking for his "15 minutes of fame.")

Minor never became a crusading journalist for integration, but a series of speeches between 1958 and 1964 show a distinct progression from a position of subtle support for integration and racial equality to a bluntly stated stance in favor of both. For instance, a speech at a 1958 education conference at the University of Mississippi carried no mention of the ongoing struggle to keep Mississippi's schools segregated. The only apparent endorsement of desegregation came in a subtle remark during the speech. "Mass education, we also seem to agree," Minor said, "goes hand in hand with maintaining a strong economy in this country." He went on to declare that "Public education in the United States is no longer a privilege. I think the people have come to look upon education as a right just as much as any of the guarantees of the Bill of Rights." No direct mention of the efforts to integrate or to continue segregation. Perhaps Minor believed that, as a reporter, taking a strong position would lead to unfair scrutiny of his news dispatches in the *Times-Picayune*.

In the early 1960s, Minor was much more bold in his speeches, as was evident during talks to the Tougaloo Science Forum in 1961 and to B'Nai B'Rith in Jackson's Beth Israel Temple in 1962, when he directly addressed desegregation and racism. Minor told the black audience at Tougaloo that ignorance was the biggest problem facing Mississippi. "Ignorance is fear, misunderstanding and distrust of others," Minor said. "Ignorance is what dominates race relations today, and has brought about a breakdown of communications between the races on basic issues." He confessed that the worsening relations between "whites and Negroes" seem to have the white community as the chief offender. But he laid blame on both sides for the unrest and tension.

> What we are drifting toward today—and there are some professionals on both sides who want it that way—is a division of the Negroes and the whites into two opposing armed camps—the citizens council on one side and the NAACP on the other. No peaceful and lasting accord between races will be reached if the leadership must come from the citizens council or the NAACP. It will be done by dedicated men and women in an atmosphere detached from the heat and fire of this emotional problem.

Minor described the Citizens' Council and the NAACP as the extremists on each side of the race issue, but failed to point out that while the Council used fear and intimidation, the NAACP largely used the courts. Minor offered advice to black members of his audience, asking them to "choose your leaders wisely, shun the radical, intemperate people who are always around to take credit when something succeeds, but disappear when things go wrong."

To an audience at the Beth Israel Temple in 1962, Minor declared that "Mississippi is in only the beginning of its toils over the race issue." He addressed the issue of what might happen when the first Negro student stepped on the campus of the University of Mississippi, running through a series of negative events that could result while at the same time saying he hoped they would not happen. He saw the integration of Ole Miss as the "first great test for Mississippi, it seems, on whether it will conduct itself gracefully or hit the panic button and reach for the most drastic weapons." (Of course Minor got his answer with the riots at Ole Miss in the fall.) Minor contended that the state legislature was filled with a "large collection of racial extremists who spend most of their energy thinking up ways to keep Negroes in their place and for harassing white persons who believe in the moderate cause." He closed by revealing a conversation with an Ole Miss professor who believed that when the first black student arrived "the students on the campus would conduct themselves peacefully and that only outside rabble rousers could destroy the peace."

Returning to Beth Israel Temple for another speech two years later in 1964, Minor observed that "Mississippi's segregation strategy has changed from one of massive resistance to gradualism, the position which formerly was regarded as anathema." Minor related what he had observed in the state. "What happened, it seems to me in Biloxi, and here in Jackson in school desegregation is the professional race groups found they no longer had their hold on the people," Minor said, "and nobody cared any longer for the fruits of bitter end resistance." Six years after his 1958 speech to educators at Ole Miss, which had not mentioned "desegregation" or "integration" and only hinted at the need for mass education, Minor spoke openly in 1964 of Mississippians' weariness of resisting integration.

But in that same 1964 speech, Minor talked about Mississippi's role in the national elections and the necessity for the state to change in order to be taken seriously by the rest of the country. Minor said that the "state cannot take part in the national political life of the Democratic Party using Mississippi ground rules." He said no state would ever again be permitted "to send a delegation to the national convention which does not include some Negroes." Minor wrote often about Mississippi's status in the nation and its effect on elections, citing irreconcilable differences between the state's beliefs and those of the rest of the country.

In 1963, three candidates vied for the Democratic nomination for governor. The campaigners, according to a 23 June 1963 column, concentrated on bashing President John F. Kennedy. Charles Sullivan, with no record as an elected public official, challenged former Governor J. P. Coleman and Lt. Governor Paul B. Johnson, Jr., for the Democratic nomination, and all ran on an anti-JFK platform. Minor complained that important issues within a governor's control "have been given a backseat to the chest-beating and fist-shaking at the 'devils' in Washington, about which a Mississippi governor can do very little."

A plan to amass a bloc of "free" presidential electors from the South to split from the Democrats was analyzed by Minor in a 30 June 1963 piece. The "free" presidential electors movement was intended to garner enough electoral votes to throw the presidential election into the House. Minor reported that legislatures in Louisiana and Florida had rejected the idea, and loyal Democratic governors from Tennessee, Georgia, and South Carolina held little hope that their states would support the effort.

The three Democratic gubernatorial candidates' hard line defending segregation angered Minor in a 4 August 1963 column. "There's no reason to assume from the words of the candidates," Minor wrote, "that Mississippi is apt to make a turn toward a softer line on the desegregation front." Minor continued, "Mississippi is being watched by the Democratic Party to determine if the cold war with the national party will continue or if there is any hope a new governor may reestablish relations with the party."

In a misreading of the coming election, Minor, in a 25 August 1963 "Eyes on Mississippi" analysis, detected a "wearied" group of Democratic candidates and described the Republican candidate as a "fresh performer" who presented to the Democrats "the most formidable threat by the Mississippi Republican party since the Civil War." The Republican candidate, Rubel Phillips, was an ex-Democratic officeholder Minor described as a "shrewd politician and seasoned campaigner, with a sizable war chest behind him." Minor believed that Republicans had built the greatest strength in the cities, where "the old hatreds for the party have largely been erased." Minor also saw Phillips' chances better than normal for a Republican. The Democratic nominee, having bashed the JFK administration, would have no hope of receiving financial help from the national party.

Johnson received the Democratic nomination for governor, "turning to his advantage the 'hate Kennedy' passions in Mississippi," according to Minor. Minor, in a 29 August 1963 news dispatch, contended that Johnson was able to "hang the 'Kennedy' label on Coleman." Johnson's role as a "staunch foe" of JFK and the National Democratic Party, Minor wrote, "was in stark contrast with his loyalty to the party in years past." Of course, Johnson went on to win the general election, with Mississippi retaining a Democratic governor for more than 100 years.

Less than a year later, during the heat of Freedom Summer, Minor followed the presidential election from a Mississippi perspective, focusing on two subjects—Goldwater versus Johnson and the state's debacle at the National Democratic Convention. Minor wrote in his 14 June 1964 column that "Great numbers of persons who call themselves 'Mississippi Democrats' . . . are attracted to Goldwater." But he cautioned that "a statement here and a statement there on Civil Rights by Goldwater" could find them "disenchanted with what they consider the senator's conservatism." Meanwhile, Minor was astonished that "something unprecedented in Mississippi politics" was happening; incumbent Governor Paul Johnson appeared to have lost control of "his first state Democratic convention to the high-riding [former Governor Ross] Barnett unpledged forces." Writing on 5 July 1964, Minor quoted insiders as indicating that Governor Johnson would not take a leading role in the state convention and would "quietly sit back and vote for Sen. Barry Goldwater, if the Arizonan makes it."

"Once 'Solid South' Era May Finally Come To End" was the headline on Minor's 23 August 1964 column. "Unless there is some great unseen change," Minor wrote, "Mississippi is going to vote Republican for the first time since the Civil War." When the Mississippi contingent walked out of the Atlantic City Democratic National Convention after the Credentials Committee offered to seat two representatives of the black Mississippi Freedom Party group as at-large voting delegates, it became apparent to Minor that the state "learned unmistakably now that it cannot take part in the national political life of the Democratic Party using Mississippi ground rules."

Less than one month before the presidential election, Governor Paul Johnson observed after the Southern Governors Conference that President Johnson was gaining support in Mississippi. Minor's 18 October 1964 analysis theorized that "no matter how enchanted [Mississippians] were with Goldwater," there still existed a "nostalgia for the Democratic Party" and the possibility also existed that Mississippians "don't dislike LBJ as much as expected." Minor also reported that although none of the five state congressmen publicly endorsed a presidential candidate, "they are thought to be leaning toward Goldwater." By late October, one Mississippi congressman did endorse Goldwater. "The fiery segregationist congressman" is how Minor described Representative John Bell Williams in the 25 October 1963 column. Minor explained that Williams had "long ago become perhaps the bitterest critic of the Democratic party" and denounced the Democratic ticket in favor of Goldwater.

Goldwater was trounced by President Johnson in the national election, but it was a different story in Mississippi. In fact, Minor reported 8 November 1964 that Goldwater received 87 percent of the vote in the state. Even bigger news was the unseating of Arthur Winstead, a 22-year Democratic veteran in Congress, by a "total unknown" named Prentiss Walker. Walker, who was "straight off the chicken farm in Smith County . . . had nothing more going for him than that he was endorsed by Barry

Goldwater." Since Winstead had more of a record in Congress of voting Republican than Democratic, apparently the mere label of Republican won the race for Walker. Minor concluded that "this result seems to serve notice to fencesitting Democratic office holders that Mississippi has reached a point where they will either have to become Republicans or do something to rebuild the Democratic Party." Clearly, LBJ's civil rights policies turned the state's voters—then still predominately white—against the Democratic Party. Minor was bemused as he described the state's political predicament.

In the year prior to the 1963 Mississippi gubernatorial election and, of course, before the 1964 presidential election, the crisis at the University of Mississippi in Oxford over the admission of Meredith as the first black student occurred. It is perhaps, along with the assassination of Medgar Evers, the most famous of the events during the civil rights movement in Mississippi. In a 12 February 1961 piece, Minor described an "abortive effort" by a black seeking admission to Ole Miss. He reported that Mississippi had no law or constitutional provision preventing blacks from enrolling in higher education institutions—the practice of segregation was "solely by administrative procedure." According to Minor, "The state's stack of segregation laws apply only to the public schools" and not to colleges and universities. However, he explained that the college board of trustees that had jurisdiction over the four-year institutions had taken action indirectly to prevent blacks from getting accepted. Minor said the policy was adopted that "requires applications for admittance to colleges to be accompanied by five recommendations from alumni . . . a move by the college board to thwart efforts of Negroes applying at white colleges." Minor suggested that "observers" believed that because there was no law against integration of higher education that the colleges and universities "may be in a better position to cope with an integration try than the public school system."

James Meredith's battle for admission to the University of Mississippi began in January 1961 with his application, which was rejected on 26 May 1961 by the Ole Miss registrar. He turned it down "officially" because Meredith wanted to transfer from a non-accredited school (Jackson State College), but of course race was the real reason. By the summer of 1962, Meredith was still trying to get accepted. Minor's 19 July 1962 article revealed that the latest order by Fifth Circuit Court of Appeals Judge Ben Cameron of Meridian "appeared to have thwarted the bid of the 29-year-old Negro Air Force veteran to register at the university for the September term." In fact, 6 August 1962 marked the fourth time Cameron refused to allow Meredith to be admitted into Ole Miss.

Then, on 10 September 1962, an Associated Press story in the *Starkville Daily News* reported the shocking news to Mississippi: "Black Orders UM Admit Meredith: Sets Aside Stay of Judge Cameron." The Black referred to, of course, was U.S. Supreme Court Justice Hugo Black. He set aside previous stays and issued a two-page opinion on the matter. Black wrote that the immediate admission of Meredith to the university could "do no appreciable harm" to the institution. Further, Black "took the unusual step" of enjoining the university from "taking any steps to prevent enforcement of the circuit court's judgment in favor of Meredith."

Meredith was headed to Oxford to enroll at Ole Miss, but the fight in the courts that led to his acceptance was minor compared to the violence resulting from white resistance to Meredith's admission. Riots broke out during the last week in September at Ole Miss, resulting in the shooting deaths of two people, 30-year-old Paul Guihard of the *London Daily Sketch* and Agence France Press and 23-year-old Oxford resident Ray Gunter. As in most of the major struggles of blacks desegregating previously all-white areas in Mississippi, Minor reported on the unrest at Ole Miss. His 1 October 1962 news story revealed a still-defiant Governor Ross Barnett. While Barnett's actions just after the shootings prompted some to believe he was "yielding" to the pressure, the governor indicated anything but that in a formal statement. Minor quoted Barnett saying he was not "altering" his stand against the admission of Meredith and blacks to Ole Miss and that "I will never yield a single inch in my determination to win the fight we are all engaged in." Further, according to Minor, Barnett said that he was "surrounded on all sides by the armed forces and oppressive power of the United States of America." Minor reported that Barnett had previously indicated that he would go to jail before a black would be allowed into a state school. Even though President Kennedy had declared a state of emergency two days earlier at Ole Miss, Governor Barnett fanned an already incendiary situation. Minor provided detailed reports about the crisis and the governor's activities.

The riots prompted the federal government to send two battalions of military police from Memphis, Tennessee, to Oxford. By 2 October 1962, Minor reported that Oxford was under "rigid control" of federal troops with "no outsiders" permitted on the school grounds, and "everyone entering the gates was searched." Meredith attended two classes 1 October 1962. Minor reported that Meredith registered and attended two classes, while Chief U.S. Marshal James P. D. McShane said "there were no incidents in the classrooms but Meredith received catcalls en route to class." Years later Minor saw the Ole Miss riots as a turning point for Mississippi. Minor said that "people came to their senses" after the violence in Oxford, and while many still opposed integration, it became apparent that integration was inevitable. The federal government was not going to back down.

Barnett, however, was not about to give up the fight. In a 3 October 1962 television address, he called for Mississippians to "be calm, patient, and control your physical and mental faculties." And, he asked the state's residents to join him in the "determination that we shall, in the end, attain victory." But Barnett's statement was again incendiary; he claimed that taxpayers throughout the nation were "being forced by the federal authorities to pay thousands upon thousands of dollars per day to keep one person, unqualified morally and mentally, at the University." He told the TV audience that he resented and deplored the situation "with every fiber of my body."

Other state officials, such as Attorney General Joe T. Patterson, were outspoken in their support for the governor and criticism of the federal government. In a 16 October 1962 speech to the University of Mississippi Law School, Patterson said that "given the ordeal that this great University has been put through," he could not imagine another college emerging with students exhibiting such "admirable conduct." He criticized the "armed might" of the federal government for interfering and called the U.S. Attorney General's actions "arrogant vindictiveness." Further, Patterson told law students that as attorney general of Mississippi, he would not allow the U.S. Attorney General "to browbeat and intimidate the officials of this University . . . regardless of the power of his office and that of the President." Finally, Patterson "frankly and emphatically" made it very clear that he "did not consider Ole Miss now integrated as a result of court ordered enrollment of classes by one individual accompanied by armed United States Marshals."

With federal marshals to ensure his safety, Meredith completed the fall semester 1962 with his grades—according to a 30 January 1963 Associated Press article—"a closely guarded secret." At a news conference, Meredith revealed only that he had received a notice from the school inviting him back "in good standing." Meredith announced that he would register for a second semester at Ole Miss, and he called it a "great tragedy for America" that whether or not a student was going to attend a university was a "big news item." In Minor's 31 January 1963 story about Meredith's announcement, he described Meredith as "nattily dressed" and "soft-spoken" and as the "son of an Attala County farmer who had cleared his land to support ten children."

Minor wrote that in fall 1962 more than 25,000 soldiers and National Guardsmen had been called in to bring peace to Oxford. Minor reported that 300 soldiers and fifteen federal marshals had "remained garrisoned in Oxford" during Meredith's attendance at the university. The thousands of soldiers called in to quell the disturbance on 30 September 1962 and after left within several days of being dispatched. As for James H. Meredith, he survived the second semester and the summer to become the first black graduate of Ole Miss on 18 August 1963. In 1966, during a "March Against Fear," Meredith was ambushed and shot. He survived and continued his efforts to help the cause of integration in Mississippi.

In the wake of Meredith's enrollment at Ole Miss and other civil rights activities in Mississippi and elsewhere in the country, conditions developed for the resurrection of a hate group that had existed but had largely been out of power since the 1920s. And on the eve of what became known as Freedom Summer in Mississippi, Minor worried about the increase in Ku Klux Klan activity in the state. In a 22 May 1964 column, Minor asserted that there was a "resurgence" of the KKK, which he described as an "organization that failed to gain a foothold in the state when it last appeared in the 1920s." While reporting that authorities calculated about 7,000 members statewide in the KKK, some Klansmen were saying that membership included people from all parts of the state and totaled 90,000. Minor observed, "The rash of cross burnings over the state—in 64 counties one weekend—prompted Mississippi's Senator John C. Stennis on a recent trip to the state to point out such efforts are damaging his position for fighting the civil rights bill in Washington."

Minor informed his readers that many of those attracted to the new Klan were unaware that the organization had been declared "subversive" by the state attorney general's office and by the House Un-American Activities Committee. According to Minor, a 1950 Mississippi law required all candidates for public office to take an oath saying they were not members of a subversive organization, just as the federal government's security program required all applicants for federal jobs to state whether they belonged to such an organization. Minor reported that a bill that had passed the Mississippi Senate related to "criminal syndicalism" was "apparently aimed in part at the Klan or similar organizations along with pro-civil rights groups in the state." The bill spelled out "violations for activities which bring terrorism, intimidation and sabotage." Minor stated that "there is real concern here that the Klan is a new force to be dealt with in keeping the shaky peace on the racial front from exploding Mississippi into a national battleground on civil rights this election year." But Mississippi indeed became a battleground in the summer of 1964.

Mississippi Freedom Summer was plagued with scores of incidents of violence in response to what Minor later described as the "invasion" of the state by people from outside of Mississippi hoping to effect change. The hot spots included McComb, Greenwood, and Jackson, but nearly every region of the state felt some effects. Minor's news dispatches straightforwardly reported on the summer's activities, but his column largely avoided specific local events, focusing instead on national and state political issues. In other words, Minor did not use his column to comment directly on the violence, but he did report these events fairly and accurately on a daily basis, again serving his readers with nonpartisan stories.

Minor closely covered the disappearance of three civil rights workers near Philadelphia in June 1964. In a 25 June 1964 article, he reported that former CIA Chief Allen Dulles had been sent to Mississippi, not specifically because of the Philadelphia incident, but to simply ensure that the state was ready to handle civil rights activities in a proper manner. Two of the youths missing were white civil rights workers and one was a black. Minor noted that one of the youths, 20-year-old Andrew Goodman, was "one of 175 out-of-state volunteers who arrived in Mississippi over the weekend to take part in Negro voter registration and education projects." A 26 June 1964 article by Minor reviewed the recommendations made by Dulles upon his departure from Jackson. Minor reported that Dulles had been urged by some black leaders to have federal marshals stationed in Mississippi to protect civil rights workers. Minor wrote that the civil rights leaders were critical of the FBI's handling of the workers' disappearance and the state authorities' reaction to the incident. There was no indication that federal marshals would be sent to Mississippi, but according to Minor, Dulles would be reporting to President Johnson about the situation.

Further details about the disappearance of the civil rights workers and the burning of their car came in a 27 June 1964 article. The workers' car was apparently driven into a swamp and burned hours earlier than authorities had originally believed. Also, Governor Paul Johnson, according to Minor, had made a "surprise visit to Philadelphia for a briefing on the developments and the conduct of the search. . . ." Minor reported that Dulles recommended "stepped-up FBI activity" as well as increased local and federal efforts to protect blacks and civil rights workers. Dulles was also quoted as saying that "joint action" was needed to "control 'clandestine groups in the state.' " Minor reported that Dulles, when pressed by reporters, identified the Ku Klux Klan and Americans for Preservation of the White Race as two of the potentially problematic organizations. And finally, Minor wrote that Dulles "did not recommend that civil rights leaders call off or discourage their program . . . but he did recommend to the President that groups sponsoring the activities—including the National Council of Churches—give clear warning to these workers that 'very, very grave danger' awaits them in Mississippi."

Minor's lengthy articles on 28 June 1964 and after provided intimate details about the case, leading up to the day when the three murdered workers were found. Again, Minor did not use his "Eyes on Mississippi" column, June through August 1964, to comment directly on the summer's activities. Rather, the columns dealt almost exclusively with politics—largely about Mississippi Democrats' strained relationship with the national party, the party's difficulties at the national convention, and the resulting effects upon the Magnolia State's standing in the country.

That fall, Minor wrote columns attempting to put the summer's violence and its aftermath in perspective. Ten Pike County white men who had been involved in sixteen McComb-area bombings over five months received sentences ranging up to five years' probation, but no time in the penitentiary. Writing on 1 November 1964, Minor saw the possibility that the "leniency" of the sentences "may actually be an important step toward raising the image that racial justice does not prevail in Mississippi." Minor reported that Circuit Judge Williams H. Watkins admitted that he was being lenient, but in effect put the entire community on probation by declaring that if other violent acts occurred during the individuals' probationary period, then their sentences would be revoked and they would be sent to prison whether they were involved in the violence or not.

Minor described the judge's decision as "drastic" and as containing a "psychological factor which has never been tried before in Mississippi—to set a pattern of behavior for a body of citizens." He also explained other significant aspects of the case. First, Minor reported that the pleas entered by the ten left no doubt that they were guilty of the crimes, putting to rest speculation that the bombings were "the work of outsiders or the invading youthful civil rights workers." It also showed that cases could be solved by the FBI, the state, and sheriff's department. Significantly, Minor observed, "The sentencing of white men for crimes against Negroes is a rarity in Mississippi." Minor, always seeking perspective in a story, documented that these arrests "were the first instances in the past several turbulent years of racial violence in the state where felony charges have been made to stick against white men involved in racial crimes." Pike County District Attorney Joseph N. Pigott, in a 3 November 1964 letter to Minor, complimented the veteran journalist for understanding "the many facets of the bombings in Pike County. . . ." Pigott expressed appreciation for the "fair manner" that Minor "treated this and past news stories concerning the courts."

Mississippi was being forced to change. Prior to the Pike County sentences in Mississippi, on 2 July 1964, President Lyndon Baines Johnson signed the Civil Rights Act. A year later, on 6 August 1965, President Johnson signed the Voting Rights Act. The Civil Rights and Voting Rights acts served as exclamation points for Mississippi, signaling that the days of segregation, when blacks were treated as second class citizens, were now over in the eyes of the law.

Minor had been in Mississippi since 1947. He recalled that in the 1960s his wife had wanted to leave Mississippi for a safer, kinder state. Minor's oldest son graduated from high school in 1964 but chose not to go to college in Mississippi because of the racial climate. The younger Minor studied at Louisiana State University, went to Vietnam, and later attended Tulane University in New Orleans. Even though Minor saw many of his colleagues and friends leave Mississippi, he remained because he wanted to "witness the improvements." Minor still resides in Mississippi and continues to "witness" the improvements in Mississippi at the turn of the century, savoring the recognition he has earned for a lifetime of outstanding journalism.

The Louis Lyons Award from the Nieman Foundation at Harvard University was given to him for "conscience and integrity in journalism." The Mississippi University for Women and the University of Mississippi have awarded him their highest honors, and Southern Illinois University bestowed on him the Elijah Lovejoy Award for his writing in his own newspaper, the *Capital Reporter*, in the 1970s. Particularly important to Minor is the John Chancellor Award, named for the late NBC reporter and anchor who once covered the civil rights movement. Minor was the first recipient of the Chancellor Award in 1997 and received a medallion, a plaque, and a check for $25,000. And, long before Minor was recognized for his work on a national level, he was a respected journalist in the South. On 3 May 1964 he was elected as chairman of the Louisiana-Mississippi Associated Press Association.

The quality of Minor's nearly 60 years of reporting and news analysis is hard to match in Mississippi or elsewhere. In the decade between *Brown* and the Civil Rights Act, Minor was consistently even-handed in his news reporting. During a time when championing the status quo or supporting the "old" Southern ways would have been easy, he instead reported straightforwardly, as best he could, the changes occurring around the country that would soon confront Mississippi. He did not back away from describing incidents and events that reflected poorly on Mississippi, its leaders, and its citizenry. As Mississippi continued its resistance to integrating the schools, Minor reported the inequities of the state's policy of "separate but equal" schools. As the 1960s began and John F. Kennedy became president, Minor's column became a stronger voice in revealing inequalities toward Mississippi blacks. The change is even more evident when reviewing Minor's speeches from 1958 through 1964. Though Minor abhorred the state's unbending resistance to integration, he did not try to solve the problem by shouting louder. His method was simple yet courageous—to report in a fair, accurate and balanced manner to demonstrate the fairness or unfairness of a situation to the reader. He did not run from controversy or danger. His legacy is that during troubled times, he accurately and compassionately respected the public's right to know by reporting in an influential regional newspaper the plight of Mississippi blacks. And Minor did that, as he revealed years later, under the threat of possible physical harm to himself and his family.

Notes

1. Whenever the author refers to Minor "recounting," "recalling," "remembering," "looking back," and the like it refers to a 15 September 1999 interview.

2. All "Eyes on Mississippi" columns, pieces or analysis, and stories written by Minor were taken from the *Times-Picayune*, unless otherwise stated.

3. At the time of this writing, Wilson F. (Bill) Minor is seventy-seven years old and still writing a syndicated column for over a dozen newspapers.

References

Barnett, Ross R. Speech. "Text Governor Ross R. Barnett Television Message." Minor Papers, Mississippi State University, Box 9, 3 October 1962.

Black, Hugo. "James Meredith vs. Charles Dickson Fair, et al." Minor Papers, MSU, Box 9, 9 September 1962.

Cassimere, Raphael, Jr. "Remembering Brown v. Board of Education." *Crisis*, May/June 1994, 10.

Crider, Bill. "Meredith Says '62 Ole Miss Clash 'Irrelevant.'" *Times-Picayune*, 17 September 1972, sec.3, 6.

Featherston, James S. "Beleaguered Bill Minor." *Nieman Reports*, Winter 1978.

Meredith, James H. "Statement by James Meredith." Minor Papers, MSU, Box 9, 30 January 1963.

Minor, W. F. Correspondence. Minor Papers, MSU, Box 9, letter from Herbert Farrell to J. M. Tubb, 9 Jan. 1962.

———. Interview with author. 15 September 1999.

———. Speeches. Minor Papers, MSU, Box 10, B'Nai B'Rith, July 1962.

———. Speeches. Minor Papers, MSU, Box 10, B'Nai B'Rith, Fall 1964.

———. Speeches. Minor Papers, MSU, Box 10, Ole Miss Education Conference, Oxford, Mississippi, 1958.

———. Speeches. Minor Papers, MSU, Box 10, Tougaloo Social Science Forum, 1961.

———. Speech. "Mississippi's "Freedom Summer Reviewed: A Fifteen Year Perspective on Progress in Race Relations, 1964–1979." Tougaloo and Millsaps Colleges, 30 October–2 November 1979.

Patterson, Joe T. Speech. "University of Mississippi Law School." Minor Papers, MSU, Box 9, 16 October 1962.

Pigott, Joe N. Letter to W. F. Minor. Minor Papers, MSU, Box 9, 3 November 1964.

Tubb, J. M. "News Release." Minor Papers, MSU, Box 9, 19 September 1962.

Hazel Brannon Smith and the *Lexington Advertiser*

Arthur J. Kaul

We know that it is to the best interest of both races that segregation be maintained in theory and in fact.

Hazel Brannon Smith, 20 May 1954

Somebody is going broke.

Smith, 4 December 1958

We had never advocated school integration at the time of the 1954 high court decision (nor since for that matter).

Smith, 14 January 1965

* * *

The editorial career of Hazel Brannon Smith resonates deeply in the popular imagination of American journalism, her story achieving a legendary status forged in the Progressive ethos of the early Twentieth Century. Academic and popular accounts of the Pulitzer Prize-winning editor of the *Lexington Advertiser* feature the plot line of a secularized evangelical salvation narrative: conservative Dixiecrat segregationist undergoes a life-changing conversion that transforms her into a crusading civil rights advocate and, eventually, liberal martyr to the cause of press freedom. For example, Mark Newman's scholarly account of Smith's career in the *Journal of Mississippi History* (February 1992) stresses a Progressive "conversion from Dixiecrat to a champion of civil rights" (p. 86). The Jackson *Clarion-Ledger* (13 April 1994) eulogized Smith as "a conservative who became a liberal advocate nearly overnight in the mid-1950s." The apogee of the legend was a Hollywood-style docudrama, "The Hazel Brannon Smith Story: A Passion for Justice," that aired on prime-time network television a month before her death.

Hazel Brannon Smith's editorials over three decades, however, belie the salvation narrative. No civil rights advocate, she repeatedly asserted that she had never advocated integration. Her editorial career mirrors not civil rights liberalism but Protestant-styled conservative American Progressivism. Just like the turn-of-the-century muckrakers, who attacked the power of economic and political combinations, trusts, "bosses,"—even the liquor traffic—Hazel Brannon Smith crusaded against illegal bootlegging in the 1940s and the respectable "bosses" of the Citizens' Councils and Sovereignty Commission in the 1950s and 1960s. Her editorial values and voice were deeply rooted in Progressivism and the craft culture of Twentieth Century American journalism that it fostered.

Richard Hofstadter described the Progressive ethos in *The Age of Reform* (1955). The "business of exposure" was the fundamental critical achievement of American Progressivism between 1890 and World War II, Hofstadter wrote. The "Progressive mind was characteristically a journalistic mind," he observed, and the exposes of the "socially responsible reporter-reformer" made the muckraker a "central figure" in the Progressive movement. According to Hofstadter, the muckrakers embodied three major Progressive themes: (1) a vision of reality that saw "evildoing among the most respectable people," (2) the mischief typically interpreted simply as "widespread breaking of the law," and (3) exhortatory appeals to "universal personal responsibility" inherited from "the moral traditions of rural evangelical Protestantism."

Smith's upbringing, and later her career, reflects this philosophy, which provides a compelling explanation for the Progressive editorials and commentary that often stopped short of the liberalism her admirers attributed to her. "Hazel, who was a nice segregationist white woman, just decided that her Christianity, her moral and political beliefs, couldn't allow her to support what was being done," Hodding Carter III told the *Clarion-Ledger* (5 January 1986). Born on 5 February 1914 in Alabama City, Alabama, near the Etowah County seat of Gadsden, Hazel Freeman Brannon's Southern middle class childhood was marked by a lovingly strict upbringing in a "Christian home." In a 5 May 1966 "Through Hazel Eyes" column, the 52-year-old editor reminisced about the influence of her parents, Dock Broad Brannon and Georgia Freeman Brannon, on her childhood:

> As a child I was taught to love everybody and not to hate anyone.... Respect and consideration for the rights of others were ingrained in me for as long as I can remember.... I never got away with anything by saying "everyone else is going to do it." My mother always said, "it doesn't make any difference. You're going to do right. Do you want to go to hell just because everyone else wants to?"

God and her parents, she wrote, gave her "the example and the strength I have to do what I must."

After graduation in 1930 from Gadsden High School at the age of sixteen, she worked for the weekly *Etowah Observer*, contributing personal items and reportage and selling advertisements on commission. She entered the University of Alabama in 1932, joined Delta Zeta sorority, became managing editor of the student newspaper, and graduated with a B.A. degree in journalism in 1935. In the midst of the Great Depression, she went in search of a newspaper to buy to fulfill a youthful ambition to become an editor and publisher. With a $3,000 loan, she bought the *Durant News*, a broken down 600-subscriber weekly in Holmes County, Mississippi, on 4 August 1936. Thirty years later, on 4 August 1966, she recalled that "the boys in the pool room were taking bets on how long I'd last and the most any of them gave me was six months." The "first important state official" to come calling on the young newspaper publisher, Lt. Gov. Billy Snider, himself a newspaper owner, solemnly told her, "Young lady, Durant has long been known as the graveyard of Mississippi journalism. If you can make a go of this newspaper, you can have anything you want in Mississippi journalism, or anywhere else for that matter." Even though the press or Linotype frequently broke down, she boasted, "We never missed an issue and were always at the post office in time—even if it did take all night to print." Three decades had not diminished her youthful enthusiasm: "But I was young and had all the energy in the world. I loved what I was doing. . . . It was fun."

The *Durant News* also was profitable, so much so that her editorial formula of the comings and goings of small town life registered in births, deaths, marriages, family reunions, and homecomings allowed her to pay off the loan in four years and make another newspaper acquisition. A front-page headline in the 8 April 1943 edition of the *Lexington Advertiser*—"Welcome to Lexington Miss Hazel Brannon"—announced that she was the new editor and publisher of the 1,800-subscriber weekly in the Holmes County seat. Two weeks later, her "Through Hazel Eyes" column on 22 April 1943 in the *Advertiser* promised, "We shall stand for upholding the traditions of the past and improving them."

In "The South's Racial Problem," a "Through Hazel Eyes" column republished as an *Advertiser* editorial on 15 July 1943 "in response to many requests from our readers," Hazel Brannon offered paternalistic Southern Jim Crow attitudes about segregation that were congenial to her white audience in a county whose population was two-thirds black. The "Negro problem," she wrote, could be solved only by Southerners, not by outsiders.

> The white man and the black man have dwelt together in peace and harmony in the south for many, many years, because each has known his place and kept it. Each has had his own ideals, customs, and habits and they have not conflicted . . . as some of our meddling friends would have us believe.
>
> The good negro is just as proud of his race and its integrity as the white man, the Indian, or the Chinese. He realizes that God must have intended for there to be a great colored race or who would not have created it. He is not fooled by loose talk concerning "social equality." He knows there is no such thing as "equality," even among white men. . . .
>
> The wise man realizes, whether he be white or black, that

as long as tastes and habits and appetites of people differ there can be no absolute "equality" among races. . . . The vast majority of the colored race in the south know that the white man is his friend; when he is in trouble the first person he goes to is a white friend. And the white friend doesn't let him down. He values the friendship of his negro friends. . . .

But the south and America are a white man's country and both races know it. . . .

Hazel Brannon had little sympathy for President Franklin D. Roosevelt and his New Deal. "Traditionally, the South has remained Democratic because of its low-tariff and white supremacy principles," she wrote on 20 April 1944. "The Democratic party has abandoned its position on the low-tariff and the principles now practiced by the Roosevelts are as repugnant to Southerners as the worst carpetbaggers of reconstruction days." On 7 September 1944, she complained that the New Deal administration had "violated every tradition held by southern people. Communists, coddled by the New Deal, have been greatly responsible for the outrages against the south." Especially vexing was a circular "put out by communists" among government employees in Washington, D.C., to outlaw the separation of blood given by whites and blacks to the blood bank. "Good negro citizens . . . no more want white blood in their veins than does the white man want negro blood," she wrote. "The communistic influences that would mix the two do not have the interest of either at heart."

A six-month law-and-order editorial campaign in the *Lexington Advertiser* launched in November 1945 challenged law enforcement officials to clamp down on illegal bootlegging and gambling. Raids on bootlegging establishments rarely resulted in the seizure of gambling devices, she wrote on 1 November 1945, prompting her to wonder "why liquor is taken at these bootlegging places and slot machines are ignored. There is a loose connection somewhere that needs tightening." A week later on 8 November 1945, Brannon complained:

> Today, however, liquor joints line the highways going in and out of most towns in the county. They don't just sell liquor quietly. They are the loudest places in town. They display

> prominently in their doors slot machines and other gambling devices. Some have combined dance halls with liquor and gambling. They flaunt it in the faces of the people . . . as well as the officers. . . . Liquor selling has now reached the state where it is the most profitable business in Holmes County.

Brannon suggested that bootleggers might be paying off law enforcement officials, including the sheriff. "The only way our officials can prove they are not being paid off, in our opinion, is to start enforcing the law now and continue to enforce it until this county is rid of the bootlegging joints that line our public highways throughout the county," she wrote on 28 February 1946. "We challenge Sheriff Walter L. Murtagh to do something about it." After the sheriff executed a search warrant, finding two and a half cases of liquor, the editor published a copy of the document on the front page of the *Advertiser* on 11 April 1946, under the headline, "What About the Slot Machines?" In the same issue, her "Through Hazel Eyes" column proclaimed that she had "no personal axe to grind with anyone" and had no "fuss or falling out" with the sheriff. "I am no lily-white reformer or crusader . . . the people of Holmes County do not want organized crime in this county with protection . . . and that is what I think we have . . . what a lot of citizens think, for that matter. I hope I have made myself very plain," she wrote. Her plain talk included a front-page "open letter" on 28 March 1946 addressed to the district attorney, county attorney, and Holmes County Circuit Court grand jury that was to convene in three days, imploring them to "do something" about the lawlessness. "If you fail to act we know a group of citizens who feel compelled to take these matters up with the Governor," she warned.

The grand jury produced no indictments for bootlegging and gambling on April 1, but Holmes County Circuit Judge S. F. Davis, responding to a petition signed by county residents, reconvened the grand jury on April 16, two days before an 18 April 1946 editorial appeared on the front page of the *Lexington Advertiser*. The whole county was "stirred up" because Sheriff Murtagh "failed to do his sworn duty" of enforcing the prohibition and gambling laws, she wrote. "He should either start enforcing those laws or resign." The next day, on 19 April 1946, the grand jury returned 52 indictments for liquor and gambling violations after hearing three days of testimony from more than 100 citizens. Hazel Brannon's stinging editorial prodding of the judge, grand jury, county attorney, prosecutor, and sheriff had yielded a victory for law and order and she was triumphant. "It all goes to prove that when people get enough of a thing they won't have anymore . . . and the people rule," she wrote on 25 April 1946. "They might let things get out of hand for a while but when they get ready to clean things up a way is found to accomplish their purpose . . . the bootlegger is definitely on the run."

Her run-in with the legal establishment continued. In October 1946, Judge Davis found Brannon in contempt of court for interviewing a witness in a murder trial after he had ordered witnesses not to talk to anyone except their attorneys. The judge ordered her to pay a $50 fine and to serve fifteen days in the Holmes County jail, sentence suspended on condition that she not violate any municipal, state, or federal law for two years. Judge Davis issued a telling reprimand from the bench that said more about the editor's earlier reform efforts that it did about contempt of court:

> I sympathize with you and am sorry you got in this mess, but you brought it on yourself. I realize you are putting on a great campaign for law and order but if you read history you will see that the only perfect being didn't make much of a hit with his reform.
>
> He reformed a few and left this advice "Before you clean up someone else clean up yourself." . . . I have been around a long time and know the job, it is to clean up Holmes County. I don't believe you can do it. I am of the opinion that when Gabriel blows his horn and rolls back the scroll of Heaven he will find the world like it is today. I am sorry this is the situation. I get no pleasure out of sentencing you. I wish you had stayed out of this mess. It reminds me of what the Irishman said when he saw the bull run head-on into the train. "I admire your spunk but doubt your judgment." You have run head-on to this Court. When called up you proceeded to give the Court a curt lecture as to his duties.

Upon appeal of the contempt conviction to the Mississippi Supreme Court, Justice L. A. Smith Jr. in *Brannon v. State* (29 So. 2d 916) on

7 April 1947 found "wholly insufficient proof" for contempt and reversed the trial court conviction.

Legal skirmishes failed to diminish the profitability of the *News* and *Advertiser*, allowing her to cultivate the image of a wealthy and flirtatious Southern belle with a taste for designer clothes, stylish hats, white Cadillac convertibles, European vacations, and the county's most eligible bachelors. "Honey, I had the most eligible bachelor in Durant and the most eligible bachelor in Lexington," she quipped in the *Clarion-Ledger* on 5 January 1986, "and my only trouble was that I couldn't have them both. That's true. I was something." She returned from a sea cruise in 1949 with a trophy, ship's purser Walter Dyer "Smitty" Smith, whom she married on 21 March 1950 in Holmes County. Thereafter, her newspapers' masthead listed the publisher as "Hazel Brannon Smith, (Mrs. Walter D.)—Editor and Publisher." "Smitty" would soon become administrator of the Holmes County Community Hospital.

Hazel Brannon's columns and editorials in the *Durant News* and *Lexington Advertiser* in the late 1940s and early 1950s often took stridently anti-communist Cold War stands that unabashedly supported U.S. Senator Joseph McCarthy of Wisconsin. She endorsed a "thorough housecleaning that will rid our national government of all pinks and reds and pro-Soviet sympathizers that have been feeding at the expense of American taxpayers for so long," she wrote on 6 November 1952. "The American people demand an end to the coddling of Russia and the pinks and reds in our state department and practically every branch of our federal government." She opposed the U.S. Senate censure of McCarthy on 11 November 1954, "We personally hope the Senate won't censure Senator McCarthy. But if it does every pink and left-winger in the country will share in the victory scored by the Communist party which has inspired and directed the campaign against McCarthy in a well-planned and officially endorsed policy . . ."

The United States Supreme Court's unanimous 17 May 1954 decision in *Brown v. Board of Education* declaring segregated schools unconstitutional sent shock waves through the South, generating "massive resistance" to integration and the formation of White Citizens' Councils. Smith's ambivalent editorial response to the ruling acknowledged the South's moral failure to make good on "separate but equal" schools while standing steadfast for segregation. "Perhaps if we had done as much as we should to improve our Negro schools throughout the South in the past decade we would never have had these cases in the courts," she wrote in "Through Hazel Eyes" on 20 May 1954.

> The Supreme Court may be morally right when its says that "separate educational facilities are inherently unequal." But we know, for practical purposes, that separate educational facilities are highly desirable in the South and other places where the two races live and work side by side. We know that it is to the best interest of both races that segregation be maintained in theory and in fact—and that where it isn't maintained trouble results. . . . The present situation has all of the ingredients necessary for a bloody revolution—if people don't keep their heads. It is a situation where a few well trained Communists could come into our section of the country and promote a revolution overnight.

She defended segregation again on 10 June 1954, declaring, "We feel that our efforts should be toward self-advancement within the boundaries of our race. . . . We believe every living person has the right to choose his or her friends—and not be compelled to associate with anyone." Her only concession was to equal protection under the law. "We believe that all men of all races and colors and creeds are the same before God . . . and should be equal before the law—should have the same protection of the law and courts."

Originating in Mississippi, Citizens' Councils sprang up rapidly throughout Mississippi and the South, publicly advocating grass roots pressure and nonviolent resistance tactics, including economic boycotts, coercion, and intimidation, to maintain segregation and thwart court-ordered integration. *Look* magazine (16 November 1965) published an account of a July 1954 effort by a "leading citizen" who solicited Smith's cooperation in establishing a Citizens' Council in Holmes County that has become part of the Smith legend. "If a Nigra won't go along with our thinking on what's best for the community as a whole, he'll have his credit cut off," the citizen said. "What do you think the Negroes are going to think when they hear that the white men are organizing?" she asked. "Well, it might be a good thing for them to be a little scared," he said. Smith responded, "No, it's not a good thing to be a little scared. People can't live under fear, and it will end up with all of us scared, and it will be a big scare. What you're proposing to do is to take away the freedom of all of the people in this community." If that was her response in a private conversation to the formation of a local Citizens' Council, her initial public expression was considerably more circumspect and veiled. "There are some who seek to stir up strife for purposes of their own," she wrote on 23 September 1954. "They appeal to prejudice and to ignorance—and their religion is the doctrine of hatred and greed implemented by the weapons of fear and distrust."

By most accounts, a signed editorial, "The Law Should Be for All" (15 July 1954), and a front page story, "Negro Man Shot in Leg Saturday in Tchula; Witness Reports He Was Told to 'Get Goin' by Holmes County Sheriff" (8 July 1954), were turning points in the Smith legend. She had crossed the color line, according to the popular media myth, and embarked on the new vocation of liberal civil rights advocate. The story said that a twenty-seven-year-old black, Henry Randall, was shot in the left leg after Holmes County Sheriff Richard F. Byrd told him to "get goin'." The sheriff drove up to where "a group of Negroes were congregated and asked one of them what he meant by 'whooping.' When the Negro replied that he had not whooped Sheriff Byrd was reported to have cursed and struck the Negro on the head." Randall fled, and Byrd fired his gun "several times, one of the bullets entering the left thigh of the victim from the rear and passing through the leg to the front." Smith concluded the story, "No charges have yet been filed against Sheriff Byrd in the shooting." "The Law Should Be for All" chastised the sheriff in uncompromising terms for "shocking reports too numerous to ignore" of similar occurrences during the previous twenty months:

> The United States of America was founded upon a Christian faith in God and the idea that Man is made in the image of God and should be free and independent—and since that time historic laws based upon the dignity of man and his rights have been held sacred in this country. The laws of America are for

everyone—rich and poor, strong and weak, white and black and all the other races that dwell within our land. . . . This kind of thing cannot go on any longer. It must be stopped. The vast majority of Holmes county people are not red necks who look with favor on the abuse of people because their skins are black. . . . In our opinion, Mr. Byrd as Sheriff has violated every concept of justice, decency and right in his treatment of some people in Holmes county. He has shown us without question that he is not fit to occupy that high office. He should, in fact, resign.

Sheriff Byrd immediately sued Smith for $57,500 in libel damages, prompting the editor to comment on 22 July 1954, "We don't know whether to be flattered at being sued for so much—or surprised that the Sheriff places the value of his reputation at so little. . . . This newspaper has in the past, and will continue in the future to print the truth as we know it to be. . . . No damage suit can shut us up so easily." The sheriff won a $10,000 judgment against Smith on 12 October 1954 in Holmes County Circuit Court. Undeterred, she continued to criticize the sheriff without naming him. "There are some sheriffs in office in Mississippi now who have lied to every man, woman and child in their counties—but they have no more remorse than an egg sucking dog."

Smith appealed the libel judgment to the Mississippi Supreme Court. On 7 November 1955, Justice Percy Lee in *Hazel Brannon Smith v. Richard F. Byrd* (225 Miss. 331, 83 So. 2d 172) vindicated Smith and reversed the libel conviction, finding Smith's *Durant News* and *Lexington Advertiser* had "substantially recited the circumstances" truthfully about the shooting of Henry Randall. Moreover, "under the facts in this record, there was no justification whatever for hitting the Negro with the blackjack or shooting him. And since the blow and the shot were both unjustified, it follows that the Negro was unlawfully assaulted in both instances." Smith announced in a four column headline on the *Advertiser*'s front page on 10 November 1955, "Editor Wins Libel Suit," reprinted the court's opinion along with commentary. "I am a firm believer in our Southern traditions and racial segregation, but not at the expense of justice and truth." *Time* magazine (21 November 1955) featured "good-looking, dark-haired Mrs. Hazel Brannon Smith" and the libel case in its press section. "I don't regard this as a personal victory," she told *Time*, "but rather as a victory for the people's right to know." On 29 December 1955, she asserted that the libel case was "not tried on its merit at all" because "prevailing tensions at the time caused by the school de-segregation ruling" had injected the "race issue" into it.

> This was accomplished by the use of the "big lie" techniques employed by enemies of the editor who wanted to shut her up—not because of the race question at all—but because she has fought for the past twelve years an unceasing battle against bootleggers and gamblers and their friends who are trying to control Holmes county.

She considered printing the "main lie" on the front page of the *Advertiser* at the time, she wrote, and "nail it for what it was—but such an action seemed so degrading." Smith issued a "fair warning" that "never again will we fail to act should that Hitler-like technique be employed against us again—on any issue . . . we will not in the future sit silently by while any individual or group attack us unfairly." Finally, she warned, "Make no mistake—There are persons who are using these tensions to their own advantage. . . . We are living in an atmosphere where citizens are honestly afraid to speak their opinions because they are afraid of being misunderstood."

Retaliation from her "enemies" was swift. Six days later, on 4 January 1956, at a special meeting of newly-elected hospital trustees, her husband "Smitty" was fired as administrator of the 45-bed hospital he had served since August 1950. The trustees' action was made public at a regular hospital board meeting on January 9 and reported in the *Advertiser* three days later. Rumors had been circulating, prompting a signed front page "Open Letter" to "The Citizens of Holmes County" from Walter D. Smith opposing any move to permit "personalities or politics in any form to become involved in the management of the hospital."

A quasi-official reason for replacing "Smitty" as hospital administrator was contained in a typewritten note given by hospital board chairman David B. Miles to a Jackson *Daily News* reporter, James Featherston, who showed up at the meeting, according to the *Advertiser*'s 12 January 1956 account. The note stated, "Mr. Smith's management of hospital personnel was unsatisfactory and his administration was unpopular with many in the county." Despite a resolution passed a few days earlier by the hospital's medical staff that praised the administrator's "absolute integrity and sound judgment," a Jackson *Daily News* story on 6 January 1956 quoted a hospital trustee who said Smith's firing "stems from the fact his wife has become a controversial figure."

An ambivalent stance on race relations that neither challenged segregation nor supported integration was controversial in the "closed society" of mid-1950s Mississippi, and Smith's editorial voice often vacillated between the competing claims of maintaining traditional segregation and moral claims of equality before the law. "Men and women of goodwill who do not belong in the extremist or radical group on either side of the racial controversy are caught in the middle," she wrote (23 February 1956), "intimidated into silence by the vocal minorities on both sides." A week later (1 March 1956), she confessed, "We have remained quiet on the worsening racial situation. Frankly, we feel that a great deal too much is being said all the time—and that every little bit added is just that much fuel to be added to the flames which will eventually engulf us all unless some semblance of sanity and reason are restored." She still endorsed segregation. "We do not believe in mixing the races in our schools, churches, social life or anywhere else," she wrote, "and we regard racial intermarriage as something rejected by God." Yet, if community leaders promoted "better feelings between the races . . . by trying to see that fair treatment is accorded everyone in our communities, particularly in our courts," she wrote, "then we will be making a contribution on the constructive side of race relations." Smith rejected both integration and state coercion in addressing a Mississippi Senate proposal that would strip churches of their property tax exemptions if they used their property for non-segregated purposes. "We do not favor integration in any form, in the churches, schools or socially," she wrote (29 March 1956). "But neither do we favor any legislative body seeking to use pressure to compel churches to do their bidding."

Smith's editorials were targets for reprisals and the Citizens' Council obliged with a smear campaign launched when her photograph appeared in the November 1957 issue of *Ebony* in an article called "The Plight of Southern White Women." The caption to the photograph stated, "U. of Alabama graduate Hazel Brannon Smith edits two crusading Mississippi papers, the *Durant News* and the *Advertiser* which have been called the 'consciences of Holmes County.' She has campaigned for equal justice for all, regardless of race." Anonymous circulars about the *Ebony* photograph popped up in Holmes County, providing so-called proof that she was an integrationist. "I have never, either in print or by spoken word, advocated integration of the races," she proclaimed in "Through Hazel Eyes" (31 October 1957), in which she reprinted her letter to *Time* asking for an explanation of how the 1955 *Time* photograph found its way into *Ebony*. She reprinted *Time*'s response a week later without comment, the letter being "self-explanatory." *Time*'s explanation was simple; *Ebony* asked for a print of the photograph and *Time* complied out of professional courtesy, just as *Time* had made similar requests of other publications.

In November 1958, thirty-five Holmes County citizens organized the *Holmes County Herald*, capitalized for $30,000 at $25 a share. The largest shareholder, Chester Marshall, hired as general manager of the *Lexington Advertiser* and *Durant News* 15 months earlier, resigned to become the new weekly's first editor. "The price of betrayal comes high these days," Smith wrote (11 December 1958). "A long time ago it was only thirty pieces of silver." Eighteen of the backers were prominent Lexington businessmen, lawyers, and public officials, many with Citizens' Council connections, including County Attorney Pat M. Barrett, Sheriff Andrew P. Smith, State Senator T. M. Williams, and State Representative Wilburn Hooker, who also served on the State Executive Committee of the Mississippi Association of Citizens' Councils. "There is not enough business in Lexington for two newspapers," Smith wrote (4 December 1958). "We have three newspapers and two job printing shops in the County at the present. Somebody is going broke."

> The only way a fourth newspaper can become financially successful in Lexington and Holmes County is for every Holmes merchant to quit advertising in the other three papers and give all their business to the new newspaper—and for every person who has job printing to take it to the new firm—and for every-

body to quit taking the other three papers—and subscribe only to the new one.

The *Four-County News* of Pickens ceased publication a year later, citing "insufficient advertising income," according to the *Lexington Advertiser* (31 December 1959).

In a lengthy front page *Advertiser* editorial, "A Free or A Controlled Press" (4 December 1958), Smith wrote that the new newspaper, according to press reports, " 'will not take a side on controversial issues.' In other words, No Hazel Eyes, no editorials." In her view, the *Holmes County Herald* would "knuckle under" to a small conspiratorial clique that controlled it, unlike the *Lexington Advertiser* whose "columns have always been and always will be open to any citizen of this county desiring self-expression." An "atmosphere of fear" hangs over Holmes County "dominating almost every facet of public and private life," she wrote. "No one speaks freely any more for fear of being misunderstood. . . ."

> Some are afraid of losing their jobs—others are afraid of losing their business. Some fear losing their friends or social standing. It is all rooted, of course, in the age old fear concerning the traditional separation of the races in our state and the South.
>
> Almost every man and woman is afraid to try to do anything to promote good will and harmony between the races—afraid he or she will be taken as a mixer, an integrationist, or worse—if there is anything worse by Southern standards. For four years now your editor has been the subject and object of vilification and worse conducted in a whispering campaign by a few misguided zealots inspired by my enemies. Such people never fight in the open. . . . I have remained silent only because I want to preserve the domestic tranquillity of Holmes County. . . . But I can no longer remain silent—I must fight back—when people try to destroy me. I am not a mixer nor an integrationist—have never been and never expect to be. All my friends know this—and most of my enemies.

A week later, "Through Hazel Eyes" (11 December 1958) bluntly told its readers, "The new newspaper is being established for one primary purpose—and that is to try to force Hazel Brannon Smith out of the newspaper business in Holmes County. . . ." A "very small group of agitators" behind the formation of the *Herald* had been "out to get me" ever since the libel suit, she wrote, and some of them caused her husband's firing. Her enemies had formed a "vicious little combine" as "a kind of Gestapo to determine how people should think and act and pressure them into it . . . these same people will next be trying to tell the free people of Holmes County what newspaper they should read, what newspaper they should advertise in," she wrote. "This attempted dictatorship based upon a lust for power and domination over the people should be stopped now dead in its tracks—before its gets us in a stranglehold and never lets go."

A few months after the *Holmes County Herald*'s founding in January 1959, the rival *Lexington Advertiser* claimed circulation superiority. "Today, the *Advertiser* has more circulation than all of the other newspapers in Holmes county," the editor boasted (2 April 1959). The *Herald* countered, claiming "more advertising than all three of the other weekly newspapers serving Holmes County combined" (18 June 1959). Merchants began diverting advertising to the *Herald*. The revenue base of the *Advertiser* further deteriorated with the loss of the county's contract for publication of legal advertising and public notices. In February 1960, the *Herald* won the two-year contract with a bid of one cent, undercutting the *Advertiser*'s bid of $30 a month, already half the maximum state-set rate. The head of the Holmes County Board of Supervisors, W. Leslie Smith, was a *Herald* shareholder. The "economic pressure" and its accompanying "gangster tactics" that she lamented in a 28 May 1959 column was taking a toll on her newspapers. "Again, for the second year in a row for us," Smith wrote (22 December 1960), "it has not been a successful year. Nor did we expect it to be."

When an *Advertiser* editorial, "Race Hatred Is Not the Answer" (4 June 1959), argued that "we do not want to see the South victimized again by the extremists. . . . We do not want the South to forever suffer for another 'Lost Cause,' " the *Herald* (11 June 1959) complained that "too many publications" were "agitating about 'Race Hatred' " to disrupt the "friendly, cooperative spirit" between the races in a "deliberate, calculated attempt to gain the interest of the reader or listener." The *Herald* offered its own race agitation in a 27 August 1959 editorial column.

(I)ntegrated schools in the North and East are hot beds and breeding grounds of pornography, rape, extortion, murder and violence of all kinds and to make matters worse are guarded by police and army troops to enforce such crime . . . neighborhoods deteriorate and rot with migrants flocking on relief and bastard babies encouraged by government agencies. To one race in this country that is their idea of Santa Claus and Utopia, a government that takes care of their offspring spawned by wandering fathers with willing wenches who know nothing of morality and care less.

The *Lexington Advertiser* called for tolerance, brotherhood and moderation. "Among Christians there should be no problem of intolerance," she wrote (29 October 1959). "Thus we grieve that 'tolerance' in Mississippi has joined the limbo of 'brotherhood' and 'moderate' in becoming dirty words—and be careful how you use them."

The siege of Hazel Brannon Smith earned national attention when she received the Elijah P. Lovejoy Award for Courage in Journalism from the International Conference of Weekly Newspaper Editors and Southern Illinois University on 17 July 1960. Named for an abolitionist editor killed by an Alton, Illinois, mob in 1837, the award cited Smith for resisting "the merciless attack of an organized pressure group . . . which sought to silence her by means of reprisals . . . personal vilification . . . economic boycott . . . and by means of the launching of an opposing newspaper." The *Holmes County Herald* reported on 21 July 1960 that the award was given for news and editorial policies "supporting integration," with both words printed in boldface. Smith published on 28 July 1960 a copy of the letter of protest she sent to her former employee and *Herald* Editor Chester Marshall, demanding a correction. "Since you know of your own knowledge, Chester, having been in my employ for some 15 months, that I have never advocated integration of the races either in my newspapers, or in any other way," she wrote in the July 26 letter, "you must have known that you were printing a lie. . . . Your story on the citation was false, malicious and libelous."

In a 4 August 1960 *Advertiser* editorial, "Our Courts Should Dispense Equal Justice for All," Smith not only chastised her local newspaper rivals but also editors throughout the state. "It is tragic, but understandable, that more Mississippi editors do not speak out when justice goes begging in our own communities," she wrote. "It seems that any editor who lifts a voice to protect [*sic*] injustice, or rank discrimination is immediately tagged 'integrationist' by the home grown variety of racial fanatics and extremists who seem to exist in almost every community."

Six weeks later, *Herald* shareholders fired Chester Marshall, hiring 22-year-old Millsaps College graduate Jack A. Shearer to take his place. "Judgment Day has come for a former Holmes County editor—and sooner or later it is going to catch up with those who were and are responsible for him," Smith wrote (20 October 1960). "The *Advertiser* will continue to expose and report fully their activities—and we'll still be around to carry their obituaries."

Several teenage boys' Halloween prank—firecrackers and a burning cross on Smith's lawn—prompted an illustrated editorial, "A Cross Burns—Symptom of a Community Illness," in the *Advertiser* (10 November 1960). Smith shot a photograph of the burning cross, took the license plate off the station wagon the boys abandoned when they fled to the nearby woods to hide. She traced the car to the home of County Attorney Pat Barrett, a *Herald* shareholder, whose son, Don Barrett, had participated in the prank. A photograph of the burning cross accompanied the editorial. Smith refused to dismiss the incident as an "innocent Halloween prank of high school boys," she wrote, because "they are all big enough and old enough to know right from wrong." She attributed their action to the baneful influence of their elders. "These young men may not have sought to inflict physical violence," she wrote. "Theirs was an intimidation much worse, a violation of the spirit, designed to incite mental and spiritual anguish. . . . The cross was burned on my lawn this time. Next time it could be yours." Objecting to the Jackson, Mississippi, *State-Times*' characterization of Don Barrett as an "instigator" of the Halloween cross burning, she asked for a correction because the error, though "slight from a reporter's standpoint" means "a great deal in the life of a 15-year-old boy." "The fact is Don was there and in his father's car," she wrote in "More about the Cross Burning" (17 November 1960), "but I do not think it is right or fair that he alone should bear the stigma of what has become a community problem."

Smith was so "shocked and revolted" by a "cheap game of character assassination" involving a University of Mississippi journalism student that she called for abolishing the state-funded Sovereignty Commission. In a three-pronged attack circulated by the Sovereignty Commission, 20-year-old Billy C. Barton of Pontotoc was falsely accused of being "actively involved in several lunch counter sit-in demonstrations" while working for the *Atlanta Journal* during the summer of 1960, being a "close friend" of P. D. East, the controversial editor of the *Petal Paper*, and being under the influence of Atlanta journalist Ralph McGill. "We have a full file on East's activities," stated the report reprinted in Smith's editorial (31 March 1961). "All those who are familiar with the key position occupied by Ralph McGill in the left-wing apparatus will recognize the significance of this fact," the report stated. Barton's aspiration to the editorship of the student newspaper made him "very dangerous." "It indicates the painstaking efforts of the pro-integration people to plant sympathizers in key positions on our college campuses, where they can exert a maximum influence on student opinion," the Sovereignty Commission report stated. The Commission was apparently oblivious to the paradox that its information came from a pro-segregation "informant planted on the staff of the *Atlanta Journal* who has had Barton under observation for some time."

"If the privately-financed Citizens' Councils want to hire spies to go around checking on people that is their affair as long as they can get away with it," Smith wrote. "But when the state Sovereignty Commission, supported with all of our tax money to the tune of a $350,000 budget, starts cooperating with these spy activities of the Citizens' Council, then it is time to call an immediate halt." Other "free citizens of Mississippi" had suffered the same type of smear but remained silent for fear of reprisals or to maintain peace in the community, she wrote.

> But the time is here when the freedom of all Mississippi people is threatened by the Citizens' Councils and the state Sovereignty Commission—and there are few people who will deny it. It is time for everyone to speak out and oppose this violation of our basic rights and freedom as American citizens. This monstrous thing will destroy us and our state as we know and love it, if we do not summon the courage not only to lift our voices

in protest but to fight it with every honorable means at our disposal. Our freedom is being taken from us in Mississippi not by Communist Russia, Nazi Germany or any other totalitarian country or philosophy—but by our own home grown variety of fascism, Mississippi born and nurtured. It should also be destroyed here.

Sovereignty Commission investigator Tom Scarbrough's 29 March 1961 report on Holmes County, prepared two days before the editorial was published, stated, "Everyone whom I talked to considered Hazel Smith, a white female, a trouble maker and integrationist." Scarbrough and other Commission investigators would eventually accumulate more than 150 documents on Smith and her newspaper.

Smith celebrated her twenty-fifth anniversary in Mississippi journalism confronting an advertising boycott, smear campaigns, and a competing newspaper founded to drive her out of business. A full-page advertisement in the *Durant News* and *Lexington Advertiser*, "25 Years of Service to Holmes County" (3 August 1961), featured the editor's photograph and a "personal letter" to readers. "I do not take myself too seriously or fancy myself as a Savior of the people of Holmes County, or even your conscience," she confided. "I flinch every time I am called a 'crusading editor.' . . . But an honest editor who would truly serve the highest and best interest of the people will not compromise convictions to support a popular cause known to be morally wrong just to incur popular favor or support." A week later (10 August 1961) she announced a "tri-anniversary" celebration during 1961 and 1962 to mark her twenty-five years as editor, the 100th year of the *Durant News*, and the 125th anniversary of the *Lexington Advertiser*. In July 1961, Pulitzer Prize winner Hodding Carter, Jr., publisher of the *Delta Democrat-Times* in Greenville, formed the Tri-Anniversary Committee to raise money for the financially struggling newspapers. Other committee members were Ralph McGill of the *Atlanta Constitution*, Mark Ethridge of the Louisville, Kentucky, *Courier-Journal*, and J. N. Heiskell of the *Arkansas Gazette* in Little Rock.

The *St. Petersburg* (Florida) *Times* saluted with "admiration" Smith's twenty-five-year "fight for the people's right to know and for law and order" in a full-page layout in the *Advertiser* (19 October 1961). Two weeks later, the *Herald* responded with a front-page editorial, "Hodding Carter to Head Drive for Holmes County Publisher; NOW, THE TRUTH IS OUT, EACH STAND IS CLEAR" (9 November 1961). "A group of out-of-state agitators, masquerading as do-gooders and moderates have begun a fund-raising campaign to buy themselves a voice in Holmes County," the *Herald* stated. The editorial described Hodding Carter as an "editor who has made a profession of selling his writings on Mississippi's racial problems to left-wing publications whose equally profiteering owners and editors describe them as 'journalistic masterpieces,' because he agrees with their warped views about his home people." On 30 November 1961, the *Herald* published a seven-column front page headline, "*Lexington Advertiser, Durant News* Receiving Assistance from Member of Top Communist Front Organization." Nelson Poynter, publisher of the *St. Petersburg Times*, was a member of a citizens' group that the U.S. House of Representatives' Special Committee on Un-American Activities in 1944 labeled "the major Communist front organization of the moment," the *Herald* reported. "This information should provide a matter of serious concern for every thinking citizen of our county." Other advertisements bearing the Tri-Anniversary logo and saluting the Cancer Society (6 November 1961), Tuberculosis Association (21 December 1961), and March of Dimes (11 January 1962) appeared—"made possible by friends of the editor."

A rancorous personal exchange between Smith and *Herald* editor Shearer filled the pages of the *Advertiser* and *Herald* in November 1961. A "Personal to Jack Shearer" in her 9 November 1961 column accused him of "taking our paper from the post office, as you well know" and "copying my stories, too." The next week, she objected to Shearer's article about the Tri-Anniversary Committee, especially that "integrationists" had bought a voice in Holmes County and that the publisher had "lost more than half her advertising revenues." "We hate to call Jack a liar this week after calling him a thief last week," she wrote (16 November 1961), "but that is exactly what we must do." Shearer's "Personal Message to Mrs. Hazel Smith" on 23 November 1961 objected to the imputation of the *Herald* being operated by "bosses." The "real would-be boss of Holmes County is yourself," he wrote. "Although you have lost practically all of your support here . . . you have accepted the support of four wealthy and powerful editors who are in the forefront of the move to integrate the South, and for some time now, the columns of your newspaper have been reflecting their views." The *Lexington Advertiser*'s editorial six months earlier, "Must Racial Turmoil Come to Mississippi?" (13 April 1961), recommended "repealing all of the statutory laws on the books that require forced segregation." The removal of "discriminatory laws" would create "no great upheaval in local customs and traditions," she wrote. "Racial preference would still prevail. Discriminating Negroes prefer their own kind just as discriminating white people do."

A sworn affidavit in the Sovereignty Commission files stoked the engine of a "vicious statewide smear campaign" against Smith that reached the floor of the Mississippi legislature, according to the *Lexington Advertiser* (11 January 1962) and United Press International (*Clarion-Ledger*, 5 January 1962). The Mississippi Citizens' Councils in Greenwood mailed copies of a 2 January 1962 affidavit in which Sovereignty Commission agents swore they saw Smith and her husband meeting with "Negro integration leaders" at the office of the *Mississippi Free Press*, "a new liberal Negro newspaper," on Lynch Street in Jackson on 15 December 1961. Former Hinds County Sheriff and Sovereignty Commission Director Albert Jones and A. L. "Andy" Hopkins, a commission investigator, swore before Secretary of State Heber Ladner that the editor had met with NAACP Field Representative Medgar Evers and "two or three other Negroes." The affidavit, accompanied by a photocopy of the 10 December 1961 edition of the *Mississippi Free Press*, reportedly was sent to all the state's newspapers and to members of the legislature. *Herald* shareholder and State Senator T. M. Williams of Lexington told his colleagues in a speech from the Senate floor that copies also were sent to "all residents of Holmes County." "If you read her newspaper you would know why we have the attitude we do toward her," Williams told the Senate (*Clarion-Ledger*, 5 January 1962). "We are no longer proud of her paper. By reading the affidavit you will understand the problems we have."

In the *Lexington Advertiser*'s front page account of the "smear campaign" (11 January 1962), Smith explained that the *Mississippi Free Press* was printed at the *Lexington Advertiser* print shop. The alleged meeting with "integration leaders," Smith wrote, was merely a delivery of newspapers. "The purpose of this affidavit was to make it appear that I was meeting and consorting with Negro integration leaders," she wrote. "Therein lies the smear. . . . There was no 'meeting' at the *Mississippi Free Press* office. . . . Nor has there been an integration meeting anywhere else at any time attended by us." Smith said that Senator Williams and State Rep. Wilburn Hooker of Lexington, a member of the Sovereignty Commission and the Citizens' Councils State Executive Committee, were two of the "principal organizers" of the Citizens' Council in Holmes County. She charged that they had teamed up to organize and to support the *Holmes County Herald* to "put me out of business simply because I will not take orders from or be controlled by Holmes County bosses, foremost of whom is Hooker."

In an accompanying editorial, "State Gestapo Rule, Personal and Press Freedom Are at Stake" (11 January 1962), Smith called for abolishing the Sovereignty Commission and state funding of the Citizens' Council. The "unholy combination" of the Sovereignty Commission's "statewide network of paid spies" and the "vicious and dictatorial Citizens' Council (which tries to destroy anyone who does not conform totally and absolutely to its line)" was a "menace to every citizen," she wrote, and "no less dreaded and feared than the Gestapo of Hitler's Germany and the paid informers of the Communist conspiracy." She pleaded for "spiritual values" that required racial problems be solved "on a basis of Christian charity and fair play." "We cannot hold down more than 42 per cent of our entire state population without staying down ourselves," she wrote, "and all intelligent people know it."

Governor Ross Barnett's strident defiance of a federal court order to admit James Meredith and to integrate the University of Mississippi created "rebellion and open insurrection" when federal troops occupied the Oxford campus to enforce the order and to quell rioting that killed two people, Smith wrote on 4 October 1962. "No infant now living will ever see the day when the stain is completely removed from the name of our once proud state." The rioting and bloodshed would have a long-standing and far reaching impact on Mississippi's image. "We must face the unpleasant fact that now we are largely regarded throughout the civilized world as an ignorant, narrow, bigoted, intolerant, people with little or no regard for human rights and Christian values." A report on the Oxford riots, issued by six members of a Mississippi General Legislative Committee—"all close friends and supporters of Governor Ross Barnett"—accusing U.S. marshals of "cruel and inhuman treatment of rioters" and other "shocking atrocities," reads like "something out of a Nazi war diary," she commented (2 May 1963).

Violence and bloodshed exploded in Holmes County in May 1963 when Tchula farmer Hartman Turnbow's house was firebombed and when World War II navy veteran Alfred Brown was killed on the streets of Lexington a month later. Three white men reportedly fired about fifteen rounds of .45 caliber bullets into Turnbow's home and tossed several "Molotov cocktails" into the living room and bedroom in the early morning hours of 8 May 1963 while his wife and sixteen-year-old daughter were sleeping, according to the *Advertiser* (9 May 1963). The reprisal came because Turnbow had tried to register to vote. The constable who investigated the incident reportedly told Turnbow that he had been keeping "the wrong kind of company with them outside agitators." The *Advertiser* editorially called the bombing a "vicious act." When Turnbow was arrested the same day for arson in the firebombing of his own home, Smith was incredulous. "It is not moral or just that any man should live in fear, or be compelled to sleep with a loaded gun by his bedside," she wrote on 16 May 1963. The *Holmes County Herald* barely noticed, except for an editorial, "Who's Excited?" (9 May 1963), that called the incident "a trumped up affair" by "outside agitators" who sought to get "local negroes" fired up for a renewed voter registration effort. "There is no news story in this paper concerning the incident," the *Herald* stated. "There is nothing newsworthy about it. We say, let 'em throw their gasoline and have their fun.... All this fuss takes up too much of the time of our law enforcement officers and this newspaper. We've got better things to do!" Brown, recently released from a Veteran's Hospital where he had been treated for mental illness, was shot twice on 8 June 1963 by two Lexington police officers who tried to arrest him on suspicion of being intoxicated, the *Advertiser* reported on 13 June 1963. The Brown killing was "senseless," a front page editorial proclaimed on 13 June 1963, and could have been avoided by "officers who either knew or cared for what they were doing." The "unprovoked arrest on a false and baseless charge" required "an honest and complete investigation," Smith wrote, "and no 'whitewash' attempted."

The murder of NAACP Field Secretary Medgar Evers was not only a "reprehensible crime against the laws of God and man," she wrote in a 13 June 1963 editorial, but also "an ignorant product of our sick, hate-filled society. Thus far it has been only a segment of our white community that has succumbed to hate. God help us when the Negro starts hating in Mississippi. . . . Time is running out for us here in the Magnolia State." The trial of Byron De La Beckwith for Evers' murder focused world attention on Jackson, Smith commented on 27 June 1963, because the civil rights activist was "more than a man—he was the living symbol of all the hopes and aspirations of Mississippi Negroes in their long struggle to throw off the shackles of discrimination existing in state law and custom." After the second mistrial in the Evers case, a sign on U.S. Highway 49 in Holmes County proclaimed "Welcome Home De la." "This crude effort to make a hero out of Beckwith is disgraceful," she wrote on 23 April 1964, "and should be an affront to every decent citizen of the state."

Hodding Carter, Jr., nominated Smith for the Pulitzer Prize in 1962 and his son, Hodding Carter III, associate publisher of the *Delta Democrat-Times*, followed with a nomination in 1963. In May 1964, Columbia University announced that Smith had won the Pulitzer Prize, the first woman to receive the prize for editorial writing. The Pulitzer committee cited her "steadfast adherence to her editorial duties in the face of great pressure and opposition." She told the Memphis, Tennessee, *Commercial Appeal* (4 May 1964), "I run my newspapers in the way I think they should be run . . . for the public interest. . . . My fight has been to defend and protect the freedom of all Mississippians to say and do what they want to do without taking dictation from the White Citizens' Council, the Ku Klux Klan or any other extremist organization." A week after winning the prize, Smith's column of 14 May 1964 observed, "Yesterday people may have fled in terror before the flaming cross carried by a hooded knight. Today a loaded shotgun by the bed is standard equipment in most every Mississippi hut and hamlet—and the hoodlum who comes to terrorize is more apt to get his hood blown off—and with it his head." She again reminded readers on 14 January 1965, "We had never advocated school integration at the time of the 1954 high court decision (nor since for that matter)."

NBC hired the Pulitzer Prize winner to cover the Democratic National Convention in August 1964. While she was in Atlantic City, New Jersey, a homemade bomb exploded in the *Northside Reporter*, a suburban

Jackson weekly she had purchased in 1956. Jackson Mayor Allen Thompson denounced the "criminal act" and announced a $1,000 reward for the arrest and conviction of those responsible. Upon her return, Smith published a front-page signed letter headlined "To the Person or Persons Responsible for the Bombing of the *Northside Reporter*" (3 September 1964). "If, by your cowardly deed, you hope to kill this newspaper, I tell you now—you are doomed to failure," Smith wrote. "It takes more than the sneak act of a criminal to destroy a free and independent press. A hundred bombs will not stop our publication. If, by chance, it was your purpose to frighten, harass, or intimidate, you'd better think again."

A month later, Smith blamed prejudiced law enforcement officials and Mississippi newspapers' "erroneous and irresponsible reporting, false information and downright malice" for the "reign of terror." "Literally hundreds of incidents . . . have never been reported in any newspaper of the state," she wrote (1 October 1964). "We have been convinced for some time the great mass of white people—the so-called good people of the state—don't actually know what is happening. We believe if they did the climate of public opinion would change overnight. . . . Our state will be literally destroyed if the newspapers of Mississippi and the law enforcement officials don't wake up and start working together for the common public good."

The Pulitzer Prize catapulted Smith into a national spotlight, the notoriety providing a springboard to bolster her sagging finances through speaking tours to raise money to keep her newspapers afloat. The advertising boycott had taken a severe toll. She was $80,000 in debt, she told the *New York Herald-Tribune* (10 May 1964), and had mortgaged personal property, cut her staff, and continued borrowing to keep her newspaper afloat. A year later, Smith was reportedly $150,000 in debt, "a respectable amount to be in debt, I think," she told the Patterson, New Jersey, *Call* on 10 November 1965, "but I'm not about to go under. I've been livin' on faith for 11 years, and, God willin', I can keep on that way until the decent people of Mississippi stop being immobilized by fear." She sold the *Northside Reporter* in 1973 and, four years later, discontinued the *Banner County Outlook* in Flora, a weekly she had acquired in 1955.

In 1966, thirty years after Smith's arrival in Mississippi, Holmes County voters legalized the sale of whiskey, the issue that had launched one of her first editorial campaigns. A month later, 130 Negro students enrolled "quietly and without incident" in Lexington's public schools, prompting a front-page editorial, "I Am So Proud of Lexington" (15 September 1966). "This facing up to reality, this courageous stand for the preservation of the public schools, deserves the highest commendation and encouragement of all people interested in the future of our community and county," Smith wrote, admonishing readers to remember a "little rule" that would offer "the solution to any and all of our problems: 'Do unto others as you would have them do unto you.'" She took a decidedly less benign view of the "little rule" eight months earlier when an anonymous late-night caller threatened "some excitement out there" at her home. She responded to the threat with a "public notice and fair warning" in her column of 17 February 1966. "The first one that put his foot on my home grounds would have been shot dead," she wrote. "The same goes for any future intruders—stay away from my home if you don't want to get killed."

The Civil Rights Act of 1964 altered the segregated dynamics of Holmes County politics. Four years later, Robert Clark of Holmes County was elected to the Mississippi legislature, the first black legislator since Reconstruction. Smith took no small credit for his election, perhaps a deliberate effort to reinforce the crusader-for-racial-justice image that had emerged by then as a popular and well-established legend. "I personally am responsible for that . . . I made certain that he got elected," she said at a fifteen-year retrospective on the press and civil rights held at Tougaloo College on 1 November 1979. In the 1970s, Holmes County's newly registered black citizens gained political power and won public offices, electing a black sheriff, superintendent of education, tax assessor, election commissioners and county supervisor. With black political power in the ascendancy in Holmes County, fewer whites, including Smith, were needed to defend their civil rights and speak up for them. "It was almost like a child coming of age who no longer needs his mother," Bruce Hill, who became publisher of the *Holmes County Herald* in the early 1970s, told the *Chicago Tribune* (27 March 1986). "Hazel was a great help to blacks for a long time, but they developed their own leadership. It was another era, and they didn't need her. It wasn't really rejection, but she didn't understand." Indeed, times had changed. The Hazel Brannon Smith who in the

1960s was praised for heroic editorializing about justice for all was criticized at the Tougaloo conference in 1979 for failing to address in the pages of her newspaper the integration of Lexington's churches, doctor's clinics, and country clubs.

Smith continued to borrow money to keep publishing the struggling *Advertiser* and to finance construction of "Hazelwood," her 14-room Greek-revival mansion on the outskirts of Lexington. Her health deteriorated, her behavior erratic, her memory fitful—signals later recognized to be the onset of Alzheimer's disease. The last edition of the *Lexington Advertiser* appeared on 19 September 1985. Two weeks earlier, the *Holmes County Herald* published a legal notice that she had filed for bankruptcy. The *Clarion-Ledger* reported on its 5 January 1986 front page that she owed more than $250,000, including a $34,000 printing bill. Her bankruptcy case was dismissed in November 1985 "after she lost her way from Lexington and did not appear at a mandatory court hearing in Jackson," the *Clarion-Ledger* reported. Banks repossessed Hazelwood; her furniture was auctioned. In February 1986, Smith's sister took her back to Gadsden, Alabama, forgotten and penniless.

In 1993, the 79-year-old Pulitzer Prize winner was named the recipient of the Fannie Lou Hamer Award at a ceremony at Jackson State University, even though many thought she had already died. She continued to suffer from Alzheimer's disease in a nursing home in Cleveland, Tennessee, where her niece was director of nursing. In April 1994, "A Passion for Justice: The Hazel Brannon Smith Story," a made-for-television movie that included several fictional elements, aired in prime time on the ABC television network. Smith and her family never gave approval for the film, and she never received any payment for the rights to her life story, a fact that prompted Mississippi political columnist Bill Minor, a longtime friend, to pen a scathing commentary in the *Clarion-Ledger* on 24 April 1994. "Considering the millions of dollars involved in the Hollywood production and the ABC network . . . there is a serious matter of righteousness and decency (if not legality) that Hazel should receive some financial benefits," Minor wrote. "More so, it is incredible that Hollywood is trading in big bucks on Hazel's life while she exists a ward of the government." Even though the film portrayed her as being more heroic than she actually was and her courage in opposing "organized bigotry" never earned the respect it deserved, he said, "she paid a high price back then, and it's wrong for Hollywood to get a free ride now."

Smith, 80, died of cancer at a Cleveland, Tennessee, nursing home on Saturday, 14 May 1994, and she was buried at Forrest Cemetery in her hometown of Gadsden, Alabama.

An epitaph to Smith's fifty-year career in Mississippi journalism can be written in terms of the Progressive ethos. The old-time religion of conservative Protestant moral fundamentalism that informed so much of American Progressivism does more to explain Smith's editorial legacy than any conversion to a new-found faith in the liberal agenda of the civil rights revolution. In the 1940s, her muckraking campaign against bootlegging and gambling was prototypically Progressive, exhorting respectable establishment leaders—sheriff, prosecutor, judge—to enforce the law and to defend Holmes County against an alien corruption that threatened to defile the small-town mythos of decency, order, and sobriety.

Her advocacy of truth, justice, and equality under the law never constituted an outright endorsement of integration. Law and order co-existed uneasily with her repeated belief in "our Southern traditions and racial segregation." Support for law and order without challenging unconstitutional racial segregation posed a paradox that Smith neither recognized nor resolved. "The Law Should Be for All," the oft-cited turning point in the salvation narrative, was actually grounded in "a Christian faith in God and the idea that man is made in the image of God" that required equal application of secular justice for everyone. The charge that she had consorted with Negro integration leaders, including Medgar Evers, was vigorously rebuffed as a "vicious smear," while Evers' murder could still be viewed as a "reprehensible crime against the laws of God and man." She took pride in the integration of Lexington's public schools in 1966, not for any profound conviction in the morality of integration but because the public schools had been preserved through obedience to the laws of God and man—without resort to violence—and she editorially reminded readers of their moral obligation in biblical terms, "Do unto others as you would have them do unto you."

Smith's editorials calling for abolition of the Citizens' Councils and Sovereignty Commission were a Progressive assault on the demagoguery of respectable people in the community who were acting as "bosses" in an "unholy combination" to deprive citizens of their freedom much as the turn-of-the-century muckrakers attacked the trusts and their conspiratorial ringleaders. The Citizens' Councils and Sovereignty Commission created in Mississippi a home-grown Third Reich whose paid spies and "dictatorial" demands for conformity spread lawlessness, she complained, and the "reign of terror" was every bit as dreadful as "the Gestapo of Hitler's Germany." The silence of the "so-called good people of the state," fearful in the face of repressive and totalitarian evil, in her editorial equation, was the moral equivalent of being a "good German." The "decent people" of Mississippi had a moral responsibility to speak out against the lawlessness, violence, and terror that threatened everyone's freedom—whites and blacks. If they wouldn't do it, by God, she would.

The rhetorical ploy of her conservative Progressive voice consistently rejected the labels of "crusading editor," "woman of conscience," and "Savior of the people of Holmes County." She told the *Christian Science Monitor* (6 July 1966), "You finally come to a point when you must decide whether you're for law and order or against it."

References

Hofstadter, Richard. *The Age of Reform*. (New York: Knopf, 1955).

Mississippi State Sovereignty Commission files. Mississippi Department of Archives and History. Jackson, Mississippi.

Newman, Mark. "Hazel Brannon Smith and Holmes County, Mississippi, 1936–1964: The Making of a Pulitzer Prize Winner." *Journal of Mississippi History* (February 1992).

Hodding Carter, Jr., and the *Delta Democrat-Times*

Ginger Rudeseal Carter

Best known as the longtime owner, publisher and editor of the *Delta Democrat-Times*, William Hodding Carter, Jr., has received international and critical attention for his editorial work during the civil rights era. Carter wrote and edited his newspaper in the Delta city of Greenville, Mississippi, his home for most of his adult life; he remained publisher until his death in 1972.

For years, the mythology surrounding Carter has cast him as an avid supporter of the civil rights movement. His biographer Ann Waldron suggested that Carter was a "reconstructed racist," one who had turned against hatred and who embraced equal rights for all. United Press International reported in Carter's 4 April 1972 obituary that Carter "steadfastly took strong stands on matters as he saw them, with particular regard for racial relations, both North and South."

Hodding Carter, Jr., in fact, was a man caught in the middle of a struggle that impacted his daily life and livelihood. Strongly committed to human rights as promised by the U.S. Constitution, yet steadfastly centered in the Mississippi planter culture, which embraced the Old South belief in white superiority, Carter's stands on civil rights put him squarely in the middle between black Mississippians pushing for change and whites opposing it. As deeply committed to his hometown and Mississippi as to his convictions, he was pained by the backlash against his editorial stands even as he steadfastly and sincerely defended them. Son Hodding III pointed out in correspondence,

> Dad alternated between trying to pretend that "our town is different" to the degree that he did not have to rise above anything there, to being certain his enemies were going to succeed in their unremitting campaign to destroy him. He hated being seen as the enemy within almost as much as he hated the bigotry, the overt racism, the dehumanizing results of segregation, the corrupted political process produced by rigid adherence to white supremacy as the guiding principle of principles. That sense of forced alienation was something he resisted from start to finish, but the effort cost him a great deal.

As Jean Folkerts noted in her 1993 *Dictionary of Literary Biography* depiction of Carter, "He took seriously the role of editor as reformer or advocate of change" (p. 21). Carter began his professional newspaper career in New Orleans fighting for the rights of unjustly fired colleagues; he later fought the political machine of Huey Long. His editorials on racial tolerance in 1945 won him the Pulitzer Prize in 1946.

Through the 1950s, Carter consistently supported the rights of black Americans in their civil rights struggle, though he stopped far short of defending integration. That Carter—a white Southern man—publicly took such positions was unusual, if not unheard of, in his era. That he did it in a leading, predominantly white Mississippi newspaper was dangerous, both to his health and his paper's existence. In fact, Hodding III told a newspaper reporter a week after his father's death that the ten-year period from 1955 to 1965—the height of the civil rights era—was the most volatile in his father's career. "He never let up," he recalled, "and neither did the threats."

This is the conundrum that is central to understanding the life and work of Hodding Carter, Jr. He was more lenient and vocal about issues of equality than most Mississippians, but he never went far enough in his advocacy of black Mississippians to satisfy civil rights advocates. This tug-of-war continued throughout the civil rights movement.

One thing is clear: Carter went further in his support of human rights issues than most white Southern editors dared to go, and he earned a national reputation and following to a degree unmatched by any other Mississippi journalist during the civil rights era. Journalists around the world, cognizant of his courage in trying conditions, held him in high esteem. Other editors profiled in this volume, particularly Hazel Brannon Smith, found Carter to be an inspiration and a help in her own newspaper struggle. As son Hodding III wrote in personal correspondence,

> He was in fact a person who served as a role model for that handful of white Southern editors who wanted to help break the South from its past without destroying their newspapers in the process. He was correctly seen as brave as hell, a believer in the duties of a free press, and a white Southerner buffeted incessantly by the demand for conformity imposed by white society. Anyone who could and did rise above that was bound to be—should have been—an inspiration to others.

Carter used this influence to explain life in the white South to the rest of the country, urging restraint and deliberation instead of civil disobedience—once again, remaining in the middle of the fray. This cautious approach was evident throughout his reporting career at the United Press and Associated Press, and in his editorship of newspapers in Hammond, Louisiana, and Greenville, Mississippi.

This chapter will examine Carter's struggle as well as his international influence as a writer, speaker, and editor during the middle of the twentieth century. His courage impacted citizens, journalists, and editors, but the backlash against his editorial stands also exacted deep personal tolls on Carter, a man caught squarely in the middle.

Hodding Carter, Jr., was born 3 February 1907 in Hammond, Louisiana, to William Hodding and Irma Dutatre Carter. He learned to read at age five, skipped grades one through three to begin his formal education in grade four, and graduated from Hammond High School as "the best, the top boy, in every sense" at sixteen. Carter idolized his parents, especially his father, Will. In "An Unforgettable Character," published in *First Person Rural* (1963), Carter recalled his father's community standing.

> During his service as a police juror, I heard two men whom I didn't know describe a third. "He's as honest," said one of the third, "as Will Carter." I think that is why in 1940 Dad got the biggest percentage of votes in the state when he ran for state legislature as an anti-Long candidate—his only real venture in politics—in the fateful election when the Louisiana voters unshackled themselves, for a time, from Longism and corrupt tyranny. (p. 9)

Carter idolized his father and wanted to be seen as one who made a difference to the community, much as his father had. He began to carve that niche for himself at Bowdoin College in Brunswick, Maine.

In *Hodding Carter: The Reconstruction of a Racist* (1993), the only existing book-length Carter biography, Ann Waldron wrote that Carter was "a racist when he entered Bowdoin College" in fall 1923" (p. 1). Carter evidenced racial prejudice, which he himself said was indicative of his upbringing. Waldron noted that Carter went to great lengths to avoid a black student, moving into a different dorm room to distance himself. He wrote an article for the Bowdoin *Quill* in December 1924 entitled "Prejudices" intended "to defend his racial views" (p. 4). In 1926, Carter became editor of the *Quill*, writing poetry and fiction for the magazine. Waldron noted that "Hodding's fiction in college foreshadowed his later journalism. It was sentimental, moralistic, often deeply passionate, sometimes very witty, just as nearly everything he would write later in his life would be" (p. 9).

Carter wrote that his four years at Bowdoin irrevocably changed him. He attributed his "great awakening" to a liberal arts education that forced him to think. "They introduced me to divine reason," Carter wrote. In the 1955 column "The Liberal Arts and The Bill of Rights," reprinted in *First Person Rural* (1963), he wrote of his upbringing, especially his reaction to the Ku Klux Klan, an earlier writing subject.

> I did not place the Klan in contradiction to the first article of the Bill of Rights, which guarantees to all Americans freedom of religion and speech and press.
>
> In that year, 1923, thirty-three persons—twenty-nine black

and four white—died by the lynch mob's rope and bullet and faggot. In my four college years, 112 human beings were similarly to die, most of them Negros, most of them in my homeland. Earlier in my boyhood, I had seen the inert body of a lynch victim. The specter has never altogether vanished. But I am sure then the Louisiana freshman at Bowdoin College did not relate that specter or the ghastly total to that article in the Bill of Rights which declares that no American should be deprived of life or liberty without due process of law. (p. 49)

Carter wrote that at Bowdoin, he discovered "that a man who differs with you—in ideas, in race, in politics, in creed—is not necessarily or even likely to be a scoundrel" (p. 51).

Carter graduated from Bowdoin in 1927—though he and his family would return regularly to Maine from 1945 on, when they bought a home there—and went to England to visit relatives. He then enrolled in Columbia University's School of Journalism from 1927 to 1928; according to Waldron, he never became a public figure as he had at Bowdoin. He did not write for the campus newspaper, and he did not stand out among his classmates. He left Columbia for Tulane, where he received a teaching assistantship in English (p. 23).

At Tulane, Carter met Betty Werlein, a friend of his sister Corrine. Carter had set his sights on a Rhodes Scholarship, but love of Betty changed his mind. Waldron wrote that he did not think Betty would wait for him, so he never left (p. 31). Instead, he took a $12.50 a week job at the New Orleans *Tribune*. From there, he joined the United Press bureau in New Orleans, only to quit in defense of a colleague's reputation. This episode left Carter temporarily unemployed, since New Orleans newspapers did not hire anyone fired by a competitor. But it also marked the first time Carter spoke out publicly against injustice and suffered as a result. Here he was emulating his father and laying a foundation for his work as a journalist in the South.

By 1931, Carter had landed a $50-a-week position as the day manager of the Associated Press bureau in Jackson, Mississippi. Two weeks later, on 14 October 1932, he and Betty were married. At the AP, Carter's young career and reputation got another test when the news agency dismissed him in 1932. According to his own account, Carter had not followed directions and was fired for insubordination by his division chief, stationed in New Orleans. Carter described the importance of this event to him and his young bride in "First, Get Fired," in *Where Main Street Meets the River*. His letter of dismissal deeply affected him.

> But the writer . . . had added another paragraph which hit me low in the stomach. I had some good qualities, he wrote, but I would never make a newspaperman, and I ought not to waste any time getting into another business. I had been a newspaperman all of three years, and with the Associated Press six months when the letter came. Betty and I had been married five months. . . . His letter was the most helpful I ever received. (p. 4)

The firing spurred the Carters to strike out on their own. As he explained in "First, Get Fired," the couple bought a ramshackle press and started their own newspaper, the tabloid Hammond *Daily Courier*, in Carter's hometown. His father, Will Carter, provided signatures for loans and other financial and moral support. The young couple spent their last $367 on the press, and a new career began. They entered an industry as "two jobless young people who started their first newspaper almost in desperation, in a year of abysmal economic depression and in a place where the first American dictatorship burgeoned in fear and evil." In Hammond the Carters took on the Kingfish himself, Huey Long, in the spring of 1932. The event that had led them to Hammond—Carter's dismissal by the AP—became a badge of courage and honor, and the editor's quick recovery following it was typical of him.

Waldron called early issues of the Hammond *Daily Courier* "lively, sometimes passionate, but often silly" (p. 42). Through the next four years hard work, good friends, cooperative advertisers, and a lot of luck kept the paper open and running. Throughout their time in Hammond, the Carters fought the Long machine, and it was one such protest that got Carter his first national attention. In summer 1934 *Literary Digest* called Carter "one of the most articulate of the Louisiana newspapermen fighting Long" (p. 58). The exposure led Carter to write a series of articles for *The*

New Republic about the Long regime. The article, "Kingfish to Crawfish," was published 24 January 1934. This and subsequent articles brought Carter national attention—and infuriated Long. Long was so enraged, according to Folkerts in her *Dictionary of Literary Biography* essay, that he removed Will Carter from the Board of Trustees of Southeastern Louisiana College. Long also refused to make the *Daily Courier* the city's legal organ. When Long was assassinated in 1935, Carter urged a return to democracy in the state, but the Long machine remained in place (p. 21).

In 1935, only a few months after the death of Carter's mother, Irma, his and Betty's first son, Hodding III, was born. His arrival was announced in a page one article.

Folkerts wrote that Carter's brave stand against Long attracted the attention of "paternalistic, although reform-minded Mississippians," who lured him to Greenville, Mississippi, with enough capital to start a newspaper there. After selling the *Daily Courier*, Carter and his young family moved to the city he would call his home until his death in 1972. In 1936, Carter established the *Delta Star*, competing with the *Daily Democrat-Times*.

The next ten years were filled with excitement and change, both personally and professionally. Carter continued to "make waves," editorializing in the *Delta Star* against lynchings and mob violence. In 1937, he ran a front-page photograph of Olympic athlete Jesse Owens, a move that was unheard of in Southern newspapers, which routinely refused to publish pictures of black people. The action was met with criticism and cancelled subscriptions, but Carter insisted he was doing what was right for journalism's sake, not for any other reason. Carter answered his critics in an editorial. "Jesse Owens is a remarkable athlete. And so we printed his picture," Carter wrote, according to Waldron. "We'll print it again when we feel like it" (p. 79). This move was decidedly bold and is an early example of how Carter stepped out in front on a key issue of race. But it is significant that the subject—Jesse Owens—was a national, not a local figure; it would be years before he made similar, and riskier, moves in his paper for local blacks.

In 1938, on the advice of his benefactors—especially William Alexander Percy—Carter bought the *Democrat-Times*, merging it with his own paper into the *Delta Democrat-Times*. In Greenville, Folkerts wrote, Carter's editorial stance on race relations "placed him to the left of the majority" of the "well-educated, conservative, entrepreneurial Delta planter faction" and in the middle of a struggle. He was representative, as Folkerts wrote, of "the style of editor who believes that journalists belong to a community and ha(s) a responsibility to move the cultural and business climate toward cautious, yet progressive, reform" (p. 22). In other words, Carter took stands on racial issues far beyond what his white readers would have preferred, risking income for the newspaper as well as his reputation. His guiding principle was that a newspaper should cover the news of the community in a way that represents the entire community while opposing what undermines the community. Or, as Carter wrote in the first issue of the *Delta Democrat-Times*, "We aspire to be the spokesman for the best that is thought and done in the South," Folkerts wrote (p. 22). Carter's national reputation continued to grow as he attacked Mississippi Sen. Theodore Bilbo, much in the same way he had fought the Long machine. This battle lasted into the 1940s.

In 1939, Carter applied for a Nieman Fellowship at Harvard University. Waldron wrote that Carter was making $150 a week in Greenville (p. 94). Carter joined the second class in 1940 for the remainder of the year after the birth of son Philip delayed his arrival. On leave from the *Delta Democrat-Times*, needing rejuvenation, Carter said the time was "the most satisfying time of my life as a newspaperman; and directly or indirectly it led to most of the agreeable happenings of the next ten years" (p. 121). What he did not say was the fellowship added to his national reputation as a journalist. The Nieman fellows were a special class of men, the "cream of the crop" in the newspaper field. The fellowship gave Carter the credentials, and perhaps the courage, to stick with editorial stands in support of improved race relations. If he did not find an audience in Mississippi, he had the credentials to write nationally.

Carter recalled that a Nieman friendship with publisher Ralph Ingersoll led him to go to work for *P.M.*, an advertising-free daily newspaper in New York City. He remained only for the summer, adding, "Betty and I were ready to go home." He did not think he could work for someone else and longed to return to edit his own newspaper. Because of savvy financial dealings in 1938, the Carters owned controlling shares of the *Delta Democrat-Times*; Carter ultimately returned as editor (p. 105).

Though Percy felt Carter lacked the temperament to be a small-town editor, the men agreed to disagree, and Carter wrote admiringly of his mentor in *Where Main Street Meets the River*. In "Gentleman Unafraid," Carter noted Percy's philosophy.

> "You can't do anything on a grand scale," he wrote of Percy's advice. "But when [the war] comes to an end, you can work again for your own people in your own way. It isn't national leaders we need so much as men of good will in each of the little towns of America. So try to keep Greenville a decent place by being a correct citizen yourself. The total of all the Greenvilles will make the kind of country we want or don't want." (p. 78)

Once again, Carter had emulated a man of character—in this case, Will Percy. Both the Wills in his life—Carter and Percy—helped shape Carter into an editor who questioned authority and fought for the rights of the average citizen. This standard would crystallize during the next ten years. But his efforts would require a constant struggle with his community and his state.

Only a few months later, Carter was called to active duty for World War II. Although he was older—33—with a wife and children, he wanted to serve. A Louisiana National Guard member since 1938, Carter was commissioned into the U.S. Army as a second lieutenant. (And as with other important times of his life, he wrote about it in "Us Mississippi Dragons," an account of how his guard unit was prepared for war.) For the next five years, Waldron wrote, Carter served as a public affairs liaison, editing the Middle East editions of *Yank* and *Stars and Stripes* and eventually rising to the rank of major (p. 109).

In 1941, an accident changed Carter's life. His right eye had been injured some time earlier while on maneuvers; he soon developed a scar on his retina, rendering the eye useless. The late diagnosis had ruined the eye—Carter had no central vision from 1941 on—and it would plague Carter for the rest of his life (p. 117). After the Japanese bombed Pearl Harbor, Betty joined the war effort, working for the Office of War Information as a writer and researcher in Washington. After his overseas deployment, Carter was stationed at the Pentagon and joined his wife and sons. Because of the damage to his right eye, Carter retired from the service with disability pay of $2,500 a year. On 28 March 1945, their third son, Thomas, was born.

He and Betty returned to Greenville at the end of the summer of 1945, and he resumed editorship of the *Delta Democrat-Times* after a stock struggle with the company that had been managing it during the war. The Carters were victorious, Waldron wrote, and with Hodding's return, "the editorials, which had been as limp as Pink Smith's, came back to life." The Carters were home (p. 150).

Without question, Hodding Carter returned from the war a well-known success in his profession. By the time of his fortieth birthday in 1947, two years after his return from World War II, Carter had won the equivalent of journalism's Triple Crown. First had come the Nieman fellowship. Then, upon his return from the war in 1945, he won a $2,500 Guggenheim Fellowship for creative writing. Then, in 1946, he won the Pulitzer Prize for editorial writing.

The 1946 Pulitzer was awarded for a series of columns written in 1945 after World War II; the Pulitzer board commended Carter for his writing "on the subject of racial, religious, and economic intolerance." Columns on local war heroes and patriotism were included in the package of entries, but one column, called "Go for Broke," advocated fairer treatment of Japanese-Americans, whose sons had fought for the United States and who were returning from battle.

> The loyal Nisei have shot the works. From the beginning of the war, they have been on trial, in and out of uniform, in army camps and relocation centers, as combat troops in Europe and as frontline interrogators, propagandists, and combat intelligence personnel in the Pacific where their capture meant prolonged and hideous torture. And even yet they have not satisfied their critics.
>
> It is so easy for a dominant race to explain good or evil, patriotism or treachery, courage or cowardice in terms of skin color. So easy and so tragically wrong. Too many have committed that wrong against the loyal Nisei, who by the thousands

have proved themselves good Americans even while others of us, by our actions against them, have shown ourselves to be bad Americans. Nor is the end of this misconception in sight.

In writing about the Nisei, Carter defended human rights and dignity for a minority race, a position that held obvious parallels for his home state. When the Nisei column was singled out by the Pulitzer committee for its brave concern for human relations, Carter was automatically vested with credibility to continue writing what he was wanted. Son Hodding III wrote in correspondence that the Pulitzer Prize was crucial to his father's editorial influence on writers and editors around the country. "The Pulitzer obviously set him apart from the herd by its very imprimatur, and it came very early," the younger Carter recalled. "You can never underestimate the power of the Pulitzer, like attention from the *New York Times*, to set the agenda for New York-based book editors."

Yet, for all those who praised Carter's prize, there were those who demeaned it. According to Folkerts, the racist Sen. Bilbo, Carter's longtime nemesis, said "no self-respecting Southern white man would accept a prize given by a bunch of nigger-loving, Yankeefied Communists for editorials advocating the mongrelization of the races" (p. 23). At one of the proudest times of his life, Carter was again caught in the middle. While his journalistic peers honored him, the segregationist establishment of his home state vilified him.

In the early 1950s, Carter continued to write editorials that upset his community and defended human rights; testing the tide of the times, Carter wrote many pieces that dealt with the rights of black Americans in the South. One of the most controversial—and one that would set an editorial example for other Southern newspapers—was entitled "Mrs. Means a Married Woman." Carter told of one woman's request that the paper use the word "Mrs." when writing about a married black woman. Reprinted in the 1952 collection *Where Main Street Meets the River*, the 1951 column described Carter's quandary over this question of editorial policy of not adding courtesy titles to the names of black Americans. Carter said she asked that he omit her name in the future if he could not give her the courtesy title on her name. Carter wrote

> For behind her request was the persistent, long-unanswered demand that we—not just we of Mississippi or of the South, but the Western white people who are an amalgam of so many anciently blended bloods—recognize that what the darker people of the world require and must get from us is a recognition of their right to human dignity and self-respect. (p. 254)
>
> ... [A]m I more afraid of what some newspaper readers might say—I knew what some readers most certainly would say—than I am of this bursting resentment, this cascading protest of the people of color against our denial of dignity? I asked myself also: What have I got to be afraid of? Afraid that somebody will write or telephone us to cancel their subscriptions to a damned nigger-loving paper? Afraid of economic reprisal or social retaliation? Afraid that our usefulness in larger matters will be impaired by our violation of the taboo against permitting a Negro self-respect? (p. 255)

Carter's answer was no, of course, in his column, but he also wrote that he had polled his entire staff before he implemented the change. As he predicted, some readers canceled their subscriptions, but he noted that the repercussions were small. Indeed it was a gutsy move on Carter's part, but it's revealing to note his justification for the editorial change—this was a move of *human* dignity, not necessarily a move in support of black rights. He would word future editorials just as carefully.

The U.S. Supreme Court's decision banning segregation in public schools, *Brown v. Board of Education*, was announced on 17 May 1954. Carter responded by crying out, "It's about time," then he saw to the placement of a banner headline reading "School Segregation Is Held Illegal," Waldron wrote (p. 234). Folkerts called Carter a "voice out of the wilderness in Mississippi." Quoting his 20 May 1954 editorial on the decision, Folkerts wrote, "Carter continually called for caution." Carter chided those who sought to destroy the public school system as a means of avoiding desegregation. "If ever a region asked for such a decision," Carter declared, "the South did through its shocking, calculated, and cynical disobedience to its own state constitutions, which specify that separate schools systems must be equal." He continued,

For seventy-five years we sent Negro kids to schools in hovels and pig pens.... And if we are to effect workable and fair compromise at the local Southern levels we have to spend dollar for dollar all down the line, for every educable child.... Most Negroes want only the same opportunities for their children as we white people want for ours." (p. 25)

But Carter never called for integration of the schools, again keeping him squarely in the middle. He called for better treatment of blacks than Mississippi segregationists could stomach, but he stopped short of integration sought by blacks and ordered by the Supreme Court. Instead, he called for equalizing the conditions in separate schools, not merging them, seeing this as a human rights issue.

Son Hodding III called the editorial one his father's finest. "Dad's best editorials," he said, "were always the ones he wrote in response to specific outrages by human beings against human beings."

White Citizens' Councils began forming across the South following *Brown*, a direct reaction to the possibility of desegregation, and Carter was vehemently opposed to the organizations. Carter and his paper continued to examine in print the issues produced by the Court's decision, and he denounced the councils in print. Yet Carter stopped short of supporting integration; in fact, he never supported desegregation of any kind, much to the dismay of civil rights advocates across the country. Carter had, in fact, solidified his position on this issue as far back as a 26 January 1947 editorial in the *Delta Democrat-Times*. Folkerts noted that Carter explained his position for those who challenged him, writing that he was against any movement for social equality, terming it "unrealistic and dangerous" to the course of improved race relations. However, Folkerts wrote, Carter supported "equal justice, the condemnation of bigots, and raising the educational and economic standards of the Negro"; he urged "a sense of Christian responsibility to fellow men" (p. 21).

John Dittmer wrote in *Local People: The Struggle for Civil Rights in Mississippi* (1994) that black leaders often saw Carter's advice as condescending. While Carter hated acts of racial violence, Dittmer noted, he did not support an anti-lynching bill. Carter hated the condition of black schools, yet he did not support bringing blacks into white schools to equalize conditions. This is the conundrum of Hodding Carter. He wanted all humans of all races to have the rights promised them by the Bill of Rights, and he made this a lifelong platform of his newspaper. Tame as this may seem four decades later, his position went much further than white Mississippians were willing to go in the 1950s and 1960s. But Carter seemed far too timid to civil rights activists, who thought he should have used his editorial influence to support integration and other goals of the black rights movement.

So throughout the 1950s, Carter's writing—and that of his paper's news and editorial staff—produced angry reaction in Mississippi, including a poem called "The Fence Rider" disseminated by leaflet all over Greenville:

> There was a young man named Fodding Harter
> Who with his scrawlings replenishes his larder
> He is world renowned by liberals and pinks
> But with his homefolks, my he stinks.
> The Yankees think he speaks for the South
> But we all know he just runs his mouth
> He thinks he's a statesman and takes many trips
> You can rest assured he's well paid for his quips . . .
> Convicts and race mixers, you're their defender
> Service to the South you do not render
> You may write your books and ride your yacht
> But express Southern sentiments you do not

The silly poem angered Carter, who responded to it on his editorial page. Carter asked that his accusers do him the courtesy of identifying themselves. "They know where we work and where we live," Carter replied, according to Waldron. "We should have the same knowledge of them" (p. 241).

Carter aroused animosity with a 22 March 1955 article published in *Look* magazine titled "A Wave of Terrorism Threatens the South," describing the resurgence of the Ku Klux Klan. The same man who had defended the Klan to Northern students thirty years earlier had refocused his stand. The article prompted the Mississippi House of Representatives to resolve 88–19, with 32 abstaining, that Carter had lied about Mississippi and the South. Carter was on a hunting trip with friends when the House passed its resolution; Betty hired a crop duster to drop copies of the newspaper near his campsite. Carter penned an editorial reply in the woods and read it over the telephone to the newspaper. In a front-page column in the *Delta Democrat-Times* titled "Liar by Legislation," republished in *First Person Rural* (1963), Carter defended himself.

"It happened on April Fool's Day," Carter wrote. "But it wasn't a joke to me or to the majority of the Mississippi House of Representatives who, by formal resolution, voted on April 1, 1955 that I had lied, slandered the state, and betrayed the South in a *Look* magazine article." Carter, heeding the advice of his hunting buddies, published "a watered down version" of the editorial.

> I did a lot of thinking about my twenty-three years as editor and publisher of small newspapers, four in Louisiana and the last nineteen in Mississippi. I have never looked upon myself as a starry-eyed crusader or an unfriendly critic of my homeland. No book or editorial or article I had ever written, including the *Look* article, would so identify me. I do like to believe that we've tried on our paper to take seriously the idea of man's equality. But we've been generally orthodox newspaper people, my wife and I. (p. 211)

Carter cited the thousands of letters of support he had received from *Look* readers and explained his stand on the *Brown* decision. He added that he was regularly misinterpreted.

> I don't mean that many white Southerners are willing to have public schools integrated now, especially in the Deep South where numerical pressures are greatest. But they know that inflammatory political behavior and the formation of vigilante groups aren't the answer any more than would be a Supreme Court edict ordering complete integration next fall. There must be a middle ground.

In the letter, Carter actually admits to placing himself in the middle of the civil rights argument, adding

> That brings up something personal. I've pretty much been a middle-of-the-roader all my life. Some of my fellow Southerners think otherwise. They've been conditioned largely by political demagogues to believe that anybody who challenges extremism is in league with the Supreme Court, the NAACP, the Communist Party, the mass circulation magazines, and everybody north of the Mason Dixon Line to destroy the Southern Way of Life. There's a lot I do want destroyed. There's a lot I want to keep. (p. 214)

He concluded by predicting "the South's braying demagogues, its Klans and Councils and Southern Gentlemen, Inc., cannot forever stand" (p. 214).

This incident with the legislature is important because it vividly illustrates exactly how Carter came to be politically misidentified during his life and career. Ultimately, terms like moderate, liberal, conservative, Dixiecrat, Southern apologist, racist, segregationist, and integrationist were all used to describe him during his career and after. Both advocates and adversaries tried to pin him with a political label, but rarely did anyone get him right.

Betty Carter, in a 1979 oral history interview, agreed that Carter was certainly no liberal.

> I think that Hodding was always a conservative, and think that his interest was simply to conserve the very best values that we had. I think the Northern press clamped that word, liberal, on him, and, of course, they started seeing him as being far more "liberal" simply because they had called him a liberal. Hodding believed in absolutely equal justice. (p. 44)

In a letter to Sarasota, Florida, student Randy Hamilton on 6 March 1960, Carter detailed the political leanings of the paper, basically describing it as being somewhere in the middle of the argument. The explanation shows how costly and difficult this editorial stand was to the paper and to Carter himself.

> We like to think of ourselves as being politically independent, with democratic leanings, and with a bent toward moderation in issues that affect the South. We have been the target of extremist groups on both sides of the racial issue, but we do not try to make that paramount.

Carter did not like to be called a integrationist. Waldron wrote that Hodding and Betty "were horrified" when the book jacket for the 1963 publication of *First Person Rural* called him "the foremost integrationist in the South" (p. 303). He forced the book's recall, and a new jacket referred to him as "one of the South's leading spokesmen." In a 28 September 1960 letter to Robert Sherrod, then editor of the *Saturday Evening Post*, Carter discussed issues he wanted to address in an upcoming piece for the magazine. Specifically, he enumerated points "that I have not seen spelled out." First, he wrote, "There is no longer a solid South, either politically or on the question of how to deal with segregation and other aspects of the civil rights struggle." He added, "The only real unity comes from the determination to hold off integration of the school as long as possible and there is a growing conviction that this can best be done at the local and national rather than the state level." On integration, Carter wrote that larger, urban centers in the South would succeed long before the small towns. Echoing his "Liar by Legislation" editorials, Carter wrote, "School integration may come in Houston or New Orleans or Atlanta but it won't have any meaning, other than token, in the Greenvilles." Always the champion of economic as well as education equality, Carter concluded his eight-point missive by writing,

> Lastly, I would want to point out that no advances in any other field will be very helpful to the Negro if his income doesn't rise. The real arbiter for the white man and the black man in the South won't be conscience. It will be cash.

Carter tried in his work to set the record straight, according to his wife Betty, who added in her oral history interview,

> What he saw himself doing was interpreting the North to the South and the South to the North. He felt that if we could understand each other and if the South would realize that the best Southern position was for the Southerner to do the things for himself. These were things that were within our tradition, they were things that we could do and should do. (p. 39)

As for his motive to explain the South to itself and the world, and as an antidote to the label apologist, Carter amplified this theme in "The Editor as Citizen," reprinted in *First Person Rural*, in which he wrote,

> (T)he editor can contribute more to a community's well-being if he thinks of himself first as a citizen of his town, who by good fortune happens to be a newspaper editor in town, rather than as a newspaper editor who happens to be a citizen, permanently or in passing, of some particular town. (p. 245)

Betty Carter said in her oral history interview that her husband had three vehicles of expression: his editorials in the *Delta Democrat-Times*, his magazine articles and books, and his speeches (p. 42). In the years following his skirmish with the Mississippi Legislature, Carter's newspaper continued to be nationally acclaimed, and it won Mississippi Press Association awards for best newspaper seven of eight years in the 1950s. Carter continued to be a prolific writer and speaker, in demand both nationally and internationally. By the mid-1950s, Carter was well known as an opinion leader for journalists in Mississippi, in the South, and across the country. The foundation for this influence may have been Carter's prolific (and Pulitzer Prize-winning) editorial writing. But this leadership position was equally supported by the publication of twenty books; by countless articles about the South in national magazines; by key speaking engagements around the country, including many at college and university convocations; by participation in international exchange programs; and by his involvement in national journalism organizations such as Sigma Delta Chi (now the Society of Professional Journalists), the Pulitzer Prize selection committee, the Nieman Fellow alumni group, and the American Society of Newspaper Editors.

Son Hodding III wrote that this role emerged from "the way he lived his professional life and the eloquent way he described his own values, his love of land and profession, and his devotion to a higher set of principles than those encompassed in white supremacy."

Carter used his influence in support of white Southern editors on more than one occasion. Hodding III said his father worked in support of many editors and reporters and noted that he never hesitated to spring to the defense of an editor or reporter who was being threatened.

> [Dad] publicly came to Albin Kreb's support when the then young man came under attack for writing in the *Daily Mississippian* in favor of the integration of higher education in Mississippi in the early 1950s. (Krebs went to the New York Times eventually.) He editorialized in support of Oliver Emmerich in McComb when Oliver was physically and economically threatened.
>
> He was a great friend, in print and privately, of Harry Ashmore when Harry was in the great war of the late 1950s in Little Rock against Faubus. He publicly lauded Ralph McGill. Actually, this is just a partial list. I think any journalist in trouble was a journalist he felt deserved his support.

More than once, Carter lobbied the Pulitzer Prize on behalf of Southern journalists. For example, Carter supported Harry Ashmore and his newspaper, the *Arkansas Gazette*, in Pulitzer nominations. Waldron wrote that Carter predicted that Ashmore and the paper would win a Pulitzer for their fight against Arkansas Governor Orval Faubus' resistance to the desegregation of Little Rock Central High School (p. 299). (Carter, away on vacation in Maine during the Little Rock desegregation crisis, editorialized by long distance in support of Eisenhower's use of the National Guard. "We go along with the first president of the United States, and with this president" [p. 270].) Carter was right—Ashmore won the Pulitzer, and the two men continued to be friends until Carter's death in 1972.

Carter's most ardent—and longest standing—support was on behalf of Hazel Brannon Smith, the editor of the *Lexington Advertiser*. Smith—

also a Pulitzer Prize-winning editorialist—had been threatened nearly out of business, her newspaper fire-bombed, her daily existence threatened at every turn. This came after she questioned law officers' treatment of blacks. Carter, his son recalled, had moved to Mississippi at the same time as Smith, and he admired his fellow journalist.

> He was ardent [in his support] because her plight aroused every one of his basic emotions: she was (like him) in a battle for survival; like him, she initially was arguing for decency rather than integration or anything close to it, yet was driven to the edge of extinction by 100 percent bigots who would not accept anything but unblinking acceptance of white supremacy; she was a "lone woman" (initially, before she married Smitty [husband Walter Dyer Smith]) being assaulted by a bunch of racist bullies who also included a number of corrupt office holders. He didn't believe the haters should be allowed to succeed in silencing any newspaper.

In 1959 and again in 1965, Carter called on Edward Barrett, dean of the School of Journalism at Columbia University, to assist in a campaign to help Smith. The first came 2 January 1959 in a letter that suggested the dean collect "a group of advertising executives with the thought of having some national advertising especially directed her way." The dean gained support for Smith from influential members of the Advertising Council. Carter himself brought publicity to Smith's plight. Reprinted in *First Person Rural* from the St. Louis *Post-Dispatch*, "Woman Editor's War on Bigots" hailed Smith's courage. Carter called his colleague a "brave woman" who "twenty-five years ago came to Mississippi with eyes shining and dreaming a dream that had to do with the rights of all men and the freedom of newspapers to speak their pieces."

> Maybe the brave bigots will stop putting up. Maybe the now silent, decent people will begin speaking up. Maybe next year the *Lexington Advertiser*, which is celebrating its 125th anniversary this year, will still be Hazel Brannon Smith's editorial

voice. If not, another light will have gone out in a shadowed state.

And perhaps the supreme irony is now that nowhere outside the Deep South would Hazel Brannon Smith be labeled even a liberal in her racial views. If she must be categorized, then call her a moderate; a churchgoing, humanity-loving newspaper woman who takes seriously her responsibility toward her fellow men. But that doesn't fit well in Holmes County where the most benighted are today also the most powerful. (p. 225)

In 1965, Carter and Barrett wrote a column in the *Columbia Journalism Review* that helped bring in more than $2,000 in cash support. According to one letter, the article prompted CBS to plan a special on Smith; an article in *Look* magazine was published in November 1965.

Carter and his paper had a reputation that brought in job inquiries from across the country. The list of reporters and editors who worked at Carter's newspaper is impressive given the size of the *Delta Democrat-Times*. In his 9 March 1960 letter to Randy Hamilton, Carter wrote that "because our policy has been aggressive, liberal, and encouraging to young newspapermen, we have attracted a considerable number of reporters who have gone on to better positions." He noted that his former reporters included Robert Brown, then editor of the *St. Petersburg Times* and a Pulitzer Prize-winner and Nieman Fellow, and Tom Karsell of the Louisville *Courier-Journal*, also a Nieman Fellow. Shelby Foote, who went on become a celebrated Civil War historian, worked for Carter in 1936. Reporter Jay Milner, who named his young daughter Carter after Betty and Hodding, joined the New York *Herald-Tribune* and later became an award-winning journalist and author in Texas. Hodding Carter III won a Nieman Fellowship in 1964, worked for presidents Lyndon Johnson and Jimmy Carter, and now heads the John S. and James L. Knight Foundation in Miami, Florida.

Carter and family—including those at the *Delta Democrat-Times*—remained in Greenville so long because they cared deeply about the town. In one of his most famous articles, the 1960 piece "I'll Never Leave My Town," reprinted in *First Person Rural* (1963), Carter reiterated that life had been difficult in Greenville at times. The article poignantly shows Carter as the man caught in the middle, and it shows how much this position bothered him. The article also showed Carter's true love for his home state. He would never leave the state he loved, no matter how politically difficult it became. He wrote,

> Sometimes I point out that politicians and newspapermen are not natural allies. But mostly I tell them whatever the spiritual, mental or democratic climate elsewhere in my state or in the South, or the nation, it is my happy lot to live in an oasis. Greenville was already an oasis when I came here from my native Louisiana. It is even more an oasis now. (p. 232)
> So, first I will tell of the kindliness and a rare toleration, a respect for the dissenter and dissimilar, which are the spiritual hallmarks of my town. These are the qualities which have made it possible for us to go our own way in Greenville—happily, hopefully, and profitably. (p. 233)

After describing the political, social, and economic developments in Greenville, Carter closed by proclaiming his affection for Greenville. "I believe a publisher should quit a town he doesn't embrace," he wrote. "I love my town." He noted that should his three sons not want to continue in the newspaper business in Greenville, he would sell the *Delta Democrat-Times* (p. 243).

By the late 1950s, Carter was one of the two most celebrated Southern spokesmen—the other was Ralph McGill. Journalists and other historians often group Carter with McGill, then editor of the *Atlanta Constitution*, in terms of influence during the civil rights era. Barbara Barksdale Clowse wrote in *Ralph McGill: A Biography* that the two were contemporaries with extraordinary influence and similar concerns (p. 182). Son Hodding Carter III agreed, writing in correspondence,

> There is no question that Dad and Ralph were the two giants among those white Southern editors who broke with their own and their region's past and, in the grinding pressure of events in the 1950s and 1960s, managed to maintain an ever more pro-

gressive course even while the demands for conformity reached almost unbearable weight and volume.

If Carter was not the single most celebrated, he was clearly one of the most daring. Every editorial stand he took throughout his newspaper career came at the expense of his very livelihood, the newspaper he and his family owned. As Hodding III noted in correspondence, Carter, unlike *Constitution* editor McGill, put his own newspaper on the line every time he spoke out against injustice.

But by the late 50s, Carter's life was also busier than ever. In deference to his busy life, by 1959, Carter began to take less part in the daily operation of the newspaper. In a letter of 5 November 1958, he asked Hodding III to return to Greenville to help with the paper. Hodding Jr., Betty, sons Philip and Tommy were heading to Africa in early 1959 on an Eisenhower Exchange Program; Jay Milner was leaving the paper. Carter suggested his oldest son and David Brown would "do the editorials, along with the stuff I will be sending home."

His father's decreasing role was "rarely known" outside of Greenville, Hodding III wrote, as his father retained the title of editor and publisher of the paper. The younger Carter explained,

> From 1959 on, I took an increasingly deep role in writing the editorials and setting editorial policy. When I got back in June, 1959, the rest of the family was still in South Africa where Dad had an Eisenhower Exchange Fellowship. Editorials were largely the province of David Brown, the managing editor who had been with Dad throughout the 1950s. Young and arrogant, I muscled in, and with no real background, began writing the major policy editorials (candidate endorsements, etc.) almost from the beginning.
>
> Dad had largely severed a day-to-day connection with editorial writing before then, and after they came back in August, he was mostly content to let me continue to play a significant role. By 1962, when he made me managing editor and David Brown had gone on (at least in part out of unhappiness with

me) to Pascagoula (which won the Pulitzer for its editor's editorials that year), I was writing the vast majority of all editorials.

When I went off to Harvard in 1965, it was widely understood in Greenville (though nowhere else) that the paper's editorial voice was mine.

Dad moved to New Orleans and his job as writer-in-residence at Tulane in 1962, which was a formal statement of an underlying reality. I went off to the Nieman as editor in all but name; it became editor in name also when I came back in 1966.

Hodding Jr., acknowledged his son's influence at the paper in a 24 June 1960 letter to E. L. "Red" Holland, Jr., editor of the *Birmingham News*.

> I am busting out all over with pride in Hodding's performance his first year which ended May 1. On that date I officially made him managing editor and two days later our paper won first in general excellence and first in community service, second in editorial writing—almost all of them Hod's—and other seconds and [thirds] in every category. It was the best showing of any state paper and the boy is responsible.

For most of the 1960s civil rights-related issues, Hodding III was the editorial voice of the paper. But his father, he recalled, continued to write columns "on occasional major issues."

> Dad would write an editorial, particularly on matters that directly concerned him or about which he was directly concerned. On those occasions, he would sometimes sign his name or initials.
>
> But I tended to write too long; he always wrote short in those days, which is another way to tell who was writing.

Hodding Jr. shifted the focus of his writing from local to national and international issues. Most of the works published in *First Person Rural*, for example, had been published in another national publication or in syndication. In addition to the *Saturday Evening Post* and the *New York Times Magazine*, articles had appeared in *Reader's Digest*, *Down East: The Magazine of Maine*, the *Princeton University Library Chronicle*, *Sales Magazine*, *Look*, *Outdoor Life*, and the Society of Professional Journalists' *Quill*. Carter also published eight books in this ten-year period, including *The Angry Scar: The Story of Reconstruction*, and *So the Heffners Left McComb*. Following the Eisenhower Exchange Africa trip in 1959, Carter wrote extensively of the similarities and differences between the struggles of Southern blacks and black Africans.

During this time, Carter also set out on the speaker's circuit, crisscrossing the country to speak at colleges, universities, churches, and civic groups. His honorarium ranged from $200 to $500, plus expenses. Wife Betty wrote a friend that by the mid-1950s, Carter was "making a lot of speeches at that time all over the country. I guess he talked in every state in the union, at every college convocation, and God knows what." One such speech to Brown University caused controversy. Carter was misinterpreted in 1963 during a speech at Brown University, and an account of his speech made the national wire services. Carter's response to accusations that he had ridiculed his home state was firm, Waldron wrote. He began a campaign to set the record straight that included a statement from the editor of the Providence *Journal*, who attested that Carter had spoken on "the role of the journalist in the South" and had not denigrated anyone—or anything—in his three speeches (p. 294). This reaction—and the forced corrections and justifications—are common of Carter in this period. He hated being misunderstood, and he hated even more being credited for beliefs he did not hold. He would go only so far, but no farther.

Through these years, the Carter family—especially its patriarch and matriarch—remained loyal to Mississippi. As Carter wrote to a Mississippi reader who'd sent him a six-page, handwritten letter,

> I would say that I know that I am guilty of occasional intemperate remarks. I rather imagine that you would be too had you and your family been subjected to the kind of anonymous abuse, threat and slander that has come our way because my points of view do not coincide with that of a majority. But I have made this state my home for going on twenty-five years

and I have no intention of leaving it or my native South. Letters
like yours encourage me in my decision to remain.

In 1962, Carter returned to Tulane as a newspaper adviser, a position he would hold for most of the 1960s. Throughout this period, Waldron wrote, Carter was losing the two things that frightened him most throughout his career—control of his newspaper and his vision. The eye problems of World War II had returned with a vengeance. Multiple operations were required throughout the decade (p. 307).

Carter faced other tragedies. In April 1964, while he was recuperating in a Detroit hospital, he and Betty received word that Tommy had died of a gunshot wound while playing Russian roulette. The day after, the family returned to Greenville to find that someone had dumped trash across their front yard. Betty Carter said in her oral history interview that Tommy's death had been reported in the newspaper, and after that, "the entire front of the place was just garbage."

> In our emotional condition and in our gardener's emotional condition, he felt that that was a deliberate thing. Whether it was or not, I don't know. But all our friends said it was deliberate. (p. 45)

An editorial in the *Delta Democrat-Times* decried the event, Waldron wrote. "Their tribute to the grief of a mother and father was an appropriate symbol of the filth-crazed haters who are today riding again in Mississippi. It was a symbol which all the complacent, comfortable citizens of this state who would passively or positively acquiesce in the resurgence of organized bigotry should mark with care" (p. 307).

After Tommy's death, Betty said in her oral history interview, Hodding "just wanted to die" (p. 46). Later that year, Carter's vision failed again, leaving him with no peripheral vision. He could barely see. He dictated his letters and columns to keep up his productivity. A year later, with Hodding III at Harvard on a Nieman fellowship, Carter returned to more regular editorial writing for the paper, but he largely was separated from the daily operation. Shortly before Hodding III returned to Greenville, Betty returned to the paper full time. By 1968, physically ill and blind, her husband was unable to take more public commitments, though he continued to receive honors and awards until his death.

Hodding Carter was exercising at the Greenville Nationwide Health Club when he died of a heart attack at age sixty-five on 4 April 1972. Condolence notes poured in from around the world. More than 200 telegrams are filed in the Hodding and Betty Werlein Carter papers at Mississippi State University, and personal letters to Betty, Hodding III, and Philip Carter number in the thousands. Some, like the one from President Richard Nixon, are short and to the point. Others, like the one from Eppie "Ann Landers" Lederer, are personal reminders of longtime friendship. Journalists, politicians, ministers, business leaders, and others wrote to describe how Hodding Carter's life had changed their own.

Carter's obituary was published in newspapers around the world. There were three basic versions—one from the Associated Press, one from United Press International, and one from the New York Times News Service—and each lauded his work as a champion for human rights. In headlines he was called an "advocate of racial harmony" and an "outspoken Mississippi editor." Headlines also noted that he "fought racism" and was "a crusader for racial harmony."

Two poignant editorials were written by Hodding III and Philip and published in the *Delta Democrat-Times* of 12 April 1972. Philip's piece, offered an intimate look at his father's life. Hodding III addressed his father's lifelong fight against injustice in the world.

> Dad never took an editorial stand lightly or without fully realizing the consequences. Knowing them so well, each deviance from the often rigid conformity of his time was a matter if wrenching personal anguish. He didn't enjoy the hatred, the public scorn, the obscene letters and telephone calls. And yet, while he never provoked a fight, he never backed away from one either. In his code, there were values much higher than the applause of a transient majority.

He ended his editorial by promising that "[w]ith God's help and in the sure knowledge that the trail Dad blazed leads toward a better land for all our people, this newspaper will answer that call as long as there is a Carter to lead it" (p. 325).

An unsigned editorial in the *Los Angeles Times* of 10 April 1972 captured Carter's influence.

> One of the several faces of courage is just being true to yourself in your own place and time. Such was the courage of Hodding Carter, publisher and editor of a small newspaper, the *Delta Democrat-Times*, in a small town, Greenville, in Mississippi.
>
> Carter loved the South and hated racism, and pungently said so in his paper, a generation ago, when it wasn't easy anywhere in the South, and not at all easy in the Mississippi Delta.
>
> Honored in the North, he was, in his early years, much abused in Mississippi, and from time to time, lived in no little personal danger. In time, the South changed, and by the end of his life—he died last week at 65—he was respected by many in his state, and indeed had come under attack in the North for being a Southern apologist.

Reg Murphy, writing on the 6 April 1972 editorial page of the *Atlanta Constitution*, noted that Carter's "sight had failed, if not his insight." Paul Greenberg wrote in the 15 April 1972 *Cincinnati Post and Times-Star* that "Hodding's style remained the same. It wasn't fancy or literary, but it was a man's voice." Greenberg also noted that "damnation from some can be the sincerest, most lasting, form of praise."

> His courage came from a deep identity, not alienation. Perhaps that's why he endured, though he knew disappointment, and bitterness and grief. Because he had a Southern comprehension of what family and community mean, of the joy in life and in fighting the good fight.

Greenberg concluded his tribute by writing, "If there is anything his courage teaches us now, it is that men make their own times, and that the good fight still beckons."

Hodding III's editorship continued "the good fight" through 1977, when he left Greenville for good to take a position in the administration of President Jimmy Carter. Waldron wrote that Betty Carter continued as publisher until the two families which owned it sold the *Delta Democrat-Times* in 1980 to Freedom Newspapers, a firm based in Santa Ana, Calif., for between $14 and $16 million. She died in 2000.

Carter's newspaper was now out of family hands. But the editor had, as the *Los Angeles Times* had concluded on 10 April 1972, played a substantial role in leading the region he loved. "At long last the new South dreamed of for so many years by Southerners of visions is coming into being," the *Times* concluded. "Hodding Carter was one of its honored builders." It was construction that took place firmly on principle, its builder always caught in the middle.

References

Carter, Betty W. Oral History Interview. The University of Southern Mississippi, vol. 150, 1979.

Carter, Hodding Jr., and Betty Werlein Carter Personal Papers. Mississippi State University.

Carter, Hodding, Jr. *First Person Rural*. (New York: Doubleday and Company, 1963).

Carter, Hodding, Jr. *Where Main Street Meets the River*. (New York: Rinehart & Company, 1952).

Carter, Hodding III. Personal interview by email.

Dittmer, John. *Local People: The Struggle for Civil Rights in Mississippi*. (Illinois: University of Illinois Press, 1994).

Folkerts, Jean. "Hodding Carter, Jr." In Perry Ashley, ed. *Dictionary of Literary Biography*. (South Carolina: Bruccoli Clark Layman, 1993).

Waldron, Ann. *Hodding Carter: The Reconstruction of a Racist*. (Chapel Hill: Algonquin Books, 1993).

About the Contributors

David L. Bennett is adjunct professor of journalism at the University of Southern Mississippi.

Ginger Rudeseal Carter is assistant professor of mass communication at Georgia College & State University (and is no relation to Hodding Carter, Jr.).

Caryl A. Cooper is assistant professor in the Department of Advertising & Public Relations at the University of Alabama.

David R. Davies is associate professor and chair of the Journalism Department at the University of Southern Mississippi.

Laura Nan Fairley is associate professor of journalism at Auburn University.

Arthur J. Kaul is professor of journalism at the University of Southern Mississippi.

Judy Smith is a doctoral student in mass communication history at the University of Southern Mississippi.

Lawrence N. Strout is the Harriet Stark Gibbons Chair of Journalism at the Mississippi University for Women.

Susan M. Weill is assistant professor of communication studies at the University of Alabama at Birmingham.

Index

ABC, 45
Accommodationist philosophy, 56, 60
Adams, Virgil, 28
Advertising, 57, 81
Alcorn College, 66
American Nazi Party, 37
American Society of Newspaper Editors, 20
Arkansas Gazette, 252
Ashmore, Harry, 177, 283
Associated Negro Press, 60
Associated Press, 24, 49, 91
Associated Press v. Walker, 49
Association for the Preservation of the White Race, 116
Atlanta Compromise, 59, 70
Atlanta Constitution, 252
Atlanta Exposition, 58
Atlanta Journal, 251

Banner County Outlook, 258
Barnett, Ross, 31, 32, 33, 34, 35, 36, 38, 72, 76, 92, 93–95, 103, 113–14, 152, 158, 162, 174, 175, 189, 190, 191, 200, 201, 221, 223, 224, 255–56
Barrett, Don, 250

Barrett, Pat M., 246, 250
Barton, Billy C., 251
Belafonte, Harry, 48
Bilbo, Theodore, 275
Black Chamber of Commerce, 62
Black Muslims, 71
Blacks, courtesy titles for, 5–6, 269–70
Blake, Eugene Carson, 90
Bond, Julian, 79
Booker, Simeon, 6, 68
Boone, Buford, 177
Boyd, J. D., 66
Boynton v. Virginia, 72
Bramlett, Sharon, 18
Brannon, Dock Broad, 235
Brannon, Georgia Freeman, 235
Brannon v. State (29 So. 2d 916), 239
Brown, Alfred, 256
Brown v. Board of Education, 7–9, 18, 19, 20, 21, 22, 23, 24, 25, 27, 28, 30, 31, 33, 34, 37, 64, 87–88, 91, 154, 161, 168, 209–11, 213, 214, 229, 276–77, 279
Brown, W. David, 39, 41, 47
Bryant, Curtis C., 118
Bryant, Roy, 69
Burt, Gordon, 121
Byrd, Richard F., 242–43

Index

Canton Citizen, 56
Carmichael, Stokely, 79
Carter, Betty Werlein, 269, 270, 273, 280, 281, 282, 293
Carter, Hodding, Jr., 25, 28, 29, 138, 139, 142, 144, 148, 150, 151, 154, 160, 165, 167, 252–53, 257, 265–93
Carter, Hodding, III, 17, 18, 29, 34, 35, 39, 41, 43, 44, 235, 257, 266, 267, 271, 277, 283, 287, 288
Carter, Jimmy, 80
Carter, Phillip, 272, 287, 291
Carter, Tommy, 274, 287, 290
Carter, William Hodding, Sr., 267–68, 270
Carver High School, 157
Cashman, L. P., 27
Cashman, Louis P., Jr., 33, 40, 43
CBS, 45, 49
Chambers, Lenoir, 177
Chaney, James, 41, 42, 43, 44, 48, 49, 77, 100
Chaze, William, 44
Chicago Defender, 64
Chicago Tribune, 259
Christian Science Monitor, 262
Church burnings, 163, 164, 165
Citizens' Council: Organized Resistance to the Second Reconstruction, 22
Citizens' Councils, 22, 32, 67, 68, 69, 70, 79, 89, 92, 107, 116, 153, 156, 158, 159, 168, 240–41, 245–46, 251, 254–55, 257, 261–62, 277, 279–80
Civil Rights Act of 1964, 38, 39, 40, 46, 47, 100–01, 112, 114–15, 128–29, 156, 209, 228, 229
Civil rights workers, 40, 41, 42, 43, 44, 45, 47
Civil War, 21
Clark, Robert, 259
Clarksdale Press Register, 19, 33, 34, 37, 45, 49
COFO. *See* Council of Federated Organizations
Colored Citizen (Jackson, Miss.), 56

Colored Citizen (Vicksburg, Miss.), 56
Colored Veteran, 61
Columbia Journalism Review, 85, 106
Columbus *Commercial Dispatch*, 19, 32, 39, 45
Commercial Appeal (Memphis, Tenn.), 257
Commission on Freedom of the Press (Hutchins Commission), 20, 50
Congress of Racial Equality (CORE), 41, 48, 71, 72, 76, 77, 91, 101, 102, 163
Corinth *Daily Corinthian*, 19, 36, 39, 42
Council of Federated Organizations (COFO), 45, 46, 47, 71, 74, 77, 111, 159
Cronkite, Walter, 49
Cunnigen, Donald, 149

Dark Journey: Black Mississippians in the Age of Jim Crow, 22, 23
Davis, S. F., 239
De La Beckwith, Byron, 73, 98, 215–17, 257
Dean, Dizzy, 118
Delta Democrat-Times, 17, 19, 25, 28, 34, 39, 41, 44, 252, 257, 271–72, 274, 282
Delta Leader, 60, 66
Democrats, 63, 77
Dittmer, John, 21, 40, 55, 66, 67, 68, 150, 277
Dixie Lumberman, 39
Du Bois, W. E. B., 59, 63
Dunagin, Charles, 114, 115, 116, 119, 133–34
Durant News, 235–36, 240, 243, 246, 252–53

East, P. D., 188, 251
Eastland, James O., 24, 99
Ebony, 246
Elijah P. Lovejoy Award, 249
Ellis, Joseph, Jr., 33, 37, 45, 49
Emmerich, J. Oliver, 27, 28, 32, 35, 36, 38, 45, 49, 111–34, 138, 160, 167
Emmerich, John, 128–29
Ethridge, Mark, 252

298

Index

Ethridge, Tom, 31
Etowah Observer, 235
Evers, Medgar, 56, 71, 72, 73, 74, 75, 98, 105, 108, 215–17, 222, 254, 256, 261
Evers-Williams, Myrlie, 108

Faulkner, William, 198
Featherston, James, 244
Featherstone, Ralph, 120
Federal Bureau of Investigation, 42, 68, 100
Fifth Circuit Court of Appeals, 30, 31, 49
Folkerts, Jean, 266, 271
Ford, Gerald R., 80
Four-County News, 247
Free and Responsible Press: A General Report on Mass Communication, 20
Freedom Democratic Party, 159
Freedom Rides, 72, 91–93, 112, 113
Freedom schools, 40, 120
Freedom Summer, 18, 19, 38, 40, 41, 43, 47, 49, 77, 99, 220, 225, 226–28
Freedom Vote, 74

Garner, Artis, 125
Gartin, Carroll, 25
Garvey, Marcus, 59
Gibbons, Harriett, 25, 35
Goldwater, Barry, 162, 220, 221, 222
Goodman, Andrew, 41, 42, 43, 44, 48, 49, 77, 100
Gordon, Charles B., 115, 123
Gray, Lloyd, 142, 143, 144, 147, 151, 157
Greene, Francis Reed, 62, 80
Greene, Percy, 55–83
Greenwood Commonwealth, 19, 33, 46, 48
Greenwood *Morning Star*, 19, 28
Grenada *Sentinel-Star*, 19
Grisham, Vaughn, 167
Guggenheim Fellowship, 274
Guihard, Paul, 37
Gulfport Daily Herald, 19
Gunter, Roy, 37

Halberstam, David, 10
Hammond *Daily Courier*, 269–71
Harkey, Ira B., Jr., 6–7, 34, 35, 39, 139, 151, 173–207
Harmon, Andrews, 27, 36
Harris, W. H., 26, 33, 42, 43, 48
Hattiesburg American, 19, 27, 36, 39, 41, 46
Hazel Brannon Smith v. Richard F. Byrd (225 Miss. 331, 83 So. 2d 172), 243
Hederman family, 22, 85, 86, 104, 115
Hederman, T. M., Jr., 31, 38
Heffner, Albert W., 122
Heiskell, J. N., 252
Henry, Aaron, 66, 78
Hereford, Robert, 157
Hewitt, Purser, 107
Hill, Bruce, 259
Hills, Charles M., 25
Hofstadter, Richard, 234, 262
Holmes County Herald, 90, 246–49, 253–56, 259–60
Hooker, Robert, 18
Hooker, Wilburn, 246, 255
Hopkins, A. L. "Andy," 254
Howard, T. R. M., 68
Howie, Bob, 99–100
Humes, H. H., 60, 66
Hurst, E. H., 113
Hutchins, Robert, 20

Imes, Birney, Sr., 32, 39, 45
International Conference of Weekly Newspaper Editors, 249
Interposition, 34, 35
I've Got the Light of Freedom, 40

Jackson Advocate, 55–56, 60–64, 69, 73, 75, 77–80
Jackson *Clarion-Ledger*, 19, 20, 22, 25, 26, 27, 31, 38, 42, 44, 68, 85, 88, 94, 95, 98, 139, 147, 234–35, 240, 254, 260
Jackson College, 61

Index

Jackson *Daily News*, 19, 20, 22, 25, 26, 27, 31, 32, 38, 41, 43, 45, 64, 68, 85–109, 244–45
Jackson, Deidra Faye, 140, 150, 157
Jackson Mississippi Freedom Democratic Party Newsletter, 75
Jackson Public Schools, 214, 215
Jackson, school desegregation, 101
Jackson *State-Times*, 19, 87, 115, 250
Jacobs, Wanda, 204
James, Folsom, 34
Jeremiad, as editorial, 176
Jim Crow laws, 23, 57
Johnson, Lyndon, 38, 42, 78, 112, 125–26, 162, 220, 221, 228
Johnson, Paul B., Jr., 38, 42, 43, 95, 112, 116–17, 128, 164, 219–21, 227
Johnston, Erle, 88–89, 114
Jones, Albert, 254

Kastenmeier, Robert, 76
Kennedy, John F., 219, 220, 223, 229
Kessler, Lauren, 56
King, Easton, 181, 187, 188
King, Martin Luther, Jr., 40, 46, 48, 56, 69, 70, 71, 89, 101–03, 158
Kneebone, John T., 168
Ku Klux Klan, 21, 22, 44, 46, 94, 116, 117, 158, 159, 163, 185, 186, 195, 225–27, 257

Ladner, Heber, 254
Lambert, James, 47
Laurel Leader-Call, 19, 25, 35, 47
Lee, Davis, 28
Lee, George W., 68
Lee, Herbert, 113
Lee, Percy, 243
Lexington Advertiser, 75, 233, 236–40, 243–50, 252–54, 256, 260
Lippmann, Walter, 20
Local People: The Struggle for Civil Rights in Mississippi, 21, 40
Look, 241
Louisville *Courier-Journal*, 252
Lowrey, Leonard, 36, 39, 46

Luce, Henry, 20
Lyceum Building, 36
Lynching, 58, 60, 64

March on Washington, 71
Marshal, Tom, 44
Marshall, Burke, 125
Marshall, Chester, 246, 249
Martin, Harry, 142, 149, 162
Mayfield, Kenneth, 150, 157
McCarthy, Joseph, 240
McComb *Enterprise-Journal*, 19, 27, 28, 32, 35, 38, 45, 49, 111–34
McComb Freedom's Journal, 75
McComb, Miss., 118–19, 120–22, 123–25
McGill, Ralph, 106, 251–52, 283, 286–87
McLean, Anna Keirsey, 140
McLean, George A., 25, 30, 35, 137–71
McLeish, Archibald, 20
McMillen, Neil R., 22, 23, 64, 80
Meredith, James, 18, 31, 33, 34, 36, 37, 72, 79, 93–97, 151–54, 174, 189, 190, 213, 222–25, 255
Meridian, Miss., 57
Meridian Star, 19, 27, 32, 41, 42
Milam, J. W., 69
Miles, David B., 244
Minor, Wilson F. (Bill), 107–08, 131, 132, 139, 209–31, 260
Mississippi Association of Colored Teachers, 64
Mississippi Free Press, 74, 75, 76, 77, 79, 80, 254–55
Mississippi Freedom Democratic Party (MFDP), 78
Mississippi Negro Democrats Association, 63
Mississippi Plan, the, 57
Mississippi Press, 187, 205
Mississippi Press Association, 182, 183, 200, 204
Mississippi Sovereignty Commission, 69, 70, 75, 88, 114, 251–52, 254–55, 261–62
Mississippi: The Closed Society, 18, 21, 23, 25, 30, 31, 37, 51, 175, 176

Index

Mississippi, University of, 18, 30, 31, 32, 34, 35, 36, 37, 38, 140, 150, 151, 153, 154, 213, 217–19, 222–25
Mississippi Vocational College, 66, 67
Mize, Sidney, 191
Montgomery Bus Boycott, 70
Montgomery, Isaiah, 58
Moses, Bob, 112–13, 119
Murphy, Harry, 96–97
Murtagh, Walter L., 238

NAACP, 23, 59, 63, 65, 66, 68, 69, 71, 73, 74, 78, 101–02, 153, 159, 163
Nash, Sherrill, 42
Natchez Democrat, 19, 29, 47
Natchez *Times,* 19
National Council of Churches, 41, 46
National Guard, 36
National Negro Business League, 62
NBC, 45
New Deal, 61, 63, 237
New Orleans *Times-Picayune,* 180, 181, 196
New York *Herald-Tribune,* 258
New York Times, 5, 8, 130, 132
New York Times v. Sullivan, 49
Newark (New Jersey) *Telegraph,* 28
Newman, Mark, 234, 262
Niagara Movement, 59
Nicholson, Ralph, 202, 203
Nieman fellowship, 272, 287–88
Northside Reporter, 257–58

Pascagoula *Chronicle,* 19, 34, 39, 41, 42, 47, 48, 49, 173–82, 184, 185, 187, 190–204
Pascagoula *Mississippi Press,* 19
Patterson, N. J., *Call,* 258
Patterson, Robert "Tut," 67, 89
Payne, Charles M., 40, 73, 74, 150
Pearson, Drew, 127
Percy, William Alexander, 271–72, 273
Petal Paper, 251
Phelps, Ashton, Jr., 196
Philadelphia, Miss., 163, 164
Pittman, Tom, 142, 146

Pittsburgh Courier, 64
Plessy v. Ferguson, 24, 64
Poll taxes, 21
Popham, John N., 8
Poston, Ted, 17
Poynter, Nelson, 253
Progressive Business League, 62
Progressivism, 234, 261
Public Opinion, 20
Pulitzer Prize, 196, 197, 198, 199, 257–58, 274, 283

Quin, Alyene, 124–25, 128

Ramsey, Claude, 195
Randall, Henry, 242–43
Randolph, A. Philip, 63
Reconstruction Acts of 1867, 21
Reed, Jack, Sr., 139
Roosevelt, Franklin D., 63, 237
Rosenwald Fund, 65
Ruml, Beardsley, 20
Rural Community Development Program, 145, 146
Rutherford, Harry, 35, 36, 43, 48, 138, 142, 143, 144, 148, 150, 151, 156
Rutherford, Joe, 151, 152, 162

Scarbrough, Tom, 252
Schlesinger, Arthur, 20
Schwerner, Michael, 41, 42, 43, 44, 48, 49, 77, 100
Shearer, Jack A., 250, 253
Shoemaker, W. C., 104–06
Silver, James W., 18, 57, 85, 113, 115, 139, 175, 176
Simmons, William J., 92
Simpson, Bill, 36, 39, 42
Skewes, James B., 32, 42
Skewes, James H., 27
Slavery, 21
Smell of Burning Crosses, 173, 180, 181, 182, 185, 197
Smith, Andrew P., 246
Smith, Hazel Brannon, 75, 177, 233–62, 283–85

Index

Smith, L. A., Jr., 239
Smith, Lamar, 68
Smith, R. L. T., 55
Smith v. Allwright, 63
Smith, W. Leslie, 248
Smith, Walter Dyer "Smitty," 240, 244–45
Snider, Billy, 235
Southern Advocate, 60
Southern Christian Leadership Conference, 41, 46, 56, 71, 78, 158
St. Petersburg Times, 253
Starkville Daily News, 19, 42, 48
Stars and Stripes, 273
States' rights, 32, 37
Stennis, John, 24
Stringer, Emmett, 66
Stroud, Bill, 142
Student Non-Violent Coordinating Committee, 71, 72, 77, 78, 99, 106, 112–13
Suggs, Henry L., 56
Sullens, Frederick, 26, 27, 32, 64, 86–88

Talbert, Sam S., 194
Thirteenth Amendment, 21
Thompson, Allen, 73, 258
Thompson, Julius, 55–59, 60–61, 64–65, 69–70, 75
Till, Emmett, 10, 68
Time magazine, 85, 243–44, 246
Tisdale, Charles, 80
Tolson, Arthur, 58
Tougaloo College, 73
Tri-Anniversary Committee, 252–53
Trimble, Elliott, 29
Tupelo *Daily Journal,* 19, 25, 30, 35, 41, 43, 48, 137–69
Tupelo *Daily News,* 142
Tupelo High School, 157

Turnbow, Hartman, 256
Turner, Henry M., 58

United Press International, 24, 48, 91
United States Marines, 42
United States Marshals, 36
United States Supreme Court, 23, 24, 25, 26, 29, 30, 33, 34, 35, 37, 49, 209, 211, 223
Urban League, 71, 163
U.S. News & World Report, 69

Vermont, in Mississippi project, 89
Vicksburg Citizen's Appeal, 75
Vicksburg Evening Post, 19, 27, 33, 40, 43, 48, 49
Vicksburg Herald, 19, 48
Vollers, Maryanne, 73
Voter registration, 40, 46, 47
Voting Rights Act, 21, 78, 209, 228

Wade, B. A., 60
Waldron, Ann, 265
Walker, Edwin A., 37, 49
Walt, Thatcher, 33
Ward, James "Jimmy," 32, 38, 43, 45, 85–109
Washington, Booker T., 56, 58, 61, 63, 76
West, Jay, 35
West Point *Times Leader,* 19, 27, 33, 42, 43, 47
White, Hugh, 24, 66
White, J. H., 66–67
White, John, 59
White primary, 57, 63
Williams, T. M., 246, 254–55
Wilson, T. B., 63
Winter, William, 167
Works Progress Administration, 61

www.ingramcontent.com/pod-product-compliance
Lightning Source LLC
Chambersburg PA
CBHW021136230426
43667CB00005B/141